CREATIVE
HOMEOWNER®

FENCES, GATES & TRELLISES

CREATIVE HOMEOWNER, Upper Saddle River, New Jersey

Editorial Director: Timothy O. Bakke
Art Director: Annie Jeon

Author: Jim Barrett
Editors: Jeff Day, David Schiff
Editorial Assistant: Georgette Blau
Copy Editor: Margaret Gallos

Graphic Designers: Michelle D. Halko, Rodney Stokes
Illustrators: Ray Skibinski, Craig Franklin, Paul M. Schumm

Cover Design: Annie Jeon
Cover Photograph: Nancy Hill Photography

Current Printing (last digit)
10 9 8 7 6 5

Fences, Gates & Trellises
Library of Congress Catalog Card Number: 97-68496
ISBN: 1-880029-96-0

CREATIVE HOMEOWNER®
A Division of Federal Marketing Corp.
24 Park Way
Upper Saddle River, NJ 07458
Web site: **www.creativehomeowner.com**

SAFETY FIRST

Though all the designs and methods in this book have been reviewed for safety, it is not possible to overstate the importance of using the safest construction methods possible. What follows are reminders; some do's and don'ts of basic carpentry. They are not substitutes for your own common sense.

- *Always* use caution, care, and good judgment when following the procedures described in this book.

- *Always* be sure that the electrical setup is safe; be sure that no circuit is overloaded and that all power tools and electrical outlets are properly grounded. Do not use power tools in wet locations.

- *Always* read container labels on paints, solvents, and other products; provide ventilation, and observe all other warnings.

- *Always* read the manufacturer's instructions for using a tool, especially the warnings.

- *Always* use hold-downs and push sticks whenever possible when working on a table saw. Avoid working short pieces if you can.

- *Always* remove the key from any drill chuck (portable or press) before starting the drill.

- *Always* pay deliberate attention to how a tool works so that you can avoid being injured.

- *Always* know the limitations of your tools. Do not try to force them to do what they were not designed to do.

- *Always* make sure that any adjustment is locked before proceeding. For example, always check the rip fence on a table saw or the bevel adjustment on a portable saw before starting to work.

- *Always* clamp small pieces firmly to a bench or other work surface when using a power tool on them.

- *Always* wear the appropriate rubber or work gloves when handling chemicals, moving or stacking lumber, or doing heavy construction.

- *Always* wear a disposable face mask when you create dust by sawing or sanding. Use a special filtering respirator when working with toxic substances and solvents.

- *Always* wear eye protection, especially when using power tools or striking metal on metal or concrete; a chip can fly off, for example, when chiseling concrete.

- *Always* be aware that there is seldom enough time for your body's reflexes to save you from injury from a power tool in a dangerous situation; everything happens too fast. Be *alert!*

- *Always* keep your hands away from the business ends of blades, cutters, and bits.

- *Always* hold a circular saw firmly, usually with both hands so that you know where they are.

- *Always* use a drill with an auxiliary handle to control the torque when large-size bits are used.

- *Always* check your local building codes when planning new construction. The codes are intended to protect public safety and should be observed to the letter.

- *Never* work with power tools when you are tired or under the influence of alcohol or drugs.

- *Never* cut tiny pieces of wood or pipe using a power saw. Cut small pieces off larger pieces.

- *Never* change a saw blade or a drill or router bit unless the power cord is unplugged. Do not depend on the switch being off; you might accidentally hit it.

- *Never* work in insufficient lighting.

- *Never* work while wearing loose clothing, hanging hair, open cuffs, or jewelry.

- *Never* work with dull tools. Have them sharpened, or learn how to sharpen them yourself.

- *Never* use a power tool on a workpiece—large or small—that is not firmly supported.

- *Never* saw a workpiece that spans a large distance between horses without close support on each side of the cut; the piece can bend, closing on and jamming the blade, causing saw kickback.

- *Never* support a workpiece from underneath with your leg or other part of your body when sawing.

- *Never* carry sharp or pointed tools, such as utility knives, awls, or chisels, in your pocket. If you want to carry such tools, use a special-purpose tool belt with leather pockets and holders.

TABLE OF CONTENTS

INTRODUCTION

This book will show you how to plan, design, and build a variety of wood, metal, and vinyl fences. You'll learn which materials and fasteners to use and how to build and install gates and latches. The last section of the book provides information and projects for adorning your yard with wood structures that encourage plant growth. And to spruce up and extend the life of existing fences, gates, and trellises, check the detailed repair and maintenance procedures.

Most of the designs and projects presented are simple, do-it-yourself structures that can be built with ordinary carpentry and digging tools. Once you've chosen a particular project or design in this book, read through the instructions carefully to see what materials and procedures are required before you begin the job. Each how-to section begins by rating the level of difficulty of the task at hand. The level of difficulty is indicated by one, two, or three hammers:

⚒ Easy, even for beginners.

⚒⚒ Moderately difficult, but can be done by beginners who have the patience and willingness to learn.

⚒⚒⚒ Difficult. Can be done by a do-it-yourselfer, but requires a serious investment in time, patience, and specialty tools. Consider hiring a specialist.

Building fences, gates, and trellises involves a range of skills from concrete work to carpentry. Although the skills are diverse, this book will show you how to build a fence that fits just right into your landscape.

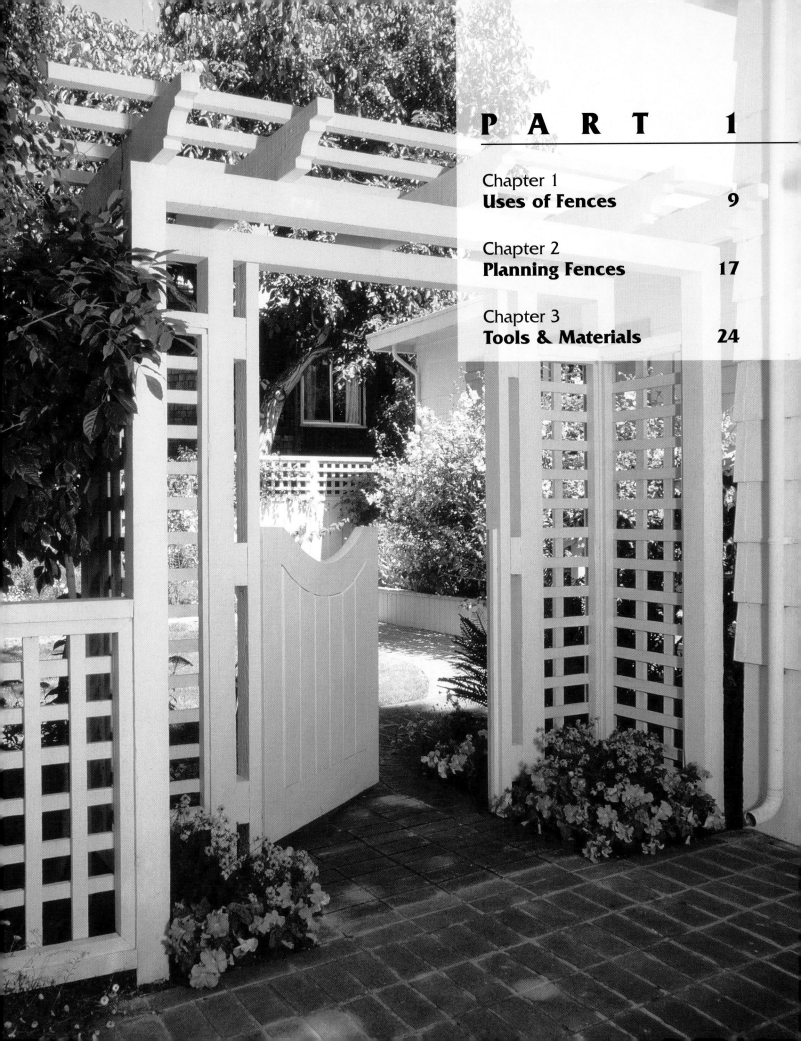

PART 1

CHAPTER 1

USES OF FENCES

Your reasons for building a fence can be entirely utilitarian: Perhaps you must delineate property lines or keep children and animals from tramping through a flower bed. Or maybe your reasons are more aesthetic: to provide support for flowering vines or to complement your home with a delicate, white picket fence and gate. Whether your reasons are practical or aesthetic, a well-planned fence can serve a variety of functions as it embellishes your home and landscape.

DEFINING BOUNDARIES

One obvious use for fences is to mark property lines so that you know what belongs to you and what belongs to your neighbors. Just about any type of fence can do this, although you'll probably want a fence that provides a certain amount of security as well. A low, open chain-link or lattice fence keeps children and animals from walking across a front lawn or trampling flower beds while allowing the homeowner to show off the yard and house to passersby. Backyard property fences are usually taller (typically 60 to 72 inches tall) and have a solid, closed design to provide privacy and security.

Most communities have height restrictions on property-line fences: typically 72 inches in backyards and 36 to 48 inches in front yards. Within the yard, low fences can define areas and keep people from crossing the

Property-line fences can provide a measure of security and privacy. This tall, lattice-top redwood fence blocks the view of the next door neighbor's house and yard. The "good-neighbor" design looks the same from both sides.

This fence is low enough to show off the colonial architecture of this New England home, yet clearly separates lawn from garden areas.

boundary lines while retaining an overall sense of openness. Such fences need only be 12 to 24 inches tall to send the message: "Stay on the path!" or "Don't walk through the flower bed!"

PROVIDING SECURITY

Security fences that use materials such as barbed wire, razor ribbon, or electricity are not covered in this book. However, security fences don't have to incorporate dangerous materials to be effective. A security fence keeps people away from where they don't belong, and any fence that is tall, sturdy, and difficult to climb will perform the job quite well. For example, a 72-inch, solid-board fence, an ornamental metal fence or a similar design that provides no horizontal handholds or footholds will discourage all but the most ambitious of fence climbers. Similarly, gates should be tall and fitted with latches that are difficult for children to operate. To prevent adults from trespassing, choose a gate latch that can be

fitted with a padlock or install a separate dead-bolt lock with a key.

Containment and Determent

Fences can contain or deter animals. The design, dimensions, and structural requirements for such fences are similar to those for security fences. To keep a large dog on the property, you'll need a fence that is at least 48 inches high. Chain link and heavy wire fences are popular for dog kennels because they aren't damaged by gnawing and scratching.

If you want to keep animals out of a garden, there are a few things to keep in mind. Install the fence before you plant the garden. Make your garden area small; deer tend to dislike small, confined spaces. Make the fence highly visible by painting it a bright color and by keeping an area of at least 10 feet beyond the fence cleared of tall brush and weeds. Make the fence at least 60 inches high, which should deter casual nibblers, but be aware that a really

Chain link makes an excellent fence for containing dogs. Chewing won't damage the chain link, and the open design allows you to monitor your dog. Most dogs won't attempt to jump over a fence that's 48 inches high.

hungry deer will leap even taller fences to satisfy its hunger.

If you want a fence that will deter burrowing garden pests, such as groundhogs, you will have to bury the bottom of it. The best way to handle this is with a kickboard, usually a 2x8 set several inches below ground, fastened like a rail to the bottom of the posts. Building a fence with a kickboard will discourage animals from digging underneath. (For

Security fences are designed without places to grab or step on, such as this solid board fence, which has no spaces between the boards. For security and privacy, gates should be solid, too, and be fitted with a locking latch that children can't reach.

With plenty to eat, this horse has no compelling reason to jump the rustic log fence. To keep animals, such as deer, from jumping into a garden area, a fence should be at least 60 inches high.

information on building kickboards, see "Installing Kickboards," page 68.) An alternative is a 6- to 8-inch wide by 4-inch deep ribbon of concrete poured at ground level along the bottom of the fence. Allow the fence siding or panels to come within 2 inches of the concrete surface, but do not set the fence boards in the concrete because they will rot.

Childproof Fences. Parents of toddlers will want an open, hard-to-climb fence that can be used to enclose a play yard while allowing them to keep an eye on the children. The fence needn't be tall; 48 inches is usually sufficient for children up to 3 years old. But avoid designs that provide holds for small hands and feet. Closely spaced wire mesh (hardware cloth), or spaced, vertical-board designs are good choices here. Avoid using splintery woods or pointed pickets because a child could be injured while trying to climb fences of such materials.

Pool Fences. Swimming pool fencing has its own set of requirements, usually dictated by local building codes and city ordinances, so check with the building inspector before enclosing a pool area. Many communities define spas, garden ponds, swimming pools, open wells, or construction sites as "attractive nuisances," and local ordinances require they be fenced off for the protection of curious children (and others) who may stray into your yard. Even if your community doesn't require pool fencing, it may be a requirement under your homeowner's insurance policy. Tall, ornamental metal fencing makes an attractive alternative to conventional chain link or wire fences for pool enclosures and is extremely difficult to climb.

Likewise, the gate or gates used with pool fencing should match the fence design and construction. A tall, imposing wall or fence won't be much of a deterrent if it's fitted with a small, flimsy gate with an easily opened latch. Swimming pool fences usually require locking gates; a variety of childproof gate latches are available for pool enclosures.

Often, fences are mandatory around pools to prevent accidents. In this case, a redwood louver fence provides intimacy rather than safety, although the design is effective because it offers no horizontal handholds or footholds.

PROVIDING PRIVACY

Any tall, solid fence will block the view of your yard and house from neighbors or passersby. Such barriers can also be used to mask unattractive sights, such as storage areas, compost bins, or trash cans. However, they can also cause landscaping problems, such as casting shade on planting beds, restricting air circulation, or making you feel like a prisoner in your own yard. In short, privacy fences don't necessarily need to be made of solid siding materials; louvered, lattice, and alternate-board fences can block views into the yard, while allowing for air circulation and daylight. Panels of translucent fiber glass or acrylic can be incorporated into a fence frame to provide light and security while obscuring the view. Another option is a welded-wire or chain-link fence on which you grow ivy or other lush perennial vines.

If you're stuck with limited yard space, the trick will be to design and locate fences that provide maximum privacy

Lattice is a good choice for privacy fences because it allows for views and ventilation. Climbing plants readily cling to lattice, enhancing privacy without imparting a boxed-in feeling.

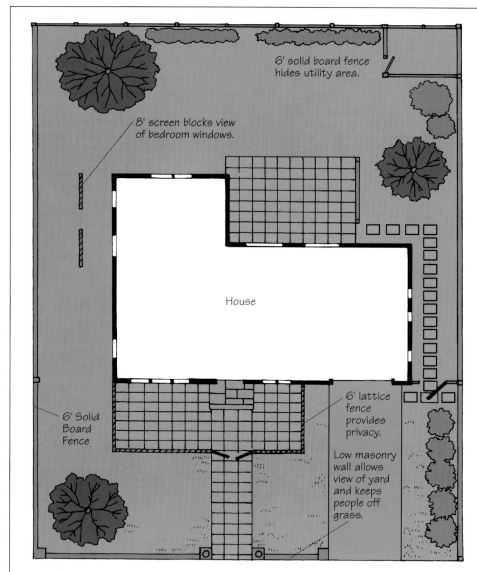

6' solid board fence hides utility area.

8' screen blocks view of bedroom windows.

House

6' Solid Board Fence

6' lattice fence provides privacy.

Low masonry wall allows view of yard and keeps people off grass.

Providing Privacy. *Use fences to control views from and to the house. Preserve views with privacy fences made from open materials, such as lattice and chain link. Vary fence heights as needed to block lines of sight into neighboring windows or private outdoor areas. Low front yard fences discourage trespassers as you show off your home.*

without creating a boxed-in feeling. By strategically placing tall, freestanding fence sections within the property (such as near bedroom windows or surrounding a deck or patio), you can create private areas, yet preserve a sense of overall openness by retaining desirable views beyond the yard. When building a continuous fence, you might choose to leave certain sections open to frame a desirable view, and install boards or panels only where they will block the line of sight from neighboring house windows. A similar effect can be achieved by alternating high and low sections along the fence line.

TEMPERING THE ENVIRONMENT

While general climatic conditions vary widely throughout the country, more subtle variations can occur within neighborhoods or even within a single yard. For example, you might have wondered why a late spring frost killed off your newly planted vegetable garden, yet left the next-door neighbor's garden unscathed. The answer has to do with microclimates, which are small areas within the yard that are affected by the amount of sun, shade, wind and moisture they

Controlling Noise

The peace and tranquility of our personal outdoor retreats can be disrupted just as much by loud street traffic, a neighbor's booming stereo, or the cacophony of children playing next door as it can from visual intrusions. As a rule, the thicker and higher the wall or fence, the more effective it will be in lowering the decibel level between you and the source of the noise. Where noise is a problem, a tall masonry wall is the best solution. Board fences and screens are much less effective in muting noise, but if you choose to go with one, make it from solid boards or plywood panels — with all cracks or gaps covered by lath or similar materials. Incorporating hedges, vines or similar vegetation is an attractive way to add another sound baffle to your design.

receive at various times of the day. You can use fences to create or modify microclimates in your yard.

Sun and Shade

Nearly every fence has a sunny side and a shady side. Depending on how the fence is oriented, you can modify the environment on either side and control sun and shade at various times of the day throughout the year. If shade is undesirable, you can build a fence with translucent panels, which admit light, yet provide privacy. Open fence designs, such as latticework panel or picket, can provide partial or filtered light.

You should also observe existing shade patterns at various times of the day during different seasons. Fences can shade areas within the property, such as decks and patios, or provide optimum growing conditions for certain types of plants. For example, a fence built along the east-west axis will cast shade on the north side throughout the year. Painting the sunny side of a fence white allows

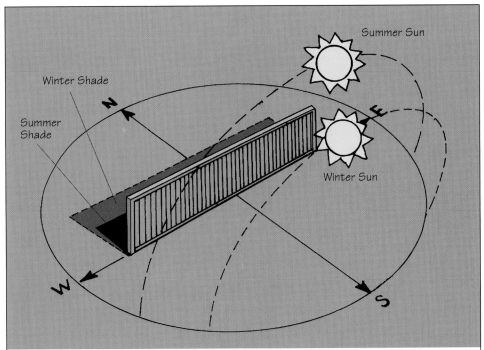

Sun and Shade. *All fences have a sunny and a shady side. You can take advantage of this by building fences to cast shade over sun-sensitive plants or onto patios, or to reflect sunlight and heat into a garden.*

it to reflect sunlight and warmth into a surrounding garden. This provides some protection against frost for plants located on the east or south side of the fence during early spring and late autumn mornings. You can also use a light-colored fence to bounce light into dark rooms in the house.

Wind

Observe how wind patterns affect your yard at various times of the day, during various seasons. In many regions, harsh prevailing winter winds blow from a different direction than do summer breezes. Strategically placed fences can serve as windbreaks to temper the force of prevailing winter winds while allowing plenty of air ventilation during the hot summer months. If you know the direction of prevailing summer breezes, you can place fences to capture and direct breezes through patios, decks, or courtyards.

Surprisingly, solid fences make the least effective windbreaks for protecting large areas of yard. Wind simply vaults over such fence designs and continues at full force several feet beyond the fence. Only a short distance directly next to the fence is protected. Open fence designs, such as lattice or spaced boards, break up the driving force of the wind into pleasant breezes, protecting a larger area behind the fence, but allowing some air circulation directly beneath them. These fences are less likely to get blown down by strong winds. Choose open designs to provide better air circulation in the yard on hot days when a cool breeze would be welcome.

The best windbreaks incorporate trees, tall shrubs, or thick vines, so you should allow such plants to grow above a fence to provide wind control, as well as security and privacy. While most communities have regulations governing the height of fences, there usually are no height limitations on trees or shrubs.

Use fences as shade screens to help cool porches or decks. In this fence, a geometric pattern of openings breaks up the solid-board design and allows air to circulate.

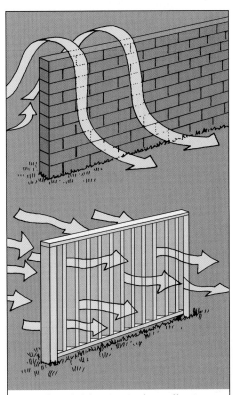

Wind. *Solid fences are less effective at blocking wind than open fences. Wind vaults over solid fences and resumes at full speed a few feet beyond them. Open fences, such as this louvered fence, allow wind to filter through at a slower velocity.*

OTHER SITE CONSIDERATIONS

Other than the environmental considerations just discussed, the type of fence you choose also will be determined by the existing and proposed architectural and landscaping features on your property. The best fence designs enhance the landscape, complement and emphasize the architecture of the house and even contribute to the overall "feel" of the neighborhood.

In planning the landscape, think of your yard as an extension of the living space in your home. Coordinate the appearance of outdoor structures and their locations with your home's colors, materials, and layout. This indoor/outdoor connection can make your house feel larger.

Architectural Accents

You can design a fence that is both functional and aesthetically pleasing by mimicking your home's architectural design. For instance, a weathered, split-rail fence perfectly accents a rustic log home in a wooded area.

With a Spanish- or Mediterranean-style house, an ornamental metal fence provides an appropriate match. For a Victorian-style home, a traditional white picket fence (perhaps accented with red roses) serves as a fitting accent.

Matching Materials and Colors. The colors and materials used for your house's exterior siding and trim can be repeated in the fence to tie together indoor and outdoor spaces. For example, the color scheme on the house can be extended to a courtyard fence to make an outdoor room, thus giving the illusion of increased floor space. Or you can install on your fence the same siding used on your house. For example, diagonal tongue-and-groove siding found on many contemporary homes makes an excellent fence siding material.

Preserving the Local Flavor. Good designs often employ regional materials that are similar or complementary to other fences in the neighborhood. Fences constructed from locally cut timbers are particularly appropriate in areas

Instead of competing with the extraordinary detailing on this Maine home, the fence's color and design help draw attention to the gingerbread woodwork.

associated with wood production, such as cedar and redwood in the Pacific Northwest or hardwood in the Northeast.

The best fence designs repeat the colors, materials, or style used in the house. Here, a weathered picket fence seems a natural extension of the simple, formal colonial home.

White picket fences help define this neighborhood's quaint, woodsy, and traditional architectural style.

Keeping Things in Scale. When designing a fence, keep in mind the overall scale of the structure. For example, a tall, vertical-board fence may look out of scale on a small suburban lot; likewise, a diminutive picket fence may get lost when surrounding a large country estate. There are no hard-and-fast rules concerning scale and proportion, and the final appearance of the fence will be governed by the aesthetic tastes of the builder. However, it might be a good idea to consult a professional landscape architect before you make your final choices. For a nominal fee, he or she can offer sound advice on keeping things in scale.

Fences that go straight from Point A to Point B are the most economical in terms of materials and labor; however, they may look out of place in an informal landscape scheme. In many cases, a curving fence, one with panels of varying heights, or one with sections staggered forward and back will look much more pleasing.

Locating Outdoor Structures

Try to anticipate how the fence location will affect interior spaces. For instance, a tall, solid fence placed near the house may obscure a view of the neighbor's house, but it also may block early morning or late afternoon sunlight through windows, making interior rooms bleak and gloomy. Consider using sections of translucent fiber glass or acrylic panels near windows to admit light while providing privacy. Alternatively, you might choose a fence with an open design, such as lattice or wire, and grow vines on the fence to provide privacy. Think of fences in terms of how they can enhance views from indoors, rather than detract from them.

When choosing a fence design, consider how it will relate to proposed plantings both on and near the structure. For example, plants can break

A low fence of light bamboo construction has the correct proportions to accompany the delicate gardens and low profile of this Japanese-style house.

An espaliered shrub is one that's been pruned to grow against a flat surface. In this case, the flat surface is a prefabricated fence panel set against a chain link fence.

The open design of an ornamental metal fence set between brick piers lets passersby enjoy the lush garden, which in turn blocks the sounds and sights of the street.

Light-colored fences provide an effective backdrop for the intense colors of flowering plants, such as these primroses. Painting a fence white also reflects light and heat into a garden for some protection from frost.

up a long, bare fence and add texture and depth. Tall shrubs, hedges, or vines can soften the institutional look of chain link or wire mesh fences while providing visual privacy and wind control.

Sections of woven wire, lattice, or chain link incorporated into solid fences and walls can provide support for climbing vines or espaliered shrubs, which are pruned to grow flat against a fence or wall. Or you can attach hanging pots, shelves, or planter boxes high up on the fence or wall to grow cascading plants or vines. On sloped sites, a series of planter boxes set atop a stepped fence provides a terraced effect that can be part of a landscape theme.

Designing a Landscape. The colors you choose for your fence should complement the color of the flowers and shrubs you place in front of it. For example, light-colored fences provide a pleasing contrast for plants with dark foliage or blooms and vice versa.

When choosing plants, find out how large or tall they will be when mature, and then consider the visual effect mature plants and shrubs will have on the fence. For example, large shrubs or hedges may eventu-

Impatiens provide a colorful, low-maintenance base that will never obscure this picket fence with massive posts.

ally obscure a low ornamental picket or wrought iron fence. Some thick, aggressive vines, such as wisteria or English ivy, can literally tear apart a thin trellis or lattice panel.

Conversely, a narrow planting bed of low annual flowers may become lost beneath a tall security fence. Choose plants that will be in scale with the fence.

CHAPTER 2

PLANNING FENCES

Now that you are aware of the functions that fences serve, you probably have in mind some attractive designs. Before you build, however, it's wise to identify hidden trouble spots in your yard that could waylay your plans. What happens on top of the soil—your yard's drainage and the location of property lines—and what's going on beneath it—buried utilities and movement due to freezing and thawing—is as important as considerations of matching fence color with plantings or creating a wind break.

Once you understand how sun, wind, rain and soil conditions affect your yard, and after you've established the locations of your property lines and any buried utilities, you can draw a site plan indicating the location, size, and type of fence you will build.

DRAINAGE PROBLEMS

If possible, observe what happens in your yard during a heavy rain. Note any existing drainage problems and determine how these problems might affect the location of fences. Also consider how the fence will change drainage patterns in the yard.

Both the type of soil and the shape of the ground influence drainage patterns in your yard. Generally, good drainage means that your lot will shed water in a heavy rain and not retain puddles in low spots. Sandy soils drain well; heavy clay soils drain poorly. Contours on the lot determine where the water will drain and collect during heavy rainstorms. The water table (natural water level in the soil) also influences drainage; if the table is high, it won't take much rain to cause flooding. If you have drainage problems on your property, determine how they will affect the fence you plan to build. Then, ask yourself what kind of drainage the project requires.

Drainage for Fences

Even if your lot drains well, consider how a new structure will alter the drainage patterns. For example, fence kickboards can block water flow, flooding the area on the uphill side. One method of handling this drainage problem is to create a shallow ditch or swale to direct runoff away from the fence. In most cases, swales have gently sloping sides and often are lined with stones or concrete to pre-

> **CAUTION**
>
> When planning grading and drainage, avoid directing runoff into your neighbors' yards. In most areas, drainage patterns in your yard are, or should be, part of a larger drainage scheme for the entire neighborhood. Be aware of how proposed landscaping changes on your property affect the overall picture.

Where fences cross natural drainage paths, it's a good idea to excavate a shallow basin or swale to allow surface water to flow beneath the fence.

vent erosion. Very shallow swales can be planted with grass or other ground covers or ivy.

Avoiding Frost Heave

In areas subject to harsh winters, wet, fine-grained soils undergo a condition called "frost heave," in which alternate freezing and thawing causes the soil to shift, often with damaging results to any structure built on it. In severe cases, frost heave will push fence posts up, weakening the fence structure.

Where frost heave is a problem, fence posts must be set in holes with a gravel subbase that extends below the frost line. The frost line is the area

In Vermont, long winters make for a deep frost line. If postholes aren't deep enough, frost heave will push the posts out of alignment. Although the fence is appropriate here, a fence in this condition won't look good around a well-maintained home.

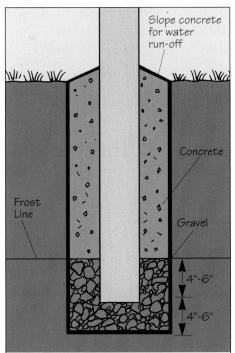

Avoiding Frost Heave. *In areas subject to frost heave, dig postholes below the frost line, fill the first 4 to 6 inches with crushed stone, set the post, add more stone, and then pour a concrete collar. Slope the top for drainage.*

below which frost doesn't penetrate in a typical winter. In areas where the frost line extends below 36 inches, consult your local building department for commonly accepted excavation practices that may save you from digging to China.

Even in areas where frost heave is not a problem, good drainage is required around fences to avoid damage to these structures. Moisture magnifies ground movement and creates erosion that will make fences sink, lean or crack; poor drainage around wood fence posts also causes rot. Gravel and sand are used to provide good drainage.

CODES AND ORDINANCES

Before you get too far along with your plans, contact your local planning council or building department to see what building codes, zoning laws, and city ordinances affect the size, design, and location of the intended fence. Most urban and

Working with Professionals

If your existing lot has serious drainage problems, or if you suspect that a fence will significantly affect drainage patterns in your yard, you should consider hiring a landscape architect, landscape designer, or soils engineer to calculate grading and drainage requirements. If large amounts of soil must be moved, or extensive trenches dug for subsurface drainage, you should hire a landscape contractor with the proper equipment to do the job.

If you are unsure of the style of fence or its location, it can help to hire a landscape architect or designer to review your plans. Most do consulting work on an hourly basis, and the money will be well-spent if the professional catches errors or omissions in the plan, points out problems you may not have considered, or recommends a more cost-efficient way to build the project.

Because fencing contractors specialize in their trade and have the equipment and crew to get the job done quickly and efficiently, you might save money by hiring a fencing contractor. Most have a portfolio of their work or can show you various jobs they've done in your area. They can build the fence to your design specifications and offer advice on structural requirements and details that would improve the design.

Typically, when hiring any contractor, you sign a standard contract that specifies what work will be done and the time frame in which it will be completed. Always make sure clean-up is in the contract.

If you plan to do a lot of the work yourself, you may opt just to hire a carpenter, mason, handyman, general laborer, or even an able-bodied college student to help you with the labor on an hourly basis. Preferably, the individual you hire should carry his own personal liability insurance; otherwise such insurance is the responsibility of the homeowner.

If you have friends or neighbors helping with the work, check with your homeowner's policy or your insurance agent to determine the limit of your liability coverage. Also remember that children like to play on piles of dirt, stacks of boards, and in wet cement. Keep the working area off limits, and make sure you are insured against lawsuits for injury if someone is hurt while in or around your construction area.

suburban communities have fence-height laws — typically a maximum of 72 inches for boundary fences in back and side yards, and 36 or 48 inches for fences bordering the street or sidewalk. In some communities, you may be able to exceed the maximum fence height if the top portion is made of wire, lattice, or other open work. If not, you can use trees or shrubs to provide privacy.

In addition to height restrictions, codes may stipulate setbacks and easements, which require that structures be built a certain distance from the street, sidewalk or property line. This is especially true if you're erecting the fence on a corner lot, where it could create a "blind corner" at a street intersection or sharp bend in the road. Usually front-yard fences more than 36 to 48 inches high must be set back a certain distance from the sidewalk; fences more than 72 inches high usually must be set back from side and rear property lines. Check local codes.

Never assume that other fences in your neighborhood meet local codes and ordinances. If you see a design that you particularly like, you might ask the owners if there are any plans for it or where they bought the materials. You might also ask permission to

In the front yard, building codes usually restrict fence heights to 48 inches or less. This homeowner planted forsythia behind a cross-buck design post-and-rail fence to block the view of the street.

reproduce the design. However, before you begin construction, check that the design conforms with guidelines set by your building department. In some cases, you'll need to get a building permit and arrange for one or more building inspections.

Check to see if there are any neighborhood covenants or restrictions that govern the style of fence. In some neighborhoods, homeowners' associations have gained the legal right to dictate what type of structure you can erect, what materials you can use, and even what colors you can paint it. Such restrictions are designed to maintain the architectural character of the neighborhood. Also, if your house has some historical significance in the community or is in a neighborhood designated as a historical area, you may have to get your plans approved by a local architectural review board to make sure the fence design is appropriate.

If your plans conflict with local zoning ordinances, you can apply for a variance: a permit or waiver to build a structure that does not adhere strictly to local property use laws. When you apply for the variance, there's usually a

fee and often a public hearing where neighbors and others involved can express their opinions. When you present your plans to the zoning commission for review, you must prove to them that you have a valid reason for requesting the variance. Even if you go through the entire process, there's no guarantee that you will be granted a variance. It's a lot easier just to keep your design within the limits of local zoning laws.

Locating Utilities

Before you start digging postholes, you must know the exact locations and depth of underground utility lines. These include water and sewer lines, as well as buried gas, electrical, and phone lines. After you've located the lines that service your own house, don't assume that more don't exist. In many housing tracts, utility companies have gained the right-of-way along front or back property lines for major underground power cables, water mains, cable TV service, or fiber-optic phone transmission lines. If you accidentally break a major phone line, TV cable, or water main while digging, you could be liable for

thousands of dollars worth of damage. If you hit a major power line, the consequences could be fatal.

Utility companies often will locate underground utilities free of charge. Underground utilities servicing your house (water, gas, sewer, and electric) may be indicated on the original deed map or site plan for your property. If your home was built recently, the local building department may have a record of utility hookup locations on your property. If your home is older, additional lines may have been added in previous remodels or landscaping jobs.

If you are uncertain where such lines exist within your property, hire a private wire/pipe/cable locating firm. These firms are listed in the yellow pages of your phone book under the heading "Utilities Underground Cable, Pipe, & Wire Locating Service" or similar heading. These services usually charge by the hour; a good firm can trace and mark all underground utilities on an average-size residential lot within one or two hours.

Locating Utilities. Before you dig postholes, ask the local utility company to check for buried water mains, electrical cables, gas lines, etc. The inspector will flag the location of any buried utility lines with a marker similar to the one pictured here.

Property-Line Fences: Know Where to Draw the Line

You need to know the exact location of the property line before you build a fence to mark it. If your fence is just 1 inch on your neighbor's side of the line, you might have to tear down the fence or face a lawsuit. In many newer subdivisions, the original survey stakes (usually a marked metal rod or wood stake driven in the ground at each corner of the property) may still be in place. If they are, show them to your neighbors and have them agree in writing that these stakes represent the actual boundaries. If you can't locate the stakes or think they may have been moved from their original position, hire a surveyor to relocate and mark the property lines, and file a record of the survey with the county. Although a simple survey of a residential tract lot can cost a few hundred dollars, it is cheap insurance against future boundary disputes, especially if you're sinking thousands of dollars into your landscape project.

Most property fences are centered directly on the property line. In this case, no matter who builds the structure, both you and your adjoining neighbors legally own it (the portion facing their yard) as tenants in common. This means that your neighbors can do what they want to their side of the fence—grow vines on it, paint wild murals on it or hang their laundry on it—anything short of actually damaging or tearing down the structure.

The best course of action is to inform the neighbors of your plans and enlist their cooperation, if possible. Then, try to come up with a design that satisfies all parties involved. With traditional board fences, it's customary (though not legally required) to build the fence so that the board side, not the frame side, faces the neighbor's property. However, there are a variety of "good neighbor" designs that look equally good from both sides. (See Chapter 5 for instructions on building these fences.) As additional insurance, you can make a written, notarized agreement with adjoining property owners that confirms the location of the property line, the type of fence that will be built on it, and who is responsible for building and maintaining it.

If you reach an impasse with any neighbor, simply build the fence 12 inches on your side of the property line. Then you can build anything you want without the neighbor's permission or cooperation, as long as the structure meets local codes and ordinances. Bear in mind that you'll be totally responsible for maintaining the fence.

MAKING A SITE PLAN

Now that you've got a better idea of what fences can do both functionally and architecturally, it's time to organize your thoughts by drawing a detailed site plan of your yard. This drawing forces you to think out your intentions and will save time and money when you integrate future projects into the overall scheme. When it comes time to build the fence, you can use the plan to help estimate materials. Even if you are hiring a landscape architect, the site plan will help you communicate your needs and desires.

The idea is simple: You start with a base map of the property that includes property lines, the house, and all other existing features. Then you use tracing-paper overlays—as many as you want—to sketch your ideas. Allot spaces within the yard for such features as lawns, planting beds, decks, patios, play areas, and storage areas. Then determine where fences, gates, and trellises will be needed. When you come up with a plan you like, you can make a final drawing of the site plan. Here's how to proceed:

1 Draw the base map. If you have an existing deed map or site plan of your property, reproduce it exactly on a large piece of tracing paper that has graph lines on it (available at stationary shops or art supply stores). For large landscape projects, draw the entire property; show its overall dimensions, its orientation (relative to North), the location of the house, and setback distances and easements from property lines, buildings, and the street. For small landscape projects, such as a backyard, just draw the portion of the property where the fence will go.

The base map should also show your house's floor plan. If you have architect's blueprints of your house, use these to show interior rooms and the location of doors and windows.

If the original site plan or blueprints aren't available, take careful measurements of the property and transfer these to a large sheet of graph-lined tracing paper. A scale of ¼ inch equals 12 inches or ⅛ inch equals 12 inches should enable you to put the entire plan on one sheet. Measure from the property lines to locate a front corner of the house. Use this corner as a starting point to measure the outside dimensions of the house and transfer them to the plan.

2 Locate additional features. On the base map, show the location of other buildings and permanent structures on the property, such as existing walks, walls, fences, detached garage, storage sheds, decks, patios, and the like. Show the location of underground utility lines, pipes and cables. Draw in the size and location of existing plantings, such as trees, hedges, and shrubs, as well as lawn areas, planting beds, and borders. Indicate which trees and shrubs are to be kept and which will need to be removed or relocated.

3 Show other factors that affect the yard. On the base map, indicate the direction of prevailing winds, and existing sun/shade pat-

With good planning, fences, gates, and trellises can be combined with other structures, such as a gazebo, and even plants and rock formations to create a beautiful, comfortable outdoor living space.

terns in the yard (direction of morning and afternoon sun). Note the existing drainage patterns, along with any outside factors that affect the yard, such as noise or privacy problems, and views that you want to retain or obscure. If you find that the base map is becoming too cluttered, you can show these features on a separate overlay attached to the map.

4 Locate new features on overlays.
Attach an overlay of tracing paper to the base map. Draw in the exact sizes and locations of new fences, along with any other proposed landscape features. Note the heights and construction materials on the overlay. If the lot will require extensive regrading, the building department may want to see spot elevations of the lot on the final plans. This work is best left to a surveyor or landscape architect. Use as many overlay sheets as needed to come up with a suitable plan. Now is the time to experiment. When you conceive a final plan, place the overlay sheet(s) underneath the base map and neatly trace in the new features on the base map. This will be your final drawing that you will submit to the building department when you apply for a permit (if necessary).

NOTE: As an alternative to drawing a site plan, there are a variety of computer programs you can buy that will serve the same purpose. Some of these landscape-planning programs allow you to view your yard in three dimensions and from all angles, enabling you to "walk through" the yard on your computer screen. Others include plant lists to help you select plantings.

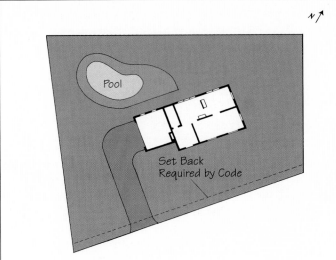

1. Use the original site plan to draw a base map showing the shape and size of the lot, the location of the house, and its floor plan. Show other major features, such as a driveway or pool, and the direction of North.

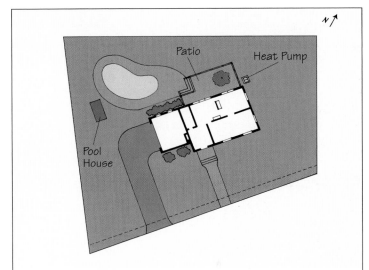

2. Add to the base map other significant details of the lot, such as large trees and shrubs, walks, patios, and outbuildings.

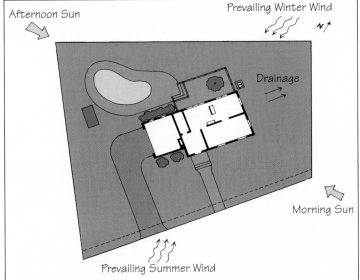

3. Complete the base map by indicating the direction of morning and afternoon sun, prevailing summer and winter winds, and views you wish to preserve or eliminate.

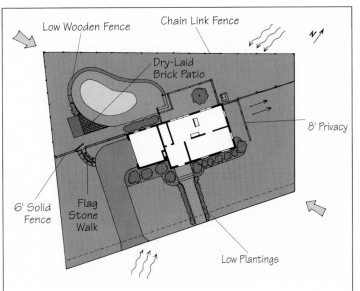

4. With the base map complete, attach separate sheets of tracing paper showing the proposed landscape, including the locations of fences, gates, trellises, and other structures.

TOOLS & MATERIALS

To build a fence, gate, or trellis, you'll need carpentry and digging tools. Most of these tools, such as shovels, hammers, and hand saws, are found in almost any home, and you can rent the tools you don't have from your local rental shop. Such tools include posthole diggers, portable cement mixers, various mason's tools, or paint spray rigs.

You'll have to choose the type and amount of lumber and related materials—fasteners, hardware, and concrete, to name a few—required to build the fence design you've chosen. Remember to order specialty items, such as decorative moldings or beveled siding, well in advance so that they'll be on hand when you're ready to start construction.

LAYOUT AND DIGGING TOOLS

To mark the fence line and determine the location of the fence posts, you'll need mason's twine (or sturdy, non-stretchable string), a 50- or 100-foot tape measure, a stick of red or other bright-colored chalk, a plumb bob, wooden stakes, and a mallet or hammer to drive the stakes. To lay out corners, extra stakes will be required to construct batter boards. (See "Setting Posts," page 51, for how to set up batter boards.)

Postholes generally need to be deep (usually at least 2½ feet) and narrow (about twice the width of the post; for

4x4 and 6x6 posts, that's about 8 to 12 inches in diameter). Digging such deep, narrow holes isn't easy with a shovel; instead, use a clamshell digger or hand auger. Clamshell diggers are better for hard or rocky soil; hand augers work best in loose or sandy soil. The depth of the postholes you'll be able to dig depends on the length of the tool's handles; generally, cheaper tools have shorter handles, so they dig smaller holes. If the soil is hard and rocky, you can use a modified clamshell digger with a lever that traps loose dirt, or you can use a pickaxe, a digging bar, or possibly a jackhammer to break up and remove the rocks. If you have a lot of holes to dig, it will be worthwhile to rent a power auger from a local tool rental shop. This tool works like a large, gasoline-powered drill for boring holes in the ground. One-person and two-person models are available. If you have a helper, you'll find the two-person model easier to operate.

If you're setting the posts in concrete, you'll need a hoe, shovel, and wheelbarrow or sheet of plywood for mixing concrete. Although you can mix the concrete directly in the posthole rather than in a wheelbarrow, you'll still need a wheelbarrow to transport the dry concrete to the postholes.

For fast and efficient joinery, put together fences, gates, and trellises with galvanized screws driven by a cordless driver drill.

Posts need to stand straight up and down, or plumb. You can plumb posts vertically with an ordinary 24-inch level, although the job will go faster if you use a special two-way post level like the one shown in the drawing "Fencing Tools." The level plumbs posts on two faces at once and is available at most large home centers and hardware stores. A line level and string come in handy for setting posts to the same height and determining rail locations on the posts. Or you might purchase an inexpensive water level—a clear plastic tube filled with colored water—to level the post tops and lay out rail locations.

Chain link fences require a few specialized tools, which can be purchased or rented at a rental shop or where you buy the chain link fencing. These tools are shown in Chapter 6. Other specialized tools required for

Fencing Tools

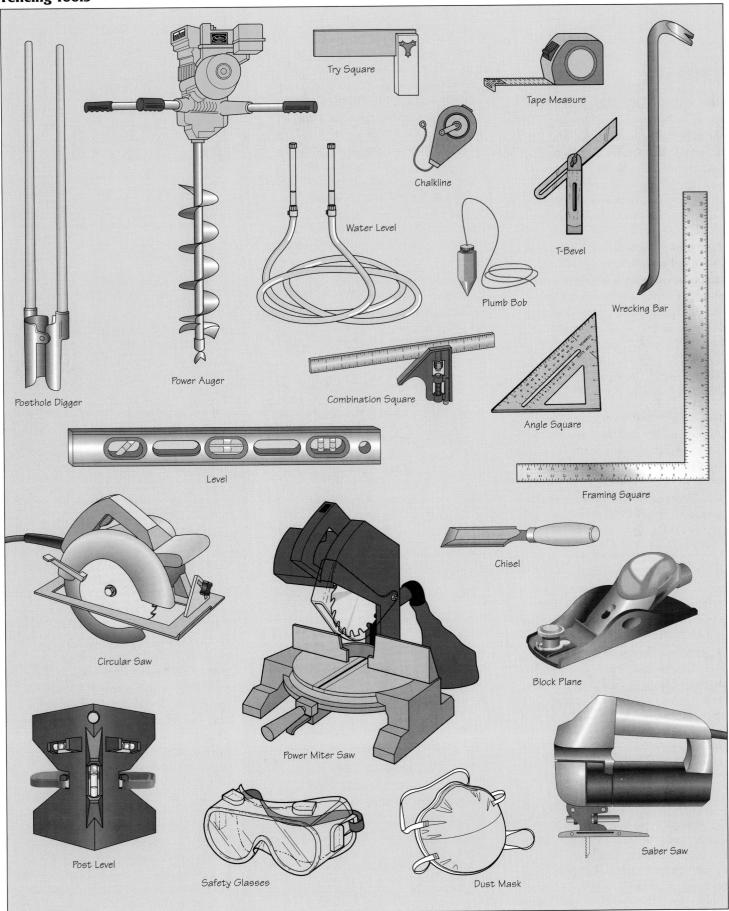

Posthole Digger

Power Auger

Try Square

Tape Measure

Chalkline

Water Level

T-Bevel

Plumb Bob

Wrecking Bar

Combination Square

Angle Square

Framing Square

Level

Chisel

Circular Saw

Block Plane

Power Miter Saw

Post Level

Safety Glasses

Dust Mask

Saber Saw

various fence projects shown in this book are listed in the step-by-step instructions for each, as needed.

LUMBER

If you're building a fence, gate, or trellis of wood, one of the most important decisions you'll need to make is what type and quality of lumber you'll use. Lumber comes in a wide variety of sizes, shapes, grades, and surface textures. For the most part, however, your choices will be limited to what's readily available at local lumberyards and home centers. Prices and quality can vary by quite a bit from store to store, so it's worthwhile to estimate the amounts you need and do some comparative shopping.

When you purchase the lumber, it also pays to hand-pick each piece because quality can vary widely within any given stack. Many dealers don't mind if you check each board, as long as you leave the remaining pile neat and orderly. If all the lumber looks like junk, find out when the next shipment will arrive and be there early to get the pick of the pile. Or try another lumberyard.

When buying fencing lumber, you'll have to make three separate, but integrated choices: what to use for the posts, what to use for the rails, and what to use for the siding, if any. Most wood fences use 4x4 or 6x6 posts and 2x4 rails. Wood siding may be boards, pickets, lath, or even plywood.

Decay Resistance

For a long fence life, choose a decay-resistant wood. Pressure-treated posts and rails are your best bet: They are widely available and typically cost less and last longer than naturally decay-resistant species, such as redwood or red cedar. Most treated lumber is preserved with chromated copper arsenate (CCA), which gives the wood its characteristic green or greenish-brown color. This type of treated lumber is easily stained. If left bare, the wood will eventually

lose its green color and weather to a silvery gray.

CCA pressure-treated wood is rated for above-ground use or for contact with the ground, based on the amount of preservative injected into the wood. Lumber labeled 0.25—which means it contains preservative in a concentration of 0.25 pound per cubic foot (pcf)—should be used only above ground. For use in contact with the ground, buy lumber rated at 0.40 pcf. You can't always find lumber that's labeled, however, so ask at the lumberyard or home center whether the lumber is rated for ground contact.

Properly installed, pressure-treated posts and rails will last as long as

Pressure-Treated Lumber's Stamp

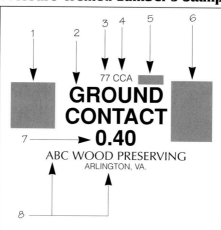

1— Trademark of building code–approved quality-control agency

2— Proper exposure conditions

3— Year of treatment

4— The preservative used for treatment

5— Drying procedure, if applicable

6— Trademark of agency supervising the treating plant

7— Preservative retention level and/or the quality-control agency procedure indication

8— Treating company and plant location

The most important information included on a treated-lumber stamp is the treatment amount (0.40), and where the lumber may be used (ground contact).

50 years, according to manufacturers. However, because the preservative does not penetrate completely through the wood, you'll need to treat any cut ends with a wood preservative. Orient posts with the uncut end down, and treat the top with preservative. You can buy wood preservatives under several common brand names in hardware stores and home centers; better preservative formulas also contain a water repellent. You can apply preservative by either brushing it on the end grain or soaking the ends of boards and posts in a container of preservative. When applying preservatives, wear heavy rubber gloves, long sleeves, goggles, and a respirator designed to filter mists and vapors.

The preservative in treated lumber will not easily leach out of the wood, so you do not need to worry about contamination of garden soil or plants from a few posts. However, the sawdust is toxic, so cut the lumber outdoors while wearing a dust mask.

Other types of wood preservatives include creosote and borate salts. Creosote should not be used because it is toxic to plants and animals. Borate-treated lumber is effective against carpenter ants, termites, and other wood-boring insects. But it has only limited effectiveness against fungus and mold.

Posts and rails made from decay-resistant species, such as redwood or cedar, often are used when appearance is a factor, such as when repeating house-siding materials in the fence. The surfaces of redwood and cedar posts and rails are either smooth (dressed) or rough-sawn for a rustic appearance.

Generally, untreated softwoods, such as fir, pine, spruce, or hemlock, should not be used for fences. If you do use these woods, keep them painted or stained with a stain-preservative to protect them from the elements. Never use these softwoods for posts or other members that come in contact with the ground.

Lumber Grading Stamp

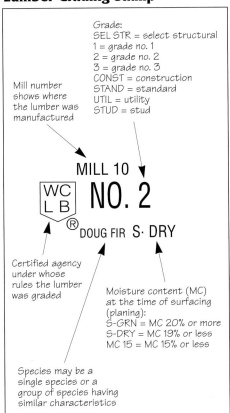

Grade:
SEL STR = select structural
1 = grade no. 1
2 = grade no. 2
3 = grade no. 3
CONST = construction
STAND = standard
UTIL = utility
STUD = stud

Mill number shows where the lumber was manufactured

MILL 10

WCLB NO. 2

DOUG FIR S· DRY

Certified agency under whose rules the lumber was graded

Moisture content (MC) at the time of surfacing (planing):
S-GRN = MC 20% or more
S-DRY = MC 19% or less
MC 15 = MC 15% or less

Species may be a single species or a group of species having similar characteristics

Lumber may bear a grading stamp to help you choose a particular quality board.

Lumber Grades

When you go to the lumberyard, you'll discover that lumber comes in many different grades, usually identified by stamps on the lumber. The best grades are also the most expensive and probably inappropriate for fence construction. Lower grades have more defects, including knots, splits, bends, and even rot. A lot of lower grade lumber is perfectly acceptable for fence construction, but you'll have to dig through the stacks to find pieces with defects that you can live with or cut off.

You can't always rely on grade stamps alone. Lumberyards often mix grades when the lumber is restacked in the yard or may apply their own designations, such as premium, economy, decking, or garden grade. Also, lumber may not be properly stacked or stored, which results in twisting, warping, decay, or the growth of mildew. You can skirt all these problems by selecting your lumber by hand. If you're using pressure-treated lumber, No. 1 grade is the best quality, followed by No. 2 grade and No. 3 grade. No. 2 grade is a good compromise between cost and quality.

Redwood Grades

The redwood trees of California and the Pacific Northwest are legendary for their size and the quality of the lumber they provide. Redwood's beautiful straight grain, natural glowing color, and weather resistance have traditionally marked it as the Cadillac of outdoor building materials.

You can usually tell sapwood from heartwood by color: the sapwood is lighter and hardly makes one think of *red* wood. Redwood heartwood is extremely weather- and insect-resistant, but the sapwood may start to rot in two or three years if it has contact with the ground or if it will remain wet for long periods of time. Treat sapwood before applying it, and use it only where it will be dry for most of the year.

Lumber Grades

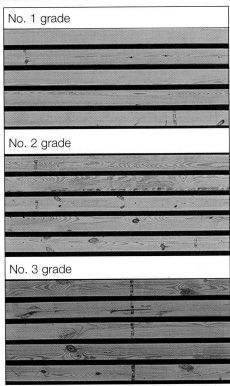

No. 1 grade

No. 2 grade

No. 3 grade

Even if the boards aren't stamped, you can tell higher grade lumber from lower by the amount of defects, such as knots and splits, in the boards.

Redwood Grading

From Left to Right: Construction Heart/Deck Heart, Construction Common/Deck Common, Merchantable Heart, Merchantable, Clear All-Heart, Clear, B-Heart, and B-Grade.

You can let redwood "go gray" by not treating it with anything; it will reach a light gray color and a slight sheen that many people find attractive. Or you can treat it with stains and a U.V. blocker to keep it close to its original color.

Redwood grades are established by the Redwood Inspection Service of the California Redwood Association. Architectural grades are the best-looking and most expensive grades of redwood. Garden Grades are more economical and have more knots. Both categories of redwood are available kiln-dried or unseasoned and are usually surfaced on four sides.

Garden grades of redwood are suitable for most fence-building applications. They include:

Construction Heart/Deck Heart.

This is an all-heartwood grade containing knots. It is recommended for work on or near the ground, such as posts, beams, joists, and decking. It is the most expensive garden grade redwood. Deck Heart looks the same as construction heart, but it is graded for strength so it can be used in deck construction. Deck Heart is available in 2x4 and 2x6 only and isn't really suited to fence work.

Construction Common/Deck Common.

Any redwood grade that doesn't have heart in its name is a mixture of heart and sapwood. Construction and deck common are cheaper than their all-heart counterparts, but a board may contain noticeable differences in color. Other than that, construction common and deck common are identical to the construction and deck heart. They cost less than heart. Construction common is a good choice for fence rails.

Merchantable Heart.

This is the most economical all-heartwood grade. It allows larger knots and smaller knot holes. It is suitable for fences and posts. It is the grade found in most prefabricated fencing.

Merchantable.

This has the same characteristics as Merchantable Heart but contains sapwood. It is suitable for fence boards and trellises as well as above ground garden and utility applications. It is usually the least expensive grade available.

Architectural grades are more expensive than garden grades and include:

Clear All-Heart.

All heartwood and free from knots, this wood is recommended for highly visible applications, and should be reserved for sophisticated, high-end fences.

Clear.

Similar in quality to clear all-heart, expect that Clear contains sapwood. Clear is ideal for highly visible applications where the wood won't be subjected to rot.

B-Heart.

Containing limited knots, but no sapwood, B-Heart is a less costly alternative to Clear All-Heart.

B-Grade.

Similar characteristics to B-Heart, but contains sapwood; same uses as Clear.

Softwood Grades

Grade	Description
Select	Highest quality, containing few or no defects. Used for finish trim and cabinetry or where high structural strength is required.
Common	Most often used for house framing, outdoor structures and general garden use. Classifications within this category range from No. 1 (best) to No. 5 (unusable for most applications). No. 1 or No. 2 Common is a good compromise between strength, appearance, and cost.

Plywood Grades

Plywood siding comes in many textures and patterns. From left to right at top are Texture 1-11 (T1-11), which has grooves, and medium-density overlay (MDO), which comes smooth or texture-embossed (both are shown). MDO comes with or without grooves. At far right is a pattern called channel groove. At bottom from left are rough-sawn plywood in panel form and rough-sawn plywood lap siding, followed by brushed-texture plywood and, at far right, Com-ply, which is a composite panel with rough-sawn face veneer.

Plywood Grades. Exterior plywood comes in various thicknesses and surface textures and often is used as an economical alternative to boards when a solid fence is desired. The American Plywood Association labels panels to show their application and grade, as well as other specifications. Panels for outdoor use are stamped "Ext." or "Siding," followed by some other numbers and/or letters. Don't use plywood designated as "x" for fences. The "x" stands for exposure, meaning the plywood is intended for house sheathing which will be exposed only temporarily.

In many cases, plywood siding used for the house, such as T1-11, is repeated in fences to provide architectural unity. Siding panels are numbered "303" and may be plain or grooved. Plywood is also available with resin-impregnated overlays, called medium-density overlay (MDO) or high-density overlay (HDO), for a hard, smooth, paintable surface on one or both faces. Other siding panels have rough-sawn surface veneers for a rustic appearance. Exterior plywood may be sanded on one or both sides or coated with resin overlays. There are no grooves or rustic surface tex-

tures. The charts show the various grades and applications of exterior plywood siding and sheathing.

Lumber Defects

Depending on their severity, lumber defects may affect a board's appearance, structural strength, or both. Lower grades of lumber have more

Plywood Siding Grades

Class	Grade	Description
Special Series 303	303-OC	Clear, so it has no patches. Recommended for staining. Limited availability.
	303-OL	Resin overlay on one or both sides is hard, smooth, paintable. Limited availability.
	303-NR	Rough veneer surface with no patches. Recommended for staining. Limited availability.
	303-SR	Rough hardboard surface veneer with some synthetic patches that mimic rough-sanded surface. Recommended for staining. Limited availability.
303-6	303-6-W	Wood surface veneer with no more than 6 patches. May be stained or painted. Limited availablity.
	303-6-S	Synthetic surface veneer (hardboard) with no more than 6 synthetic patches. Recommended for painting. Limited availability.
	303-6-S/W	Surface veneer combines hardboard and natural wood with no more than 6 wood or synthetic patches. Recommended for painting. Limited availability.
303-18	303-18-W	Wood surface veneer with no more than 18 patches. Recommended for painting, but may be stained.
	303-18-S	Synthetic surface veneer with no more than 18 synthetic patches; recommended for painting.
	303-18-S/W	Combination wood/synthetic wood surface veneer with no more than 18 patches of either material. Recommended for painting.
303-30	303-30-W	Least expensive all-wood surface with no more than 30 patches. Not recommended for stain.
	303-30-S	Least expensive all-synthetic surface with no more than 30 patches. Recommended for painting.
	303-30-S/W	Least expensive grade. No more than 30 wood and/or synthetic patches. Paint only.

Exterior Plywood Grades

Grade	Description
A-A Exterior	Highest quality, has good appearance on both sides; usually no knots or defects. No "voids" (missing wood) in interior. Easy to paint and stain. Use on fences where you want the same appearance on both sides.
A-B Exterior	One side good (no knots or knotholes); back is smooth, but may have some tight knots. Larger knots or knotholes may be cut out and plugged with wood patches, called "footballs." Few or no voids in plies. Can be used for same applications as A-A, if sanded, primed, and painted.
A-C Exterior	One side is good; back has knots, small knotholes, other minor defects; larger knots may be plugged. Some small voids between plies. Use when attaching panels to one side of fence framework, good side facing out.
B-B Exterior	Both sides reasonably smooth; may contain small splits, knots, knotholes, or other minor defects in surface plies; some voids between plies. Usually easy to paint with minor patching required.
B-C Exterior	One side rough; other side reasonably smooth with small, tight knots, minor splits, and patches. Use as a base for exterior coatings such as stucco or shingles.

defects than higher grades. For example, you can expect to find plenty of knots in lower lumber grades. A knot occurs where a limb joins the tree trunk. Knots usually affect appearance only, but large, loose ones can weaken the lumber. Knots may be sound (tight), loose, or missing, resulting in a knothole.

Checks, splits, and shakes are cracks in wood caused by improper seasoning or natural defects in the tree. Even in lower grades of lumber, these defects usually don't run the full length of the board, so often you can cut off the damaged portion and use the good part. Wane is the lack of wood, or presence of bark, on the edge or corner of a board cut too close to the outside of a log. Again, you might be able to cut off the affected area. In some cases, you can orient the board or framing member to hide the defect, such as placing the defective side of a rail toward the boards, provided there's enough nailing surface.

Warped Lumber. Warped boards might be twisted, bowed, crooked, cupped, or any combination of these distortions. Because they aren't flat, warped boards make it harder to assemble fence components accurately, and they affect the appearance of the finished structure.

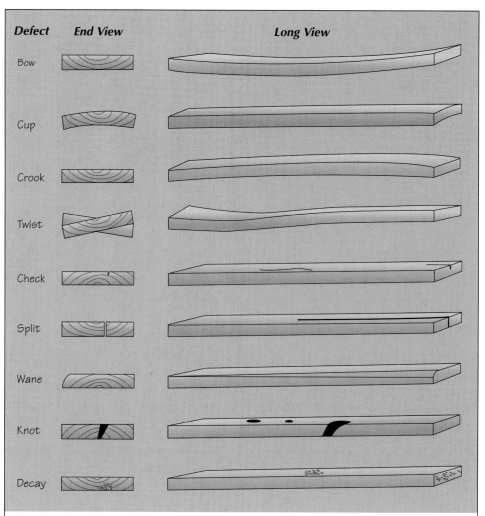

Defect	End View	Long View
Bow		
Cup		
Crook		
Twist		
Check		
Split		
Wane		
Knot		
Decay		

Lumber Defects. Here are examples of common problems with lumber. You can avoid many of them by handpicking your own lumber and storing it in stacks off of the ground with spaces between the boards.

Warped Lumber. Check that the board is straight by holding it on edge and looking down the top edge.

To avoid having to deal with warped boards, pick straight boards from the lumberyard by "sighting" every board. To sight a board, pick up one end, hold it so the narrower dimension is facing up (with a 2x4, for example, a 1½-inch side will face up), and with one eye, look down the top edge. If the board is warped, you'll see it. Detecting a cupped board is a simple matter of looking at the end. It should be flat, not U-shaped.

If you opt to have the lumberyard pick and deliver lumber to your site, you'll get your share of warped boards. In this case, sort through the pile and pick out the best boards for use in the most important positions. For example, choose the straightest posts for corners and ends, and the truest siding boards for the most visible areas of the fence, such as in the front yard. Stack these straight, true boards neatly until you're ready to use them. Once the lumber is integrated into the fence structure, it's less likely to warp because it will be held in place with nails or other fasteners. Sometimes, minor bows or crookscan be "worked out" of the board when you fasten it in place if you've got something to nail to at the middle of the board.

Parasite Problems. Another factor affecting lumber grade is the presence of parasitic damage or rot. Some common forms manifest themselves as holes—white speck, honeycomb, and wood-boring insect damage—and decay or dry rot. Mildly damaged low-grade boards may be acceptable for wood-fence construction and are an inexpensive alternative to premium-grade lumber. Holes can be filled with wood patch, decay can be scraped away, and the sound wood can be painted or treated with a preservative.

Lumber Sizes

The term "nominal" refers to the dimensions of lumber at the time it is cut at the mill; for example, a 2x4 measures a full 2 inches by 4 inches. However, after the lumber is dried (usually in a kiln) and surfaced or planed to a uniform width and thickness, the actual dimensions are less. For example, a surfaced, kiln-dried 2x4 has an actual size of 1½ inches by 3½ inches. A rough-sawn, unseasoned 2x4 will measure much closer to the nominal dimension. The chart shows a comparison of nominal versus actual lumber dimensions.

Lumber Size

Dimensional lumber is dried and planed, so it is smaller than its nominal size. These sizes are industry standards; slight variations will occur.

Lumber	Nominal Size (inches)	Actual Size (inches)
Boards	1x3	¾" x 2½"
	1x4	¾" x 3½"
	1x6	¾" x 5½"
	1x8	¾" x 7¼"
	1x10	¾" x 9¼"
	1x12	¾" x 11¼"
Dimension Lumber	2x2	1½" x 1½"
	2x3	1½" x 2½"
	2x4	1½" x 3½"
	2x6	1½" x 5½"
	2x8	1½" x 7¼"
	2x10	1½" x 9¼"
	2x12	1½" x 11¼"
Posts	4x4	3½" x 3½"
	6x6	5½" x 5½"

Lumber Surfaces

Surfaced (dressed) lumber is planed to create one or more smooth sides. Fence boards or lath may be surfaced on one side (S1S); two sides (S2S), one edge (S1E), two edges (S2E) or all four sides (S4S). Generally, the more surfaces that are planed, the more expensive the lumber. Most framing lumber and pressure-treated lumber is S4S. If you want a finished appearance or if you plan to paint the fence, use S4S for posts and rails, and S1S or S2S for siding.

Rough-sawn lumber has not been planed. It has a splintery appearance, often showing saw marks, and it lacks the uniformity of surfaced lumber (width and thickness may vary slightly from one board to the next). Usually, you can buy rough-sawn lumber at large lumberyards. Rough-sawn costs less than surfaced lumber, making it a good choice for rustic-looking fences. To preserve rough-sawn wood, paints or stains can be applied with a brush or a spray gun.

Moisture Content

In living trees, wood moisture content can be well over 50 percent; that is, more than half the tree's mass is water. After it is cut, wood dries and shrinks, which can cause splits, checks, and warping unless drying conditions are carefully controlled. For this reason, most lumber is air dried or kiln dried to remove moisture before it is sold.

In some lumberyards, kiln-dried lumber is placed under cover, while green lumber (sometimes called garden-grade lumber) is stacked out in the yard. Remember, "green" lumber isn't green in color. The only green-colored lumber you'll find is pressure-treated stock, which is kiln-dried. No matter what the designation, you often can determine moisture content simply by hefting the board: Green boards will be heavier than dry ones. Green lumber is usually less expensive than kiln-dried or air-dried lumber and is generally easier to nail, but green lumber will shrink as it dries, causing nails to loosen and gaps to appear between fence boards. Splits usually occur at board ends if the lumber dries out too quickly.

Therefore, the use of kiln- or air-dried lumber is recommended. However, in an outdoor environment, even kiln-dried lumber will swell and shrink with changes in humidity, which can cause boards to warp and board ends to split at nail-hole locations. Treating the wood with a water repellent or wood-stabilizing treatment (available in gallon cans at paint stores and home centers) will minimize warping and splitting. Predrilling nail or screw holes near board ends also will help prevent splitting.

Estimating and Ordering Lumber

Most lumberyards sell precut lumber by the running foot, typically in 24-inch increments. Precut fence boards are an exception; many are sold in 60-inch lengths. Lumber may also be sold by the board foot, especially if you're buying very large amounts. A board foot is equal to the amount of wood contained in a board 1 foot wide by 1 foot long by 1 inch thick. Remember that board-foot sizes are nominal, not actual, and are used for ordering purposes only; you'll need to take this into account when estimating the actual number of boards required to cover the fence.

To help estimate the actual amount and lengths of posts, rails, and siding materials, measure the overall length of the fence line, then plot and mark the locations of the posts. To figure rail sizes and amounts, measure the distance between each post to get rail lengths. (If the rails will be set in mortised or dadoed posts, add the extra length to the rails.) Next, determine the number of fence sections needed, and multiply this figure by the number of rails in each section to get the total number of rails required.

To determine how many boards, pickets, or other siding pieces are required to cover one section, divide the length of the section by the actual width of the board or picket. Then, multiply this figure by the number of sections in the fence. Remember to use actual board widths in your calculations, not nominal widths. Buy one or two extra posts and rails and a few extra boards or pickets to allow for cutting errors. If you're using fancy pickets or trim pieces, order a few extra for future repairs.

To avoid wasting lumber, it's best to lay out the fence to take advantage of standard lengths. For example, you can space posts on 72- or 96-inch centers, rather than 60- or 84-inch centers. If you must use odd spacings, determine how to make best use of standard lengths. Plan your cuts to maximize the use of wood.

If you're cutting shorter boards from longer ones, but you don't have access to a truck with a lumber rack, have the lumber delivered. There may be a delivery fee. If delivery works out to your advantage, be prepared to have a stack of lumber dropped in your driveway or on an accessible part of your property.

FASTENERS

Nails and screws are the most common fasteners used in fence construction. Sometimes, bolts and various metal connectors are used where additional strength is required, such as in areas prone to high winds or seismic activity.

Nails

For fences, nails make the weakest connections, but they're inexpensive and more than adequate for most applications. Box nails and common nails are used to fasten rails to posts and some types of siding to rails. Common nails are slightly thicker than box nails and have better holding power, but they're harder to drive and are more likely to split the wood at board and rail ends. To avoid splitting wood, blunt nail ends with a hammer, and predrill nailholes near board ends. Galvanized exterior finishing nails and casing nails are used to attach decorative moldings, lath, and similar features where exposed nailheads would detract from the appearance of the fence. These nails have less holding power than box or common nails. Spiral-shank nails (also called screw nails) and ring-shank nails hold better than do box or common nails, but are harder to drive, tend to split wood, and are extremely difficult to remove if you make a mistake. Commonly, spiral-shank nails are used for plywood siding. Duplex nails have double heads for easy removal; use these for temporary nailing, such as when attaching temporary braces to fences posts.

Nails used for fencing should be rust resistant. Galvanized nails are most often used for outdoor applications. Aluminum nails also resist rust, but they bend easily and are more expensive than galvanized nails. Stainless steel nails offer the best rust protection, but they're even more expensive than aluminum nails.

Nails are sold by the pound, and their lengths are designated by the symbol "d" which means "penny." For example, an 8-penny or 8d nail is 2½ inches long. Half the length of the nail should be in each of the pieces you are nailing together. Typically, you would use 8d or 10d nails to toenail 2x4 rails to 4x4 posts; use 6d nails to attach 1-inch boards to

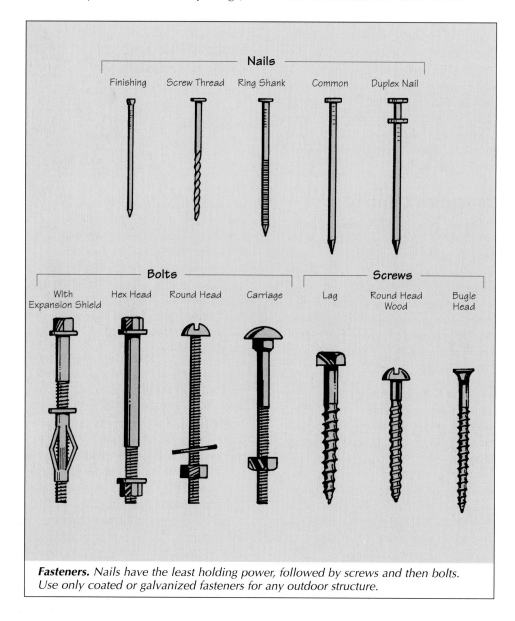

Fasteners. *Nails have the least holding power, followed by screws and then bolts. Use only coated or galvanized fasteners for any outdoor structure.*

Nail Sizes

Penny Weight	Length (inches)	Approx. Number per Pound (Common Nails)
60d	6	10
50d	5½	15
40d	5	20
30d	4½	25
20d	4	30
16d	3½	50
12d	3¼	65
10d	3	70
8d	2½	105
7d	2¼	160
6d	2	180
5d	1¾	270
4d	1½	315
3d	1¼	570
2d	1	875

2x4 rails. The "Nail Sizes" chart shows the sizes of various nails and how many are in a pound.

Screws

Screws provide much greater holding power than nails. Wood screws fall into three categories: roundhead, flathead, and buglehead. Usually, roundhead and flathead screws are slotted and require predrilling. Bugleheads, which have sharp points, and Phillips heads, which are self-tapping (they don't require pilot holes), come as either fine-threaded black all-purpose screws or coarse-threaded galvanized deck screws. Deck screws are used often in fence and deck construction. They can be driven easily with a Phillips screwdriver bit chucked in a variable-speed electric drill or power screwdriver. Screws should be driven flush with the wood surface or slightly countersunk. As with nails, use galvanized screws for all outdoor applica-tions. Choose #8 or #10 gauge screws long enough to reach through the top board and three-quarters of the way into the bottom board. If part of the screw shank is unthreaded, that part should extend completely through the top piece of wood. The "Screw Sizes" chart below shows the various sizes available.

Before driving screws near the ends of boards, it's a good idea to drill pilot holes to avoid splitting wood. Some drill bits also countersink the holes so that the screw head can be recessed below the wood surface. In this case, you can create a fine finished fence by gluing a dowel plug in the countersink hole or filling the hole with wood putty to hide and protect the screw head.

Other Fasteners

Bolts, masonry anchors, and various metal connectors sometimes are used in fence construction. Bolts, for example, are appropriate for joining heavy wood-framing members, such as 6x6 posts and rails. Masonry anchors and screws are used to attach wood members to masonry surfaces, such as brick or concrete walls and columns. Metal connectors can reinforce connections between posts and rails and are used for special applications, such as attaching posts to existing concrete patios. Common types of fasteners are shown in the drawing on page 32.

Concrete and Gravel

Even if you're setting posts in concrete, you should first place a few

Screw Sizes

Length (inches)	Available Shank Number (approx. diameter in inches)
½	2 (1/16) 3 (1/16) 4 (1/8) 5 (1/8) 6 (1/8) 7 (1/8) 8 (3/16)
⅝	3 (1/16) 4 (1/8) 5 (1/8) 6 (1/8) 7 (1/8) 8 (3/16) 9 (3/16) 10 (3/16)
¾	4 (1/8) 5 (1/8) 6 (1/8) 7 (1/8) 8 (3/16) 9 (3/16) 10 (3/16) 11 (3/16)
⅞	6 (1/8) 7 (1/8) 8 (3/16) 9 (3/16) 10 (3/16) 11 (3/16) 12 (3/16)
1	6 (1/8) 7 (1/8) 8 (3/16) 9 (3/16) 10 (3/16) 11 (3/16) 12 (3/16) 14 (1/4)
1¼	6 (1/8) 7 (1/8) 8 (3/16) 9 (3/16) 10 (3/16) 11 (3/16) 12 (3/16) 14 (1/4) 16 (1/4) 18 (5/16)
1½	6 (1/8) 7 (1/8) 8 (3/16) 9 (3/16) 10 (3/16) 11 (3/16) 12 (3/16) 14 (1/4) 16 (1/4) 18 (5/16)
1¾	8 (3/16) 9 (3/16) 10 (3/16) 11 (3/16) 12 (3/16) 14 (1/4) 16 (1/4) 18 (5/16) 20 (5/16)
2	8 (3/16) 9 (3/16) 10 (3/16) 11 (3/16) 12 (3/16) 14 (1/4) 16 (1/4) 18 (5/16) 20 (5/16)
2¼	9 (3/16) 10 (3/16) 11 (3/16) 12 (3/16) 14 (1/4) 16 (1/4) 18 (5/16) 20 (5/16)
2½	12 (3/16) 14 (1/4) 16 (1/4) 18 (5/16) 20 (5/16)
2¾	14 (1/4) 16 (1/4) 18 (5/16) 20 (5/16)
3	16 (1/4) 18 (5/16) 20 (5/16)
3½	18 (5/16) 20 (5/16) 24 (3/8)
4	18 (5/16) 20 (5/16) 24 (3/8)

inches of gravel in the posthole. Ideally, the stone sizes should be ½ to 1 inch. Gravel is sold either in sacks or by the cubic yard. If you have only a dozen or so posts to set, it's more convenient to buy gravel in sacks; if you're setting many posts, it's less expensive to order gravel by the yard and have it delivered to the site. One cubic yard equals 27 cubic feet, or enough for about 18 to 54 posts, depending on your method of installation. In most cases, you'll need about 1-½ cubic feet of gravel for posts set in earth-and-gravel fill, or ½ cubic foot of gravel for fence posts set in concrete.

It's usually more convenient to buy dry concrete in sacks, rather than mixing your own from separate components or having wet concrete delivered by truck. For most situations, you can figure one bag of concrete mix per posthole. Simply drop a bag next to each posthole, then mix and pour each bag separately. Some fence contractors pour the dry mix into the hole, a little at a time, mixing it with water as they go. Some lumberyards sell a less expensive fence-post mix, which contains less cement in proportion to sand and aggregates. This mix is preferred for most situations because it is designed to provide better stability against lateral stresses (leaning).

Concrete needs time to set up and develop strength before you can start nailing rails to posts. If you don't allow for some set up time (usually at least one or two days), any pounding on the posts may break up the concrete collar, rendering it almost useless. If you don't have the time to allow for the concrete to set up, you can buy a more expensive fast-setting concrete mix, which sets up in two hours or less. This enables you to add rails and siding the same day the posts are set. Ask your masonry supplier which mixes are best suited for your purposes.

Safety Equipment

Common sense should tell you not to do carpentry without first having some basic safety equipment, such as eye and ear protection.

Wear safety goggles or plastic glasses whenever you are working with power tools or chemicals… period. Make sure your eye protection conforms to American National Standards Institute (ANSI) Z87.1 or Canandian Standards Association (CSA) requirements (products that do will be marked with a stamp). Considering the cost of a visit to the emergency room, it doesn't hurt to purchase an extra pair for the times when a neighbor volunteers to lend a hand or when you misplace the first pair.

The U.S. Occupational Safety and Health Administration (OSHA) recommends that hearing protection be worn when the noise level exceeds 85 decibels (db) for an 8-hour workday. However, considering that a circular saw emits 110 db, even shorter exposure times can contribute to hearing impairment or loss. Both insert- and muff-type protectors are available; whichever you choose, be sure that it has a noise reduction rating (NRR) of a least 20 db.

Your construction project will create a lot of sawdust. If you are sensitive to dust, and especially if you are working with pressure-treated wood, it's a good idea to wear a dust mask. Two types of respiratory protection are available: disposable dusts masks and cartridge-type respirators. A dust mask is good for keeping dust and fine particles from being inhaled during a single procedure. Respirators have a replaceable filter. Both are available for protection against nontoxic and toxic dusts and mists. Whichever you purchase, be sure that it has been stamped by the National Institute for Occupational Safety and Health/ Mine Safety and Health Administration (NIOSH/MSHA) and is approved for your specific operation. When you can taste or smell the contaminate or when the mask starts to interfere with normal breathing, it's time for a replacement.

Work gloves are also nice for avoiding injury to the hands—catching a splinter off a board or developing a blister when digging postholes is not a good way to start a workday. Similarly, heavy-duty work boots will protect your feet. Steel toes will prevent injuries from dropped boards or tools. Flexible steel soles will protect you from puncture by a rogue nail.

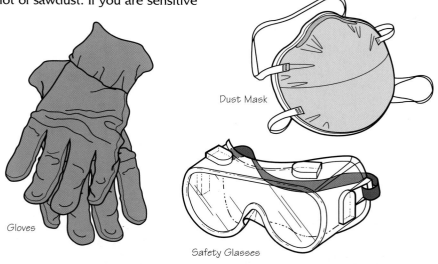

Dust Mask

Gloves

Safety Glasses

PART 2

The fence and gate at left also work as an arbor. The curved tops and dramatic posts of these two fences are variations on a theme.

The post-and-rail fence shown above allows an open view, while providing a barrier. In the same way, the board fence shown at left allows light and air into the yard, while protecting the owner's privacy.

The Victorian picket fence at left provides a barrier between a busy street and a tranquil yard. Though far from a busy street, the suburban picket fence shown below creates a similar sense of security.

In the early days, fences could be as simple as a post and rail (above, left). By the Victorian era, whitewashed picket fences set off the house (above, right). Today, many fences are made of metal or vinyl as shown at left.

Structurally, the elaborate Greek Revival fence shown to the left is only a few steps removed from a simple utility fence along the shore like the one shown above.

Depending on how it is situated, a fence can guide you along a path (above) or keep you out of a yard (below).

A security gate doesn't have to be ugly. You may even want to call attention to a well-designed gate by framing it with trim or an arbor as shown above. Nor does a gate have to be a solid wall. A security gate can let in a bit of air and light, and still act as a barrier as shown below.

This gate frames the house—the pickets allow you to see in and see out, and the posts echo the columns of the house. The picket points, meanwhile, discourage all but the most determined trespasser.

A gate makes a statement about the yard and its owner. It can indicate a desire for privacy (above). It can keep out casual traffic while leaving the yard open to view (right). Or it can be a transition from one area of the yard to another (below).

TRELLISES

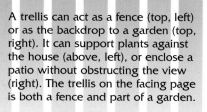

A trellis can act as a fence (top, left) or as the backdrop to a garden (top, right). It can support plants against the house (above, left), or enclose a patio without obstructing the view (right). The trellis on the facing page is both a fence and part of a garden.

ARBORS

An arbor can be a freestanding architectural element in your yard (above, left). Combined with a fence, an arbor can accent an opening, making it easy to find (above, right and below, left).

Arbors were originally structures designed to support plants (above and overleaf), but an arbor can also be a plant-free transition from one part of the yard to another as shown at left.

SETTING POSTS

The first step in building a fence is marking the fence location with stakes and string. Once you've done that, mark post locations along the string with tape or bright-colored chalk. If you're installing the fence on a property line or if the fence must meet certain setback requirements, you'll need to establish the exact location of the line to avoid disputes with neighbors or to make sure the fence meets local ordinances. Once you've located your property lines, mark the corners with surveyor's stakes or other markers.

If you're building a fence within the property, first you'll need to establish the locations of end posts and corner posts. Usually, this is done by measuring out from one or more existing reference points on the property, such as the house, the driveway, an existing fence, or other landmarks. If you haven't already done so, draw up a site plan, as discussed in "Making a Site Plan," page 22, and use the plan as a guide.

After plotting the fence line, you can mark the post locations on the ground, dig the postholes, and install the posts. Once the posts are set, you'll add the rails and siding for the particular design you've chosen. (If your design calls for rails that are notched or dadoed into the posts, you might want to dado the posts before setting them. See "Dadoing Posts," page 68, for details.) If you haven't chosen a design yet, thumb through the wood fence projects in Chapter 5.

PLOTTING A STRAIGHT FENCE

This section explains how to locate posts for a straight fence built on flat ground with corners meeting at 90 degrees. It is likely your situation is not so ideal, but with these instructions and a little common sense, you can lay out posts for just about any fence design. For instructions on laying out fences along slopes, see "Fences on a Slope," page 56. To plot a curved fence, see "Curved Fences," page 55.

1 Mark the end posts. Drive a 1x2 stake firmly into the ground, marking each end of the fence line. Drive a small nail into the top of each stake marking what will be the center of the fence posts. Stakes typically project 4 to 6 inches above ground; however, taller stakes may be required for the string to clear low obstructions along the fence line.

Digging the postholes will obliterate all your layout marks. Erect batter boards to make it easy to reestablish them. To build batter boards, drive two stakes about a foot apart, a few feet beyond each corner stake. Connect them with a crosspiece. Stretch mason's twine from crosspiece to crosspiece, positioning it so that it crosses the nail on the corner stakes. (Use mason's twine because it does not sag as much as ordinary string.)

2 Establish a 90-degree corner. If the fence will enclose a square or rectangular area, you'll want the corners to form an exact 90-degree angle. Lay out the corner using the triangulation method. Begin with the side you have laid out, which has the corners A and B in the drawing. Put a batter board about 12 inches beyond the approximate location of the third corner and another one about 12 inches beyond the opposite corner—corner B in the drawing. String a line from crosspiece to crosspiece so that it crosses the nail in the corner stake at point B. From the same corner stake, measure out 3 (or 6) feet along one string and 4 (or 8) feet along the other, and mark these measurements on the strings. Have a helper slide the string along the far batter board until the diagonal distance between the marks equals 5 (or 10) feet. Mark the string location on the batter board. Mark the location of the end post on the string, hang a plumb bob or use a level to transfer this point to the ground, and drive a stake at this point (C).

3 Establish additional corners. To enclose three sides of the property, run a second string out from a batter board at point A, attach it to another batter board, and repeat the above procedure. To form a complete enclosure (fenced on all four sides), drive two batter boards slightly

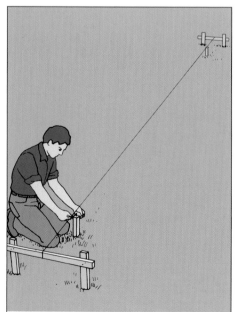

1. Lay out the course of the wall with mason's twine stretched between batter boards.

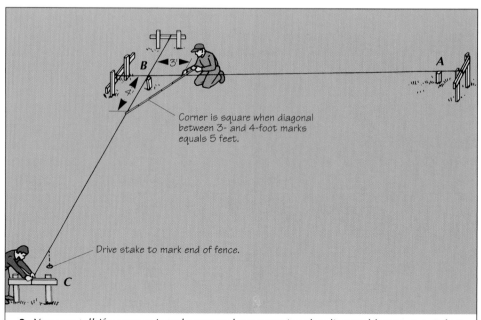

Corner is square when diagonal between 3- and 4-foot marks equals 5 feet.

Drive stake to mark end of fence.

2. You can tell if a corner is truly square by measuring the diagonal between a 3-foot and a 4-foot leg (or 6-foot and 8-foot leg). The corner is square if the diagonal measures 5 (or 10) feet.

beyond each of the corner locations, adjust the strings until they intersect at 90 degrees at all four corners, then drive stakes where strings intersect.

4 **Locate the posts.** Once you've established the fence line with stakes and string, measure the total length of each side from corner to corner. Then, measure and mark post locations along the string, either by dividing the total length into equal intervals (do not exceed 96 inches between posts) or to make best use of precut lumber lengths (48-, 72-, or 96-inch rails). Apply small pieces of tape to the string that mark the center of each post.

Unless you divide the overall length into equal sections, you will probably end up with a short section at one end. For example, if the total length of the fence line is 34 feet, you can either divide it into six equal sections measuring 68 inches, or you can divide the fence into five 72-inch sections, with a short 48-inch section at one end. If the fence includes a gate, you can place the short section at the gate location and build the gate to fit in the short section.

If you are using precut lumber for rails that will fit snugly between the posts, remember that the mark on the string indicates the center of the post, not the edge. Be sure to allow for the thickness of the post when doing your layout work. If you're using prefabricated fence panels, locate post centers so that the panels either fit snugly between them or butt together on the center-line of the posts. The method you choose depends on the particular panel design; consult manufacturer's instructions.

5 **Transfer post locations to the ground.** Use a plumb bob to transfer the marks from the string to the ground, as shown. Mark each post location on the ground with a nail stuck through a piece of paper or with a stake. Once all of the marks are in place, remove the string.

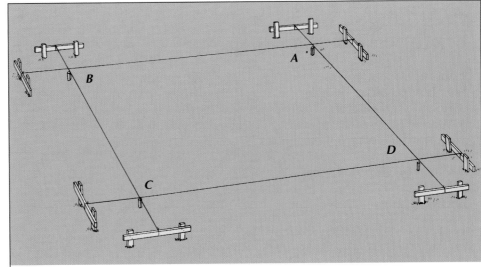

3. *To enclose an area completely, first lay out one corner, and then set up batter boards and strings to lay out additional corners.*

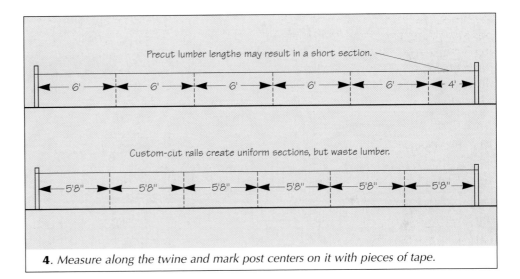

Precut lumber lengths may result in a short section.

6' · 6' · 6' · 6' · 6' · 4'

Custom-cut rails create uniform sections, but waste lumber.

5'8" · 5'8" · 5'8" · 5'8" · 5'8" · 5'8"

4. *Measure along the twine and mark post centers on it with pieces of tape.*

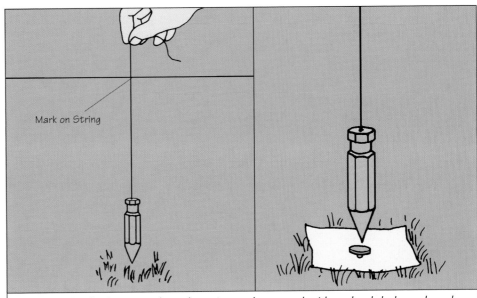

Mark on String

5. *Transfer the locations from the string to the ground with a plumb bob, and mark each location with a nail, stuck through a piece of paper.*

Dealing with Obstructions

In some instances, you may find large barriers or obstacles, such as trees, boulders, or drainage areas, interfering with your chosen fence line. In such cases, you can remove the obstacle, move the fence line, or build the fence to skirt or incorporate the obstacle. The drawings show four common solutions for dealing with these obstacles.

If a tree stands in your fence line and you've decided to incorporate the tree into the fence, you should set the posts several feet away from the tree to avoid damaging its roots. Install the fence rails and then the siding so that they extend beyond the posts and toward the tree. To keep these

sections from sagging, install diagonal braces made from siding material, as shown. Cut the nearest boards to match the trunk profile. You can do this by placing the last board or boards against the tree and scribing a line with a compass to follow the trunk profile. Leave about 2 inches between the board and trunk to allow for tree growth. Cut along the marked line with a saber saw, then attach the board(s) to the rails. You can use the same technique to incorporate a boulder into the fence.

Where a fence crosses a low area, extend boards below the bottom rail to follow the contour, as shown. Do

not extend boards farther than about 8 inches below the bottom rail or the ends will tend to warp.

If the fence must cross a swale, ditch, or small stream that contains water during the rainy season, construct a grate from lengths of No. 3 rebar or $\frac{1}{2}$-inch galvanized pipe, spaced about 6 inches apart, to keep people and large animals from crawling underneath the fence. Drill holes through a rail made from two 2x4s. Attach the rail to the fence, insert the pipe or rebar through the holes, and drive it into the ground. For extra measure, you can set the grate into a ribbon of concrete.

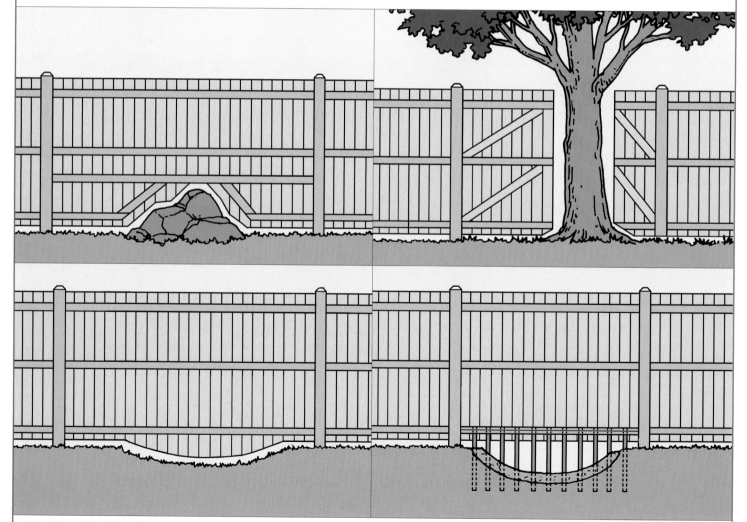

Dealing with Obstacles. *Trees and boulders can be incorporated into the fence by setting the posts a few feet from the obstacle and extending the rails and siding from the posts. Cut the siding to match the profile of the obstacle, leaving a few inches of space. Extend siding below the bottom rail to cover low spots.*

CURVED FENCES

A gently curving fence can add architectural interest to an otherwise dull landscape. Also, curved fences are naturals for front yards of corner lots.

When building a curved fence, you have two basic construction options: a true-curve fence with curved rails, or a segmented fence with short, straight sections fastened together to mimic a curve. The construction method you choose can affect the post spacing and the size of the postholes, so before you start digging, decide which style of curved fence is best for you. Then lay out the curve and plot the posts at intervals along the curve. Here are step-by-step instructions for installing rails and siding on curved fences.

Plotting a Curved Fence

The trick to laying out a curved fence is to plot the curve symmetrically. To do this, all you need is a short length of copper pipe, a piece of heavy, nonstretchable cord, and a pointed stick. With these, make a simple compass to mark the curve on the ground. The following instructions describe how to lay out posts to make a fence with a curved, as opposed to a square, corner.

1 Establish a reference line.
First, lay out the fence to a corner. Drive stakes at the points where the curve will meet the straight sides of the fence. Run a string between the stakes. Then measure to the exact middle of the line and drive a stake at this midpoint. Run a perpendicular line from the stake, using the 3-4-5 triangle method. (See "Establish a 90-degree Corner," page 52.)

2 Make the compass; draw the arc. Drive the copper pipe into the ground at a point along the second, perpendicular line. The closer the pipe is to the first line, the deeper the arc will be. Tie one end of the nonstretchable cord to the pipe. Extend the cord to one of the stakes marking the end of the first layout line, and at this point, tie the pointed stick to the cord.

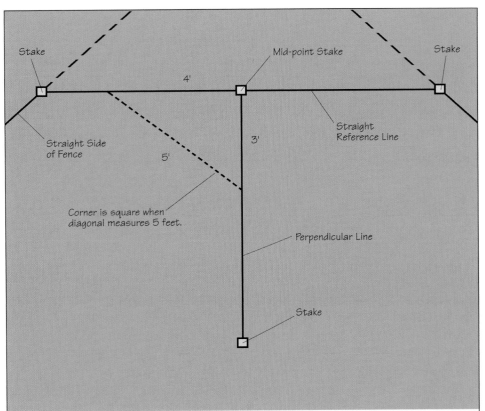

1. *A curved fence begins with a straight line connecting the ends of the curve. Drive a stake at the midpoint of the line, and draw a line perpendicular to it.*

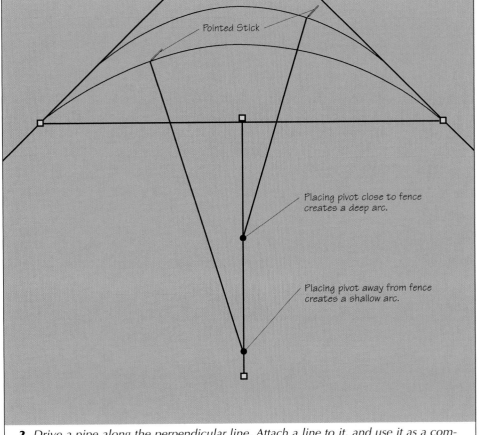

2. *Drive a pipe along the perpendicular line. Attach a line to it, and use it as a compass to draw an arc.*

Now use the stick to etch the arc on the ground, as shown. Reposition the pipe to get the arc you want.

3 Locate the posts. Locate posts by marking their position on a piece of cord. First, lay the cord out straight and use a tape measure and felt-tip pen or pieces of tape to mark the desired post intervals on the cord itself (every 72 inches, for example). Then lay the cord over the arc drawn on the ground, and transfer post locations to the ground.

The post spacing will depend mostly on how tight the arc is and how much weight the posts must support. Generally, the tighter the arc, the closer the post spacing. In general, space posts between 48 and 72 inches apart. There's no rule here; simply space the posts to meet the design requirements of the fence, as you would for a straight fence.

4 Orient the posts. If you're using square posts to build either a true-curve or segmented fence, orient each post so that the outside face falls along the curve. You can check this by running a piece of twine out from the original pivot point to a nail in the center of each post, as shown. Then use a try square or framing square to orient one side of the post perpendicular (90 degrees) to the twine. After setting the posts loosely in the holes, have a helper backfill the hole with earth and/or concrete while you keep the post aligned. If you're using concrete, make any final adjustments before the concrete hardens.

FENCES ON A SLOPE

You have two basic design choices for hillside fencing: contoured fencing and stepped fencing. On a contoured fence, the rails run parallel with the slope, so the fence follows the contour of the ground. These fences are easier to construct than stepped fences, especially on the uneven slopes or rolling terrain that is typical of rural landscapes. Board fences, discussed on page 65, are a popular choice.

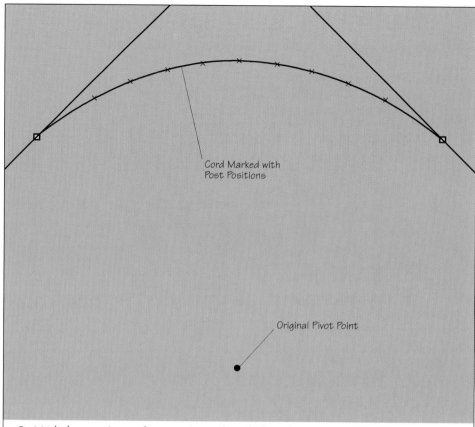

3. Mark the post intervals on a piece of cord, then drape the cord along the arc of the fence to determine post locations.

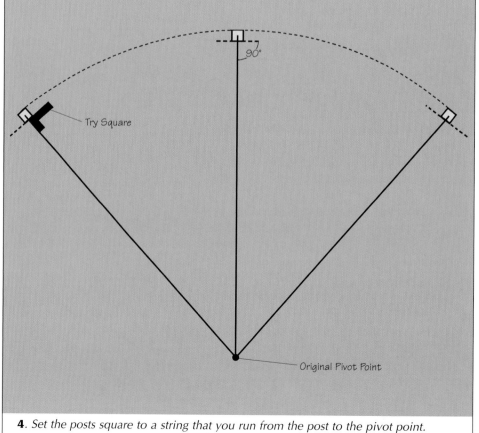

4. Set the posts square to a string that you run from the post to the pivot point.

As the name implies, each section of a stepped fence steps up the hill like a stairway, usually in equal intervals. The top rail of each section is placed level; the bottom rail may be placed level or, more rarely, parallel with the slope. Stepped fences work best when the slope is fairly straight and even from top to bottom, so they're generally preferable in urban or suburban settings, where the topography has been smoothed by grading and other landscaping. Also, the geometry of stepped fences reflects the strong horizontal and vertical lines of surrounding houses and other buildings.

Practically any fence design can be adapted to stepped fencing. On some solid-board or panel designs, however, the space beneath the bottom rails must be covered by extending the boards or panels below the rail to ground level. Such designs aren't recommended for steep slopes; if the boards extend more than about 8 inches below the bottom rail, they're likely to warp.

Plotting a Contoured Fence

This type of fence is laid out similarly to a straight fence along level ground. The only difference is that you may need extra stakes to keep a very hilly landscape from interfering with the layout lines.

1 Plot the fence line. Drive a stake at each end post location and run mason's twine between the stakes. Make sure the stakes are tall enough so that the twine clears any obstructions or minor changes in terrain. If the terrain is very uneven, you may need to install intermediate stakes to keep the twine from touching the ground.

2 Locate the posts. Measure along the line and mark intermediate post locations with chalk or small pieces of tape. Then use a plumb bob to transfer post locations to the ground, and mark these spots with stakes or nails stuck through paper scraps (see "Transfer Post Locations to Ground," page 53).

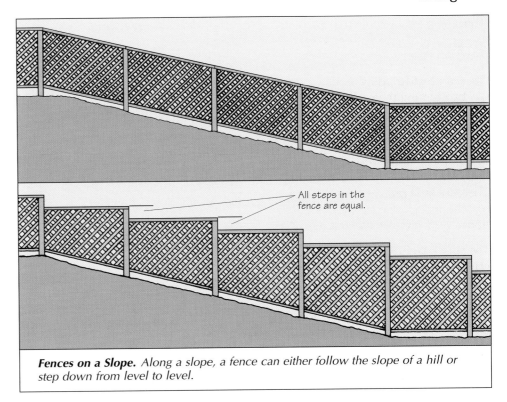

Fences on a Slope. Along a slope, a fence can either follow the slope of a hill or step down from level to level.

All steps in the fence are equal.

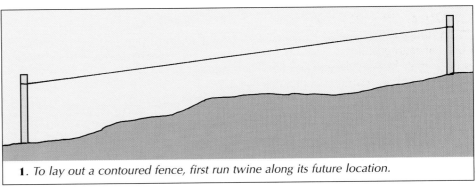

1. To lay out a contoured fence, first run twine along its future location.

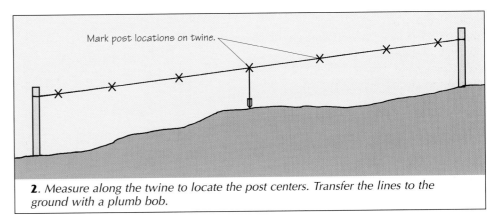

Mark post locations on twine.

2. Measure along the twine to locate the post centers. Transfer the lines to the ground with a plumb bob.

When installing posts for contoured fencing, set each post to exactly the same height above the ground (72 inches, for example). Fasten each rail at the same height along each post, so they follow the contour of the slope. (The top rails might meet the posts at 70 inches above the ground.

The bottom rails meet the posts at 6 inches above the ground.) Install picket boards so that they are plumb, rather than perpendicular to the slope of the rails. Extend the boards several inches below the bottom rail, and cut the ends to follow the contour of the ground.

Plotting a Stepped Fence

A stepped fence is more difficult to plot than a contoured fence because you must work from a level reference line. Having a level line to work from is an efficient way to locate posts for a fence with level rails. If the slope is very steep or the fence run is very long, you may want to hire a fence contractor to plot the fence for you. For gradual slopes or shorter sections of fence, proceed as follows:

1 **Establish a level line.** Drive a short stake marking the post location at the top of the hill and a tall stake marking the location at the bottom of the hill. The lower stake must be tall enough so that you can stretch a level line between the two stakes. The lower stake must also be plumb, so check it with a level to be sure it is standing straight up and down. Attach mason's twine to the stakes and use a line level to level the twine.

2 **Mark the post locations.** Measure along the leveled string and mark post locations with chalk or pieces of tape. As mentioned earlier, you can space the posts evenly by dividing the fence into equal sections, but to make the best use of precut lumber sizes, consider spacing the posts 72 to 96 inches apart. Transfer the post locations to the ground with a plumb bob, then mark them with stakes or pieces of paper stuck with nails.

3 **Determine the step size.** The most attractive stepped fences have the same step height between sections. To figure out the step height,

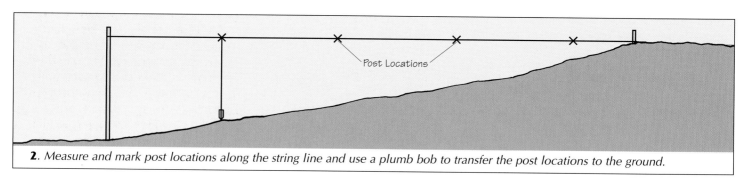

1. Begin layout of a stepped fence by running a level line between two stakes.

Line Level

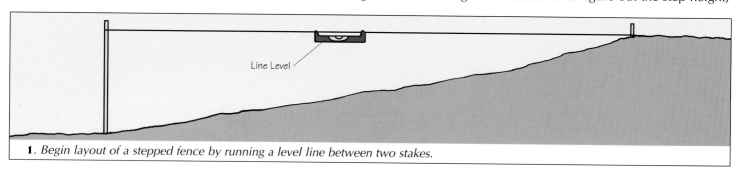

2. Measure and mark post locations along the string line and use a plumb bob to transfer the post locations to the ground.

Post Locations

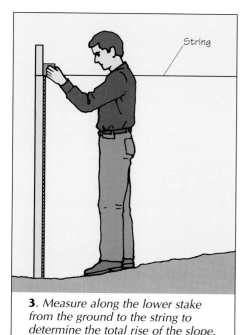

String

3. Measure along the lower stake from the ground to the string to determine the total rise of the slope.

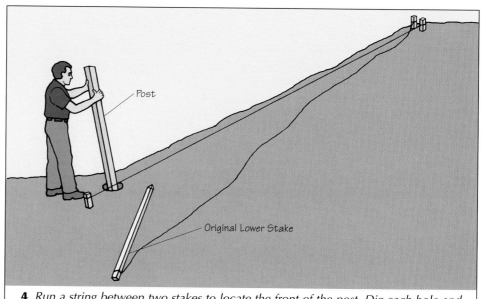

Post

Original Lower Stake

4. Run a string between two stakes to locate the front of the post. Dig each hole and install each post starting from the bottom of the slope.

first you must determine the overall height of the slope. Measure the distance from the ground to the string at the lower end post. This measurement is the overall height or rise of the slope. Divide the rise by the number of sections (the areas between the posts) to determine the size of the step. For example, if the total rise is 48 inches, and the fence contains four equal sections, there should be 12-inch steps between posts.

4 **Set the first post.** Before you dig holes for the posts, run twine between two small stakes so the posts form a neat line stepping up the hill. (The twine will be half the thickness of the fence posts away from your original stakes.) Begin digging at the bottom of the hill. Dig the hole and insert

the post, as described in "Installing Posts" below. The height of this post depends on the fence style. With some fence styles, the posts are as high as the siding. With other styles, the siding projects above the posts. In this example, the top rail will be fastened across the top of the post, and the siding can either project above the rail or be installed level with it.

5 **Mark the step heights.** Before setting the rest of the posts, mark the step heights on the posts. From the top of each post, measure the distance of the step height (12 inches in this example) and mark the point with a pencil and a square.

6 **Set the line posts.** Set the successive uphill posts (the line

posts, as opposed to the end posts) so that the step-height marks you penciled on them are level with tops of the previous posts. Use a line level or a level and a long, straight board to set the posts to the correct height.

7 **Set the end post.** If the fence levels off and continues at the top of the hill, set the top post as you did the other posts. If the fence ends at the top of the hill, set the post temporarily and mark a cut-off line that is level with the previous post. Remove the end post, cut it, and set it permanently as described below.

INSTALLING POSTS

As a rule of thumb, fence posts are set with at least one-third of their total length in the ground, at a minimum of 24 inches deep. In areas subject to frost heave, it is recommended that you set the bottoms of the posts at least 6 inches below the frost line, if that is practical. However, check local codes and standard practices in your particular area. The one-third rule applies especially to gate, end, and corner posts, and ones that support heavy siding materials. Solid-board or panel fences subject to high winds may also require deeper posts. However, the rule doesn't always make best use of standard precut lumber lengths (a 72-inch fence would require a 9-foot post, for example). For this reason, most 72-inch fences

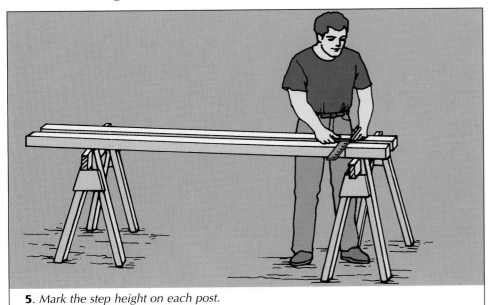

5. Mark the step height on each post.

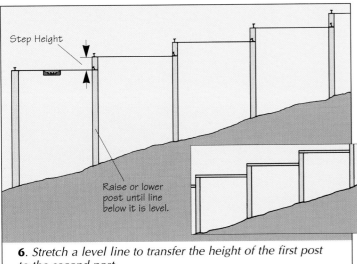

6. Stretch a level line to transfer the height of the first post to the second post.

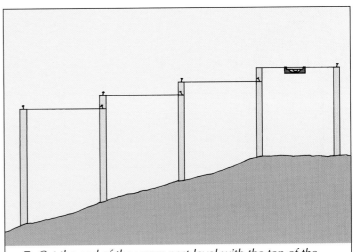

7. Cut the end of the upper post level with the top of the previous post.

can use 96-inch posts sunk 24 inches in the ground. The end posts, corner posts, and gate posts on such a fence should still be the full 9 feet long.

1 Dig the postholes. Use a post-hole digger to dig postholes 4 to 6 inches deeper than the intended post depth. The extra depth will be back-filled with gravel or rubble to facilitate drainage beneath the post. The gravel also prevents concrete (if used) from sealing off the post bottom, trapping water beneath the post.

Keep the holes as narrow as possible; usually about twice the width of the post. In boggy soils or heavy clay soils subject to frost heave, you may need to dig wider holes, and backfill with com-pacted sand and gravel or gravel and concrete. (To help you decide which backfill material to use, see "Choosing Backfill Materials," page 63.) If you're adding a stabilizing concrete collar in very loose or sandy soil, make the hole diameter about three times the width of the post (12 inches for a 4-inch post). Dig all of the postholes before you start setting the posts. To dig all holes to the same depth, measure from the end of the tool's digger blade to a point on the handle equal to the desired hole depth and mark with a felt-tip pen.

2 Set the first post. First relocate the layout twine to mark the face of the posts instead of the center. If you used batter boards, simply move the string sideways half the thickness of the posts. (Remember that a 4x4 post measures only 3½ by 3½. Move the twine half the thickness—1¾ inch-es.) If you used stakes, drive new stakes that are centered roughly half the post thickness away from the original layout line. Drive nails in the stakes marking the faces of the posts, and run twine between them.

No matter what type of backfill you're using—earth, gravel, or concrete—start by shoveling 5 to 6 inches of coarse gravel into the hole and tamp-ing it firmly. If an ordinary tamper is too wide, you can use the post itself as a tamper.

Set the post in the hole and check the height. Add gravel as necessary to raise

Mark post hole depth on handles.

1. *Dig postholes 4-6 inches deeper than the bottom of the post so that you can put gravel in the hole for drainage. The hole should be three times as wide as the post.*

2. *Stretch a line between stakes or batter boards to position the faces of the posts.*

the post top to the desired height. Then hold the post gently against the layout twine, while a helper shovels in about 4 to 6 inches of gravel.

To plumb the posts, hold a 24-inch level on adjacent faces and move the

post into plumb while a helper back-fills the hole with the desired material.

3 Tamp the earth and gravel fill. If you're using earth-and-gravel fill, add the backfill several inches at a time, tamping vigorously with a length of 2x4 as you go. Periodically check that the post is plumb.

4 Backfill with concrete. If you're using concrete, first moisten the hole with a garden hose to prevent the soil from sucking water out of the wet concrete. The best mixing method is to stir dry ingredients in a wheelbarrow or other clean container, and then add water and stir again. Some do-it-yourselfers mix everything in the hole, but this generally folds dirt and debris into the concrete and weakens it. It's better to shovel a clean, stiff mix into the hole, and then plunge a length of reinforcing rod or your shovel handle into the wet concrete several times to remove any air pockets and to ensure a consistent mixture (make sure you hose off the handle as soon as you're done).

5 Temporarily brace the post. Slope the top of the concrete collar to help shed water. Be careful not to knock the post out of alignment while the concrete is setting up. Then set up temporary 2x4 braces nailed with duplex nails to the post and to stakes in the ground to keep the post plumb. Leave the braces in place until the concrete has cured sufficiently (about 2 hours with a fast-

3. *If you choose to backfill the hole with dirt, tamp it with a 2x4, and check the post for plumb while you work.*

4. *You can mix some types of concrete right in the hole, but it's better to premix. Moisten the surrounding area, and then pour in the mixed ingredients. Plunge the shovel handle in the hole to remove air pockets.*

5. *Brace the post to hold it plumb while the concrete dries.*

setting mix, or 24 to 48 hours with a conventional mix). It's best to set and brace all the fence posts, and install the rails and siding after the concrete has cured.

6 Set the other end post.
Measure the height of the first post, and set the other end post to the same height, making sure it is plumb as you add the backfill. To keep the posts aligned, run mason's twine from the face of one end post to the other. Tack the twine in place so that it is 6 inches from the tops of the posts.

7 Set the line posts. Just as you set the corner or end posts, set the intermediate or line posts. Position the posts so they just touch the strings. Measure from the upper length of string to the top of the posts to keep the line posts at the same height as the end posts. Check the posts with a level as you work.

6. *Set the other end post, and adjust its height with a line level and string. Backfill the hole and brace as needed.*

7. *Align the remaining posts with the string; then backfill and brace. Measure to keep the posts at the same height.*

Choosing Backfill Materials

Typically, posts are set in tamped earth, earth and gravel, or concrete and gravel. You can use a flat base stone 4 to 6 inches thick as a footing. Whether or not you decide to use concrete depends largely on the fence design and soil conditions. Generally, you can use earth-and-gravel fill if the soil is not too loose, sandy, subject to shifting or frost heaves, and if the fence posts don't have to support much weight. Post and board fences, lattice, spaced pickets, or fences under 60 inches tall are all light enough for earth-and-gravel fill. In extremely loose or sandy soils, you can attach 1x4 pressure-treated cleats to the bottoms of the posts, as shown, to provide lateral stability. A base stone is not required in this procedure.

For added stability, use concrete, especially in areas with deep frost lines. You can even drive 16d nails partially into the post before placing the concrete to lock the post and concrete together. If precise post spacing is required (such as when dadoing or mortising rails into posts, or attaching prefabricated fence panels or sections), you'll need to set the posts successively, fitting in rails or sections as you set each post. Fast-setting concrete mixes are preferred for this type of construction. After pouring the concrete and attaching the first set of rails or panel, install temporary braces at post locations to keep the fence section plumb while the concrete sets. As you fill in successive sections, occasionally recheck the entire fence for plumb, and adjust the temporary braces if necessary.

If you're unsure of local building practices, seek advice from the building department or ask several local fence contractors for recommended practices in your area.

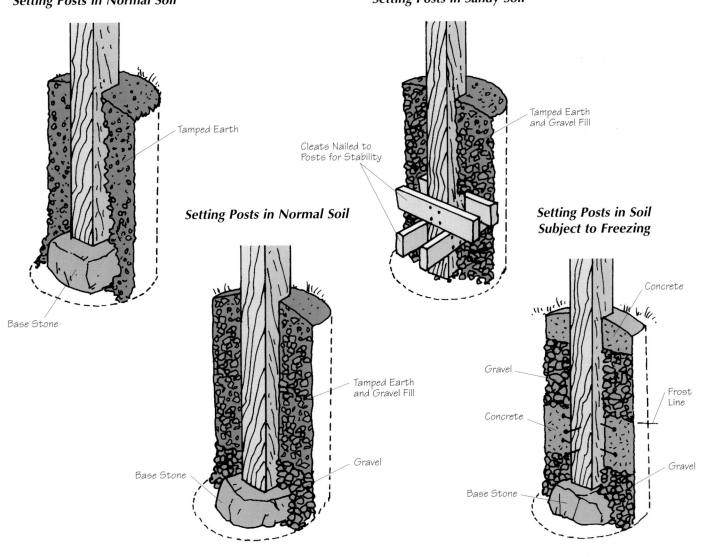

Setting Posts in Normal Soil

Tamped Earth

Base Stone

Setting Posts in Sandy Soil

Cleats Nailed to Posts for Stability

Tamped Earth and Gravel Fill

Setting Posts in Normal Soil

Tamped Earth and Gravel Fill

Base Stone

Gravel

Setting Posts in Soil Subject to Freezing

Concrete

Gravel

Concrete

Frost Line

Base Stone

Gravel

WOOD RAILS & SIDING

Rails and siding give a fence both its character and strength. Rails are the horizontal parts of the fence frame. The siding includes things like pickets, boards, or paneling, and is usually supported by the rails. Many localities have strict rules that apply to fences. Before you begin to build, check with the local building department to see if your wood fence meets ordinances and restrictions regarding setbacks, height, and structural requirements.

In most cases, the basic framework for wood fences consists of 4x4 posts and 2x4 rails to which you attach boards or panels. Make sure you use wood suitable for outdoor use. The least-expensive solution depends in part on where you live. The most durable timber is pressure-treated lumber. In the Northwest, however, redwood and cedar may be significantly cheaper than pressure-treated wood and could be more cost effective. Elsewhere, however, it's a good idea to use pressure-treated wood at least for the posts, if not the rest of the fence. If your budget allows, you can still use redwood or cedar for the more visible parts of the fence, such as caps, rails, and siding. Avoid untreated pine or douglas fir. They don't hold up well, even when painted. For more on selecting fence materials, see "Decay Resistance," page 26.

BOARD FENCES

Board fences are the most common wood fence in urban and suburban yards. The design options for them are virtually limitless.

Most board fences use ¾-inch thick siding in widths ranging from 3 to 12 inches. Boards 6 or 8 inches wide are popular because they're usually more economical than narrower boards. They're also less likely to cup and split than wider ones.

Board fences can also use house siding such as shiplap, clapboard, channel rustic, and others.

Typical Construction. Most board fences consist of siding boards nailed to one side of the frame, creating a "board" side and a "frame" side. In front or side yards, you typically place the board or "good" side toward the street because it looks better. On property-line fences, it is customary to face the good side toward your neighbor's yard to avoid ill feelings.

Some fences look the same on both sides. You might want to build one of these fences for marking property

Prefab Fences

If you want to avoid the design process and save a considerable amount of time and effort building a fence, consider buying prefabricated fence panels. Made of wood, metal or PVC plastic, the panels come preassembled in 36-, 48-, 72-, and 96-inch sections, in heights from 36 to 96 inches. Some designs also come with matching gates and other features, such as prefabricated arbors. Most lumberyards and home centers stock a few popular designs. You can order others through catalogs or brochures available at the service desk.

To build a prefab board fence, set the posts at the proper spacing, depending on the length of the panels, and fasten the panels to the posts. Installation techniques vary among manufacturers, but most panels with horizontal rails and vertical siding are fastened to the posts with fence brackets. Complete installation instructions are provided by the manufacturer.

Most stores sell a variety of prefab picket fence panels, as well as several other popular styles. Prefab wood panels are the closest thing to an "instant fence." The panels don't cost much more than if you had bought everything separately and built the fence from scratch. Quality of materials and factory assembly are sometimes mediocre. Check the panels carefully for defects in materials and workmanship, and make sure they're sturdy enough to meet your needs.

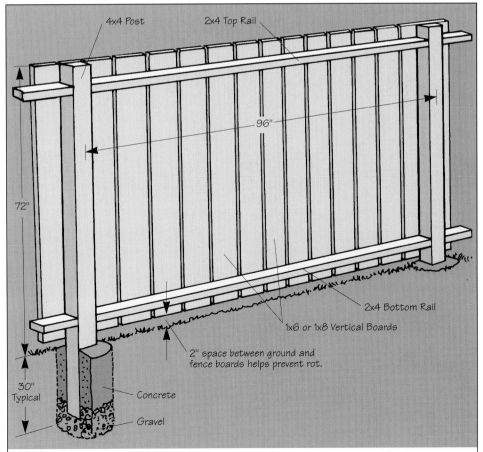

Board Fences. *A typical board fence consists of 4x4 posts and 2x4 rails. Posts are typically spaced on either 72- or 96-inch centers.*

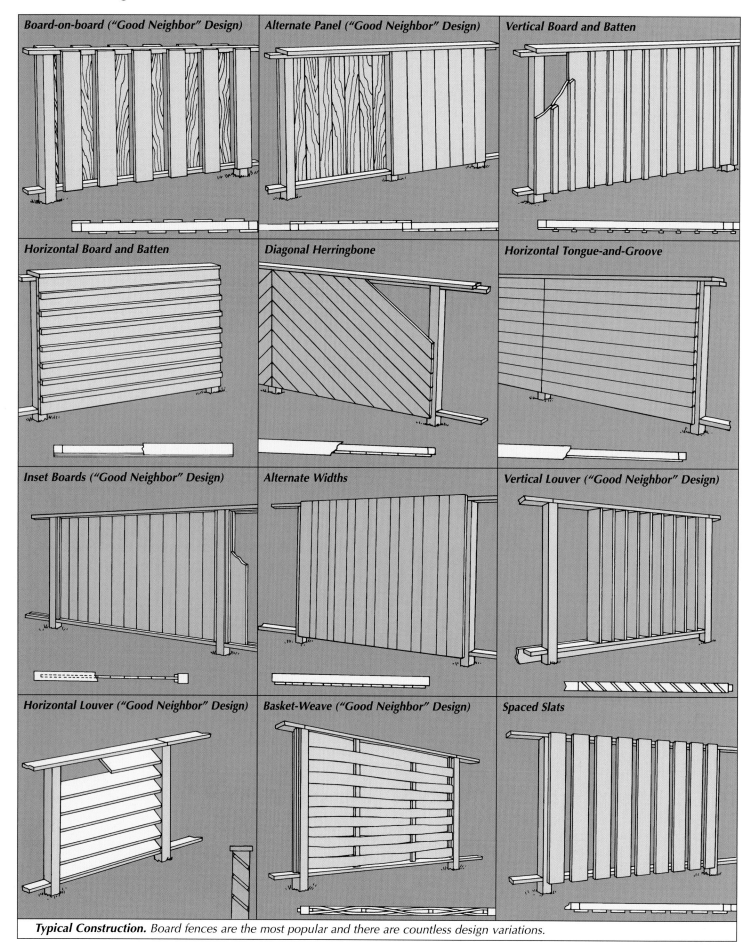

Board-on-board ("Good Neighbor" Design)

Alternate Panel ("Good Neighbor" Design)

Vertical Board and Batten

Horizontal Board and Batten

Diagonal Herringbone

Horizontal Tongue-and-Groove

Inset Boards ("Good Neighbor" Design)

Alternate Widths

Vertical Louver ("Good Neighbor" Design)

Horizontal Louver ("Good Neighbor" Design)

Basket-Weave ("Good Neighbor" Design)

Spaced Slats

Typical Construction. *Board fences are the most popular and there are countless design variations.*

lines. Some of these "good neighbor" designs include the "Vertical Board-on-Board Fence," page 72, "Alternating Panel Fence," page 74, and "Louver Fence," page 75.

Board-Top Variations. Many siding materials can be oriented horizontally, vertically, or diagonally to match the house style. On vertical-board designs, the board tops can be cut at angles to shed water, prolonging the life of the boards. Decorative cuts also add interest to the fence design, as does altering board width and direction. Using other types of wood or incorporating lattice, battens, or exterior moldings also adds visual appeal.

Post and Rail Variations. Many board fence designs incorporate a 1x6 or 2x6 cap rail nailed across the post tops to help protect the fence below. Angling the cap rail discourages young fence climbers from walking along the top of the fence. To angle the cap rail, cut the post tops at a 30-degree angle. Then set all the posts to the same height by adding or removing gravel below the post. You can also set untrimmed, long posts: Strike a chalk line to mark the post tops, and cut the angle with the posts in place. To mark the angle on the first post, carry the chalk line to the opposite face with your square. Measure down to mark the bottom of the slope. Mark the angle on the other posts by setting a T-bevel to match the angle on the first post.

Joining Rails to Posts

Depending on your fence design, you can join the rails to the posts in several ways. The following instructions are for joining 2x4 rails to 4x4 posts—the basic framework for many fences.

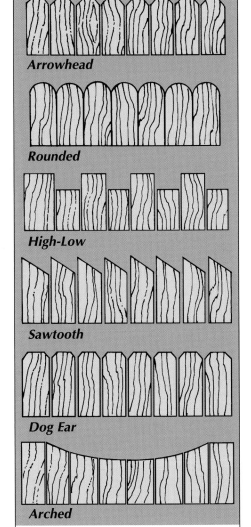

Arrowhead

Rounded

High-Low

Sawtooth

Dog Ear

Arched

> ***Board-Top Variations.*** *You can add interest to vertical-board fences by changing the shape of the top. Except for the arched fence (bottom), all board tops are cut before you attach them to the fence. For an arched design, attach boards with tops flush, and cut them to shape later.*

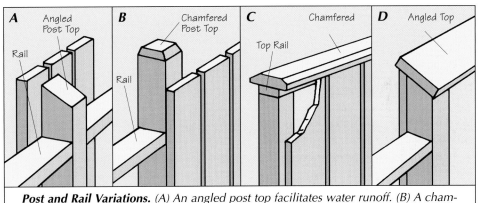

> ***Post and Rail Variations.*** *(A) An angled post top facilitates water runoff. (B) A chamfered post top helps water run off and gives the post a finished appearance. (C) A chamfered cap rail protects the structure beneath. (D) An angled cap rail discourages children from walking along the top of the fence.*

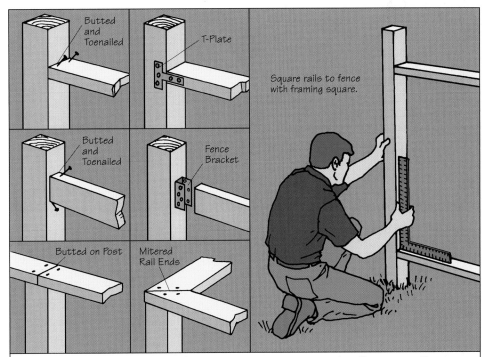

> ***Joining Rails to Posts.*** *Shown here are various ways to attach rails to posts. Butt joints are the weakest; you can strengthen these joints with metal connectors. Always check to make sure rails are square with posts.*

In most cases, top and bottom rails are simply butted between the posts. As a rule, the bottom rail is placed 2 to 8 inches above ground level and the top rail is placed 4 to 8 inches below the post top. Add a center rail if you're building a fence with heavy siding materials, or if the rails span more than 72 inches. Mark where the rails meet the posts with a chalk line and line level. Cut the rails one by one to fit snugly between the posts. Attach with nails or screws. This type of construction depends entirely on the strength of the fasteners to support the sections of fencing, so consider using fence brackets or T-plates to beef up the connection between rails and posts. The connectors add strength but you may consider them unattractive.

In some fence designs, the top rails are fastened to the tops of the posts (see the drawings on page 66). For strength, top rails should span at least three posts. Butt the joints halfway across the post where they meet. Drill pilot holes in the top rail ends before fastening them with nails or screws. Where post rails butt together on a post, drive two 10d nails or two 3½-inch galvanized deck screws in each end of the rail. When the rail runs across a post, attach it with four fasteners.

Dadoing Posts. For increased strength and a more traditional appearance, cut notches in the posts to house the rails. Although you can cut these notches (called dadoes) after setting the posts, it is easier to cut them with the posts laying flat across two sawhorses. Mark the dado locations carefully, and be sure to set all of the posts to exactly the same height or the dadoes—and therefore the rails—won't be level.

To cut dadoes, measure from the top of the post, and mark the top and bottom of each dado with straight lines. Then make a series of ½-inch deep cuts between the lines with a hand saw or circular saw. Remove the waste with a chisel. Cut the bottom of each post to the exact length before setting it in the posthole.

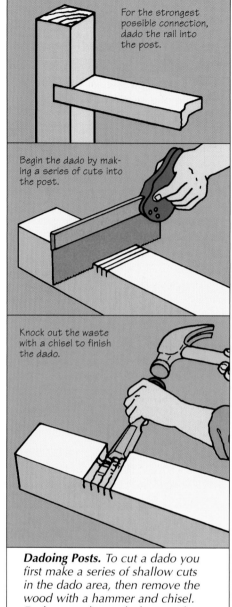

For the strongest possible connection, dado the rail into the post.

Begin the dado by making a series of cuts into the post.

Knock out the waste with a chisel to finish the dado.

Dadoing Posts. To cut a dado you first make a series of shallow cuts in the dado area, then remove the wood with a hammer and chisel. Dadoes can be cut before or after setting posts.

Making the Connection. Although nails are easiest to use and least expensive to buy, many fence builders prefer screws for joining rails to posts (and sometimes boards to rails). That's because screws make a stronger connection. They are also more easily removed if you make a mistake or want to repair the fence later. No matter which fastener you choose, however, it's best to predrill holes to avoid splitting the rail ends. Make the holes about ⅔ the diameter of your nails or screws.

If your fence is not dadoed and you're not attaching the rails with fence hardware, simply butt the rails between the posts. To attach them, toenail 10d galvanized nails or similar-sized screws through the top and bottom edges of the rail. Start by placing the rail flat on the ground. Start a screw or nail about 1½ inches from the end of the rail and drive it at an angle. Have a helper hold the opposite end of the board level while you nail one end to the first post at the mark you made. Then, go to the opposite end and nail it to the post. With a framing square, make sure the rail is square to the post.

Installing Kickboards. To prevent decay and termite infestation, keep the bottom ends of the siding at least 2 inches above the ground. If you don't want a gap under the fence, you can attach a horizontal 1x8 or 1x10 kickboard along the bottoms of the posts. Notch the kickboard to fit around major obstructions, if necessary. The kickboard adds strength to the fence and is one way of correcting a fence sag. Attach the kickboard before you attach the siding, and make sure you leave enough room for a gap between the two. Allow a ¼- to ½-inch gap between the bottoms of the pickets and the top edge of the kickboard to help prevent decay.

Although you can simply set the kickboard on the ground, burying the bottom edge several inches below ground level will block water runoff from the neighbor's yard and discourage animals from digging underneath. Make sure the kickboard material is designated for below-grade use.

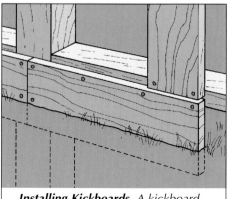

Installing Kickboards. A kickboard strengthens the fence and keeps animals from crawling under it.

POPULAR BOARD FENCES

The following projects show how to add a variety of siding materials (boards, pickets and plywood) to the post-and-rail frame, and in several cases, how to modify the frame to accept the siding. Also included are projects for simple post-and-rail and post-and-board fences, in which the rails also serve as the siding. All of these designs can be modified to suit your particular requirements.

Solid-Board Privacy Fence 🔩🔩

Solid-board privacy fences are easy to build and go well with practically any style house. The most common solid-board fences are 72 inches high and use 1x6, 1x8, or 1x10 siding. Board tops can be cut in a variety of patterns (see "Board-Top Variations" on page 67). A dog-ear fence is shown here.

1 Build the frame. Set the posts and attach the rails. This design calls for a middle rail, installed halfway between the top and bottom rails, to keep the boards from warping.

2 Cut the board tops. This step is optional. You might choose to make decorative cuts on the board tops for appearance or to shed water. To speed cutting, clamp several boards together with the top board marked for cutting, and cut three

Preventing Sagging Rails

With time, many fences begin to droop or sag, especially toward the middle of a section that spans more than 72 inches. Placing the rails on edge, rather than flat, will help prevent sagging. Another way you can prevent sagging rails is to nail or screw a 2x4 vertical support midway between posts. First, cut a support long enough to fit under the top rail and extend about 24 inches into the ground. Then cut half-lap notches in the bottom rail and in the support, as shown, so that the outside edge of the support is flush with the outside edge of the rail. Set the support in concrete and gravel, as you would a fence post.

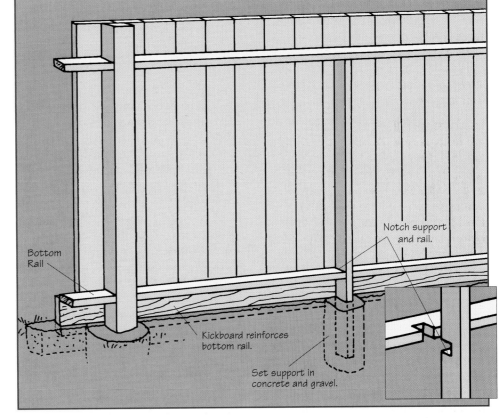

Bottom Rail

Notch support and rail.

Kickboard reinforces bottom rail.

Set support in concrete and gravel.

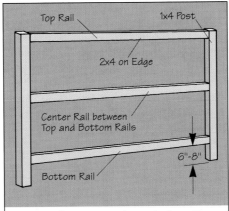

Solid-Board Privacy Fence. *This fence has a board side and a frame side. With vertical boards butted together, the fence provides complete privacy.*

Top Rail

1x4 Post

2x4 on Edge

Center Rail between Top and Bottom Rails

Bottom Rail

6"-8"

1. Set the posts and attach the rails, making sure the rails are square with the posts.

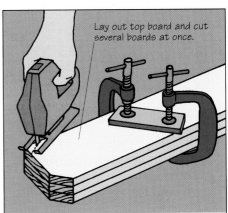

Lay out top board and cut several boards at once.

2. Decorative cuts make a fence more appealing. Save time by cutting several boards at once.

or more boards at a time with a hand saw, saber saw, portable circular saw, or power miter saw. Save the top board as a template for marking and cutting additional boards.

3 **Attach the boards.** Start by attaching strings to the end posts about 2 inches above the ground on the face of the posts that will hold the siding. Level the string with a string level, and align the bottoms of the boards with it as you install them. If you want to conceal the post, begin

by holding the board flush with the outside edge. If you don't want to conceal the post, hold the board flush with the inside edge of the end post, as shown. Then attach the board to the frame. For boards up to 6 inches wide, drill two pilot holes for either 8d galvanized nails or 2-inch galvanized deck screws. For wider boards, drill pilots for three nails or screws. Leave a $\frac{1}{16}$-inch gap between boards as you install them to allow for swelling in wet weather. (Use 4d nails as spacers).

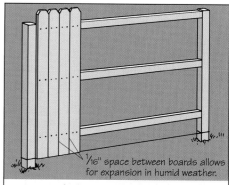

$\frac{1}{16}$" space between boards allows for expansion in humid weather.

3. Attach the boards about 2 inches above the ground. Use a string level as a guide.

Making Curved Fences

Sometimes, a sharp corner can evoke an objectionable, boxed-in feeling, or create a dangerous blind spot for drivers. Curves soften sharp angles in fences and are less likely to obstruct views. To build a curved fence, you must set the posts on 48- to 72-inch centers along an arc. You can apply either straight or curved rails, depending on the look you are trying to create. It takes curved rails to make a truly curved fence, but making curved rails is not as difficult as you might think. As shown in the drawing, each rail consists of two separate pieces of 1x4 redwood strung across several posts and screwed together to form a laminated rail. The rails must span at least three posts—they won't form a curve if they span only two. Stagger the joints so that a joint on the top rail is not on the same post as a joint on a bottom rail.

In the design shown, the rails are let into 3½-inch wide by 1½-inch deep dadoes cut into the posts. Soak rails in water before use to make them more flexible. Attach the first piece to the posts with 3-inch galvanized deck screws, using two screws at each post. Then screw the second piece over the first, using 1¼-inch galvanized decking screws, spaced about 8 inches apart. Stagger the screws so that one is near the top of the rail, the other near the bottom.

For tighter arcs, you can laminate thinner redwood strips, called benderboards, or cut a series of ¼-inch deep saw cuts, called kerfs, about 2 inches apart in the one-by-fours to make them more flexible. Place the kerfed side against the posts. In all cases, the laminated rails should be a total of 1¼ to 1½ inches thick to support the weight of the siding. True-curve fences look best with narrow, lightweight boards, slats, pickets, or rough-split redwood "grapestakes" attached vertically to the rails. Wide boards may split when attached to curved rails.

Segmented Fences. Instead of curved rails, you can attach short, straight fence sections to posts plotted along a curve. Technically, this type of construction does not result in a smooth curve. Instead, you get a series of short, straight chords that roughly follow an arc. On this type of fence, you miter the rail ends and the siding before fastening them to the face of the post, as shown. Drive the fasteners at the point where the rail touches the post for the strongest connection. Because the rails are straight, you can use wide boards or plywood for the siding.

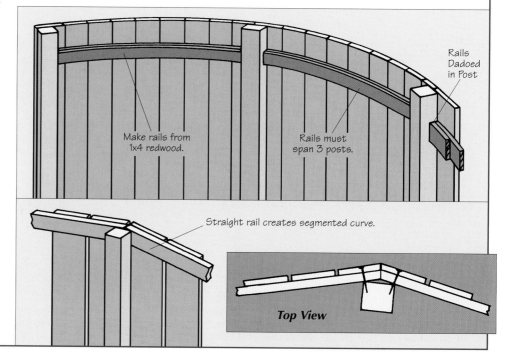

Make rails from 1x4 redwood.

Rails must span 3 posts.

Rails Dadoed in Post

Straight rail creates segmented curve.

Top View

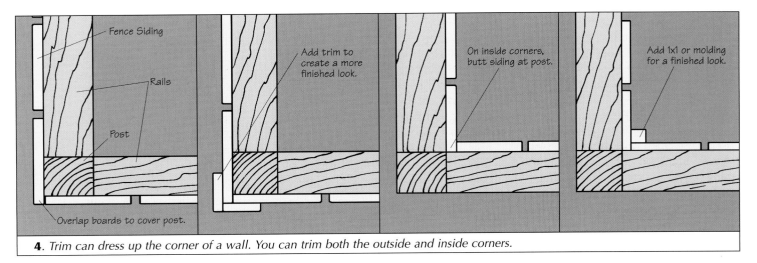

Fence Siding

Rails

Post

Overlap boards to cover post.

Add trim to create a more finished look.

On inside corners, butt siding at post.

Add 1x1 or molding for a finished look.

4. Trim can dress up the corner of a wall. You can trim both the outside and inside corners.

Attach the corner boards.

Where two fences meet at a corner, overlap the end boards, as shown, to hide the post. This often requires ripping one or both siding boards to a narrower width so that they fit. Rip boards on a table saw or with a portable circular saw equipped with an edge guide. For outside corners, attach the corner boards to the posts with 8d galvanized nails or 2-inch deck screws, spaced about 18 inches apart and 2 inches in from the corner. For a more finished appearance, you can cover the exposed board edge with 1x3 battens.

For inside corners, simply overlap the boards. Attach them to the rails as you did the other boards. The joint formed by the lapped boards can be covered with a 1x1 or 2x2 strip or other molding. If desired, finish the corner with a mitered cap rail (see "Joining Rails to Posts," page 67).

Horizontal-Board Fence

This solid horizontal-board fence has a formal appearance that's well-suited to contemporary home designs. The fence shown uses 96-inch 1x6s attached horizontally between posts on 96-inch centers. In this design, all posts should be exactly the same height. This design does not work well on sloped or uneven terrain.

Attach 2x4 nailers midway between posts to provide additional nailing surface for the boards. A 2x4 vertical center support keeps the boards from bowing and the bottom rail from sagging. Drop siding, V-groove siding, shiplap, and other conventional house siding materials work well to make a fence that complements the wood siding on your house.

Attach the cap rail and bottom rails.

Install the 1x6 cap rail across the tops of the posts. Position the cap to overhang the front and back of the posts by 1 inch. Attach 2x4 bottom rails to the posts so they are level and at least 2 inches above ground level.

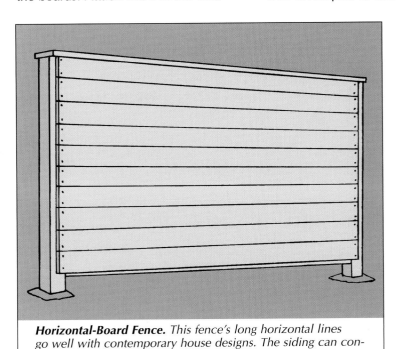

Horizontal-Board Fence. *This fence's long horizontal lines go well with contemporary house designs. The siding can consist of boards or wood siding to match your house.*

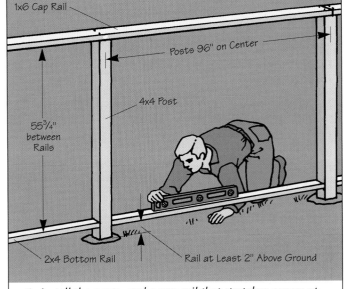

1x6 Cap Rail

Posts 96" on Center

4x4 Post

55³⁄₄" between Rails

2x4 Bottom Rail

Rail at Least 2" Above Ground

1. Install the posts, and a cap rail that stretches across at least three posts. Cut the bottom rail to fit.

2 Attach the center support.

Cut the 2x4 center supports to fit between the rail and cap. Fasten the supports midway between the posts. The support should be flush with the face of the bottom rail, but recessed 1 inch from the front edge of the cap rail. Drive two galvanized 16d nails or 3½-inch deck screws through the cap rail into the support. Toenail the support to the bottom rail with 10d nails or 2-inch galvanized deck screws. Put a block under the bottom rail to hold it steady when toenailing the center support.

3 Attach the boards.

Cut the siding boards to span at least two posts. All ends should fall at the middle of a post face. Starting at the top, position the first board tightly under the cap-rail overhang. Attach the boards with two galvanized 8d ring shank nails at the posts and the vertical support. Install the remaining boards, leaving 1/16 inch between the boards to allow for expansion in wet weather. You might have to rip the bottom board flush with the bottom rail. If you are using tongue-and-groove siding, position the first board so the groove faces down. Slip the tongue of the second board up into it, and so on.

4 Attach the kickboard (optional).

You can choose to nail a 1x8 or 1x10 kickboard along the bottom rail to cover the gap and prevent animals from digging under the fence. If so, leave the bottom ¾ inch of the rail exposed when attaching the siding. Notch the kickboard to fit around any concrete collars. Nail it to the exposed section of bottom rail. Kickboards can be placed on the ground, but are more effective when they extend 6 to 8 inches into the ground. If you're going to set the kickboard in the ground, dig a trench for it when you're digging the posts.

Vertical Board-on-Board Fence ☂☂

This 72-inch fence provides a modicum of privacy while not completely blocking sunshine and wind. It works well along a property line because both sides have siding. The fence is covered with 1x6 siding boards, spaced one board width, or 5½ inches, apart. Note in the drawing how boards are staggered: A gap on one side of the fence is filled by a board on the other side.

1 Build the framework.

Set the posts 60½ inches apart. This spacing allows for six 1x6 siding boards, spaced one board apart. Alter to fit your needs, but the maximum distance between posts should be no more than 96 inches. Cut 2x4 rails to fit between the posts. Position them so that you'll be nailing the siding into the wide face of the rail. Center the rails on the face of the post. Fence brackets will make

2. The center support gives the fence rigidity. Slip a block underneath it to support it when nailing.

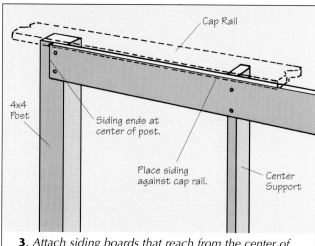

3. Attach siding boards that reach from the center of one post to the center of another. The fence will be stronger if the boards span at least two posts.

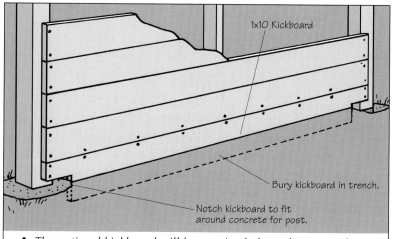

4. The optional kickboard will keep animals from slipping under the fence. Use pressure-treated wood, and cut it to fit around any obstructions.

positioning easier. The top rail can be attached flush with the top of the posts, as shown, or several inches below it, depending on the effect you want to achieve.

2 Attach the boards to the front side.
Drill two pilot holes to avoid splitting the siding boards at each rail location. Butt the rail against the end post and attach the first 1x6 board to the rails with galvanized 8d nails or 2-inch deck screws. Then, using a 1x6 block as a spacer, attach the next boards to the front side of the fence. Lay out the spacing with a piece of 1x6 scrap as shown. If necessary, adjust the spacing so that there's no more than a full board width between the last board and the post. Use a carpenter's level to make sure the boards are plumb as you attach them.

3 Attach the boards to the back side.
On the other side of the fence, temporarily tack one of the boards to the rail so that it is snug against the post; this will be the spacer board. Butt a second board against the first and attach it to the rails. Remove the first board and use it as a spacer to attach remaining boards. Adjust the spacing if needed, and check for plumb.

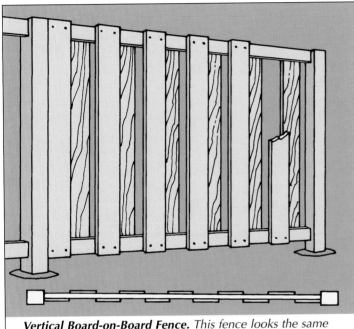

Vertical Board-on-Board Fence. This fence looks the same on both sides, so it's a good choice for marking property lines. The boards are spaced one board width apart; for more privacy, you should reduce this spacing.

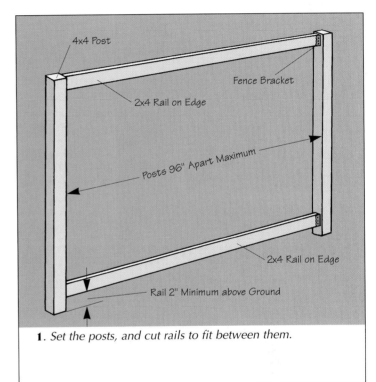

4x4 Post

Fence Bracket

2x4 Rail on Edge

Posts 96" Apart Maximum

2x4 Rail on Edge

Rail 2" Minimum above Ground

1. Set the posts, and cut rails to fit between them.

Position boards using 1x6 scrap as spacer.

Board is flush with rails and tight against posts.

2. Attach the boards, using a cut-off to lay out the spaces between them.

Spacer Temporarily Tacked in Place

Nail this board permanently in place.

3. Attach boards to the other side of the fence. Start by temporarily nailing a board next to the post, then permanently nailing another board next to it.

Alternating Panel Fence 🔩🔩

This variation of a solid-board fence has 1x6 boards to the neighbor's side of the fence from the middle of the span to one post and on your side of the fence between the middle and the next post. It enables you to share an attractive fence with your neighbors while providing privacy and good wind control. The fence shown has posts set on 96-inch centers with top rails fastened to the post tops. Bottom rails are toenailed between posts. The fence is 72 inches tall, which is typical of boundary fences. You can build it lower if desired.

1 Build the framework. Set the posts and install the rails. Attach a 2x4 center support midway between each pair of posts, as shown. Drive two 16d nails or 3-inch galvanized deck screws through the top rail into the center support, and screw or toe-nail two 10d nails through the support into the bottom rail. Put a block under the bottom rail while you're nailing, and make sure the center support is square to the rails.

2 Fill in the first panel. Position the first board so that it covers the post. Drill two pilot holes at rail heights, and fasten the board with 8d galvanized nails or 2-inch deck screws. With a carpenter's level, make sure the board is plumb. When you add the remaining boards, space them so that the last one will be set flush with the edge of the center support. Leave ⅛ inch between boards. If necessary, rip the last board to width on a table saw.

3 Attach the alternate panel. Move to the rails between the center support and the next post. Cross to the other side of the fence, and attach 1x6 siding boards to it. When finished, work your way down the length of the fence, alternating sides between sets of posts.

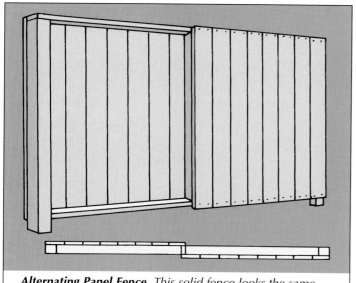

Alternating Panel Fence. *This solid fence looks the same from both sides. The alternating panels create a textured surface that other fences don't have.*

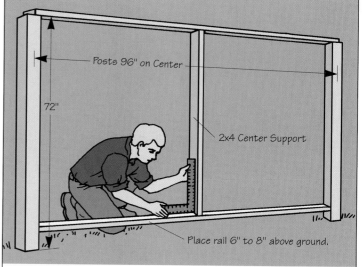

1. Set the posts and rails, and attach a center support between the rails. Make sure the center support is square to the rails.

2. Attach boards to one side of the fence.

3. Cross to the other side of the fence, and attach boards to it.

Louver Fence 🔩🔩🔩

Although a louver fence requires more lumber than a conventional board fence, it makes an attractive enclosure for patios and pools. A louver fence filters sunshine and wind without completely blocking them; this fence also offers privacy. Louvers are commonly set at 45 degrees, although you can set them at another angle to provide more (or less) privacy and wind control. The fence shown here is just over 72 inches tall and has posts set on 96-inch centers. The louvers are 1x4 boards nailed at an angle to 2x4 rails.

1 **Cut the louvers.** Build the framework, setting posts, and cutting the rails to fit. Note the rails are different

lengths: The bottom rail is dadoed into the posts, while the top rail sits on top of them. After building the framework, cut the fence boards to fit between the top and bottom rails.

2 **Attach the first louver.** Put the first louver between the rails near a post. Set it at the proper angle with the 45-degree face of a combination square or speed square. Center the louver on rail so that any gap between the louver and rail edges is uniform. Slide the square until the louver butts against the post. Double check the angle and mark the location by tracing a line along the louver. Drill pilot holes and toenail the first louver to the bottom rail with 10d galvanized finish nails. Drive two 2½-inch screws or nails through the top rail into the louver.

3 **Make a spacer.** For accurate spacing and angle of the boards, make a spacer block by cutting one end of a 1x3 scrap to the desired angle. (This spacer block will space the boards 2½ inches apart. If you want wider spaces, use a 1x4 block; use a 1x2 block for thinner spaces.) Lay the spacer block on the bottom rail with the mitered end flush with the edge of the rail, and guide each board into position.

4 **Attach the remaining louvers.** Attach the remaining louvers between the posts to fill out the section. Put a block under the bottom rail to keep it steady as you are toenailing. Adjust the spacing of the last few louvers to allow enough room for the final louver.

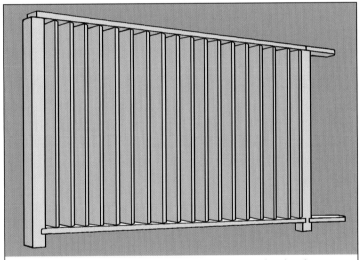

Louver Fence. With boards installed at an angle, this fence filters wind and sunlight. Louvers can be installed horizontally as well.

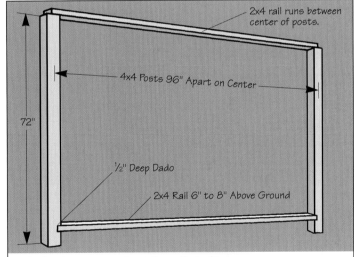

1. Set the posts and cut the rails to fit.

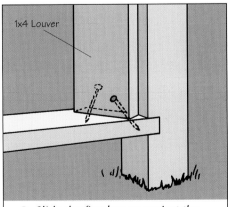

2. Slide the first louver against the post, and adjust its angle with the 45 degree face of a combination or speed square.

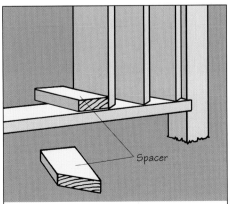

3. Cut a piece of scrap and use it as a spacer to position the remaining louvers.

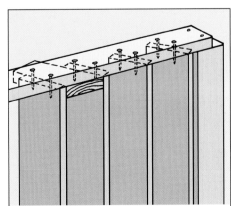

4. Fill in the rest of the section. Attach the louvers with nails or screws through the top. Toenail louvers to the bottom rail.

Lattice-Top Fence 🔨🔨🔨

Board-and-lattice fences offer privacy and good wind protection while retaining an open feeling. The lattice-top fence shown looks the same on both sides. It uses prefab 12 by 96-inch lattice panels sandwiched between 1x1 strips on the top and middle rails. The 4x4 posts are set on 96-inch centers, and the lattice is cut to fit between posts; use an old saw blade and wear eye protection because your saw is bound to hit the staples that hold together prefab lat-tice panels. The bottom portion of the fence consists of 1x8 boards centered between the posts and rails, also held in place with 1x1 strips. For a nicer appearance, you can substitute tongue-and-groove boards for square-edged ones.

1 **Build the frame.** Attach the bottom and middle rails to the posts so that the top edge of the middle rail is 12 inches below the post top. For the 72-inch high fence shown here, the distance between the middle rail and the bottom rail should be 53½ inches—enough to leave a 2-inch gap between the ground and the bottom rail.

2 **Attach the 1x1 strips and boards.** Attach four 1x1 strips (available at most lumberyards) to the rails and posts with 6d nails so that the strips are set back about ⅝ inch from the faces of the posts and rails. The strip corners can be butted, or, for a better appearance, mitered. Predrill nail holes near the ends to avoid splitting.

Starting flush against one post, attach the boards as shown by toenailing through them into the rails with 8d galvanized finish nails. Leave ½-inch spaces between the boards or space evenly so that the last board is a full one. If you need to, rip the last board to width on a table saw. After filling in each section, attach a second set of 1x1 strips set back ⅝ inches from the opposite side of the fence.

3 **Attach the top rails and lattice.** Nail the 2x4 top rails with 16d galvanized nails across the post tops; 96-inch 2x4s should reach from the center of one post to the center of the next. With 6d galvanized finishing nails, attach one set of 1x1 strips to the inside of the posts and to the top and middle rail, positioned so there is 1 inch between the strip and the front

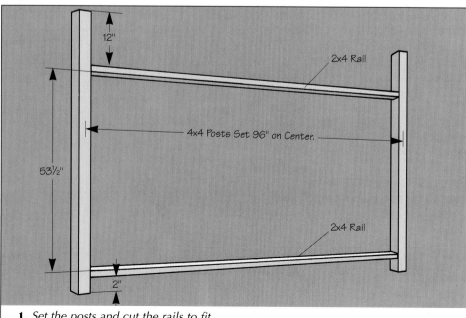

Lattice-Top Fence. *This is another fence that looks the same from both sides. The prefab lattice top panel makes it less imposing than a solid board privacy fence.*

2x4 Rail

4x4 Posts Set 96" on Center.

2x4 Rail

12"

53½"

2"

1. Set the posts and cut the rails to fit.

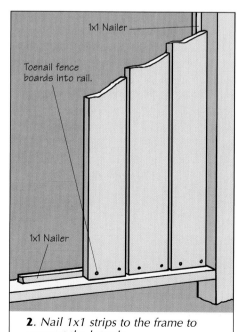

1x1 Nailer

Toenail fence boards into rail.

1x1 Nailer

2. Nail 1x1 strips to the frame to support the boards.

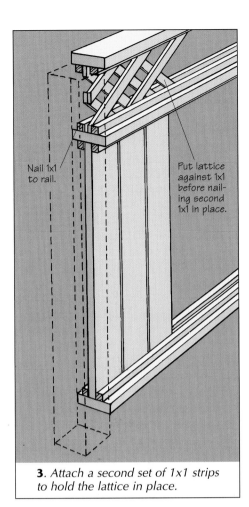

Nail 1x1 to rail.

Put lattice against 1x1 before nailing second 1x1 in place.

3. *Attach a second set of 1x1 strips to hold the lattice in place.*

of the rail. Trim the ends of the lattice strips to fit between the posts. Place the lattice against the strips, then install a second set of strips to hold the lattice in place. It is not necessary to nail the lattice to the strips.

PICKET FENCES

Picket fences are often found gracing the front yards of Colonial, Victorian, and other traditionally styled houses. A picket fence is in fact appropriate for almost any house, especially houses with formal gardens. As opposed to solid-board fences, the open design of a picket fence shows off plantings within the yard, yet provides a definite boundary to discourage casual trespassers.

Planting low shrubs, vines, or perennial plants, such as red roses, next to the fence helps soften the repetitive design, although you'll need to prune plants back when it comes time to repaint the fence.

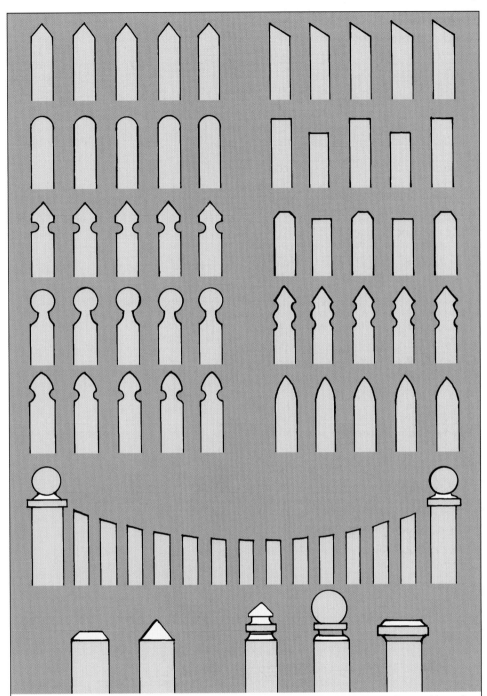

Picket-Top Designs. *The look of a fence depends on the style of the pickets. Although you can buy precut pickets at lumberyards, you can customize your fence by designing and cutting your own pickets. You can also buy or make custom posts to match your pickets.*

Picket-Top Designs

Some lumberyards and home centers carry precut pickets, but the designs are often limited. To make your own simple pointed pickets, clamp two or three boards together and cut the tops with a hand saw or circular saw. To make fancier top cuts, clamp together a pair of boards and cut the pattern with a saber saw.

Many lumberyards also sell precut posts with decorative tops. Some of these tops, called finials, embellish the classical beauty of a picket fence; lumberyards sell separate finials, too, that can be attached to 4x4 or 6x6 posts. If you have access to a band saw, you can cut your own post top designs. A few examples of post and picket tops are shown in this section.

Building a Basic Picket Fence

Most picket fences are 36 to 48 inches tall, and use a framework of 4x4 posts on 96-inch centers with 2x4 rails, just like the board fences on the previous pages. On some designs, the posts extend above the picket tops, in which case you can use a decorative post top. On other designs, the top rails are attached across the post tops, and the pickets extend 4 to 6 inches above the framework.

The pickets themselves usually consist of evenly spaced 1x3s or 1x4s attached to the outside of the rails. A couple of tips: The pickets are often the same width as the posts. And the bottoms of the pickets should be at least 2 inches above the ground level to prevent decay and make it easier both to paint the fence and to remove weeds.

1 Build the frame. To make the picket fence shown, build the frame so the bottom rail fits between the posts, and the top rail overlaps the posts. For strength, use a top rail that spans at least three posts. Cut the rail so that it meets the next rail in the center of a post. Cut the 1x4 pickets so that they will extend about 6 inches above the top rail.

2 Attach the post pickets. Starting at one end of the fence, attach the first picket to the end post with two 6d galvanized nails or two 2-inch galvanized deck screws at the same height as the rails. Make sure the edge of the picket is flush with the edge of the post, as shown. Install a picket over every post in the fence.

3 Space the pickets evenly. The best picket fences have uniformly spaced pickets. You can get uniform spacing with some simple math:

First, choose the number of pickets you want between the posts. Multiply the number by the width of a picket to find out the total distance occupied by pickets. (Round up to a whole number, if necessary.) Subtract the answer from the distance between posts to find out how much unoccupied space there is.

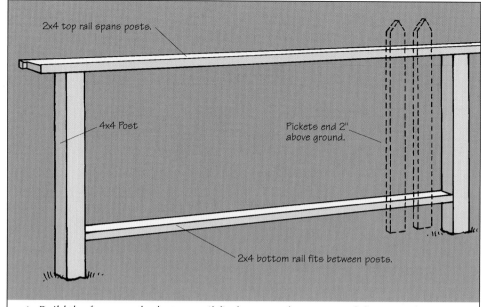

2x4 top rail spans posts.

4x4 Post

Pickets end 2" above ground.

2x4 bottom rail fits between posts.

1. *Build the frame so the bottom rail fits between the posts, and the top rail overlaps the posts.*

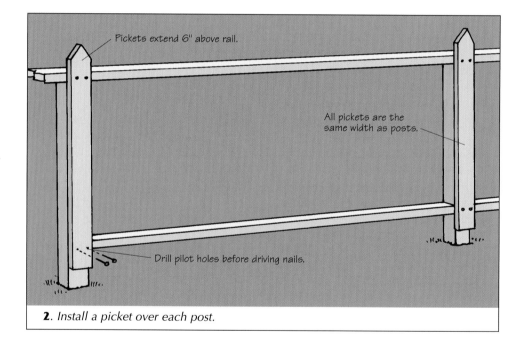

Pickets extend 6" above rail.

All pickets are the same width as posts.

Drill pilot holes before driving nails.

2. *Install a picket over each post.*

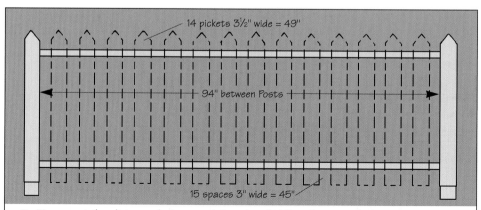

14 pickets 3½" wide = 49"

94" between Posts

15 spaces 3" wide = 45"

3. *Figure out the distance between pickets by dividing the cumulative space between pickets by the number of spaces.*

To find out the space between pickets, divide the amount of unoccupied space by the number of spaces per section. The total number of spaces will be one more than the total number of pickets.

4 Attach the remaining pickets. Rip a board to the width you just computed and use this spacer board to space the pickets. A wood cleat nailed to the top of the spacer board makes it easier to use.

Set up stakes and a level string 2 inches above ground, and set the pickets to this height. Place the spacer board against a post picket, then butt the second picket against the board and nail or screw it in place. Repeat for remaining pickets, checking them for plumb with a carpenter's level. Make sure the spacing will work by marking the last few boards and spreading any discrepancy over several pickets.

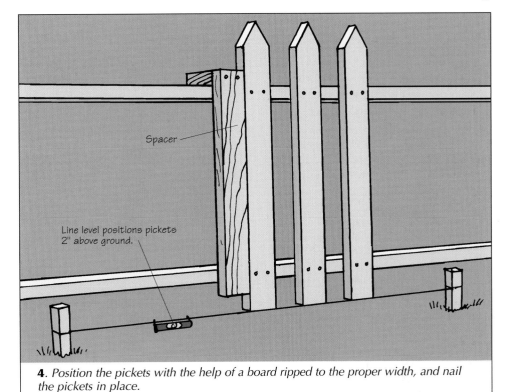

Spacer

Line level positions pickets 2" above ground.

4. Position the pickets with the help of a board ripped to the proper width, and nail the pickets in place.

Curved-Top Picket Fence

The undulating shape of a curved-top picket fence nicely complements a natural setting or a gingerbread house style, such as Victorian. You can make the curved top by cutting the pickets after they've been fastened to the fence frame. The only pickets that should be cut to their exact length are the post pickets; you can let the intervening pickets "run wild" as long as they extend at least 6 inches above the top rail and are even along the bottom.

You will need soft, heavy cotton rope cut about 12 inches longer than the span between posts. Attach the rope to the top of the post pickets, allowing it to sag freely across the picket faces. After making sure that the rope does not sag below the top rail, carefully trace the rope on all of the picket faces except the post pickets. Remove the rope, cut along the line with a saber saw, and sand the picket tops smooth. For a finished appearance, top off the posts with decorative caps or finials, available at lumberyards and home centers.

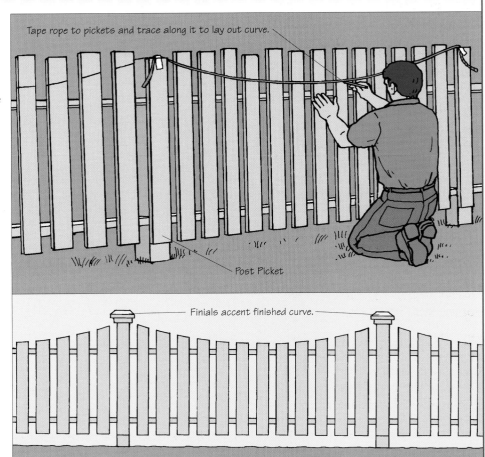

Tape rope to pickets and trace along it to lay out curve.

Post Picket

Finials accent finished curve.

OTHER WOOD FENCES

In addition to the board-fence designs shown so far, wood can be used in other ways to create attractive fences. The following pages show some of the more popular types.

Rustic Post-and-Rail Fence 🔩

If you're looking for a fence that works well on uneven terrain, and has rustic charm, a rail fence is a good choice. Rails are readily available at lumberyards and garden centers. The rails may be square or roughly wedge-shaped, just like a piece of firewood, and are typically from 72 to 96 inches long. In some areas, round, unsplit "palings" are available, with or without the bark attached.

Rails generally fit into a mortise in the post. They can overlap, they can be tenoned, or they can simply butt together. Fences with two or three rails per section are the most common. Some lumberyards carry premortised posts and tenoned rails, sold as kits, or you can buy the rough stock and cut your own mortises and tenons.

1 Mortise the posts. Use a pencil and a try square to mark the size and locations of the mortises. Rail fences are somewhat crude (which is part of their rustic charm), so you don't need to be too exact. Make the width and length of the mortise ⅛ to ¼ inch larger than the width and thickness of the rails. Cut the mortises in the same locations on each post: Make the top edge of each upper mortise about 2 inches below the post top, for example. Lay out the bottom mortise so that bottom rail will be at least 6 inches above ground level after the post is set. To rough out the mortise, drill a series of 1-inch holes all the way through the post, then clean up the edges with a hammer and wide wood chisel.

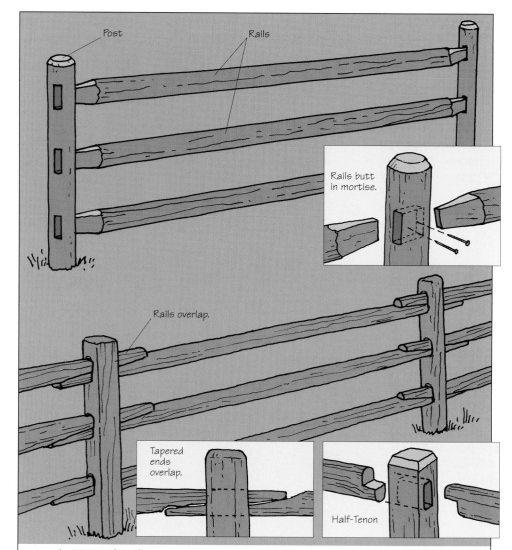

Rustic Post-and-Rail Fence. *The look of post-and-rail fences is well suited to rustic houses on hilly terrain. There are three typical construction techniques. One involves cutting a mortise through the posts, and butting the rails in a mortise. You can also taper and overlap the rails or cut half-tenons in the rails and insert them in a mortise.*

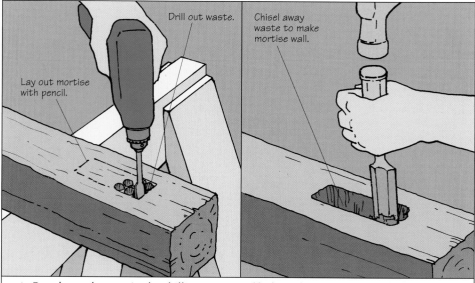

1. *Rough out the mortise by drilling a series of holes. Clean up the edges with a chisel.*

2. *Cut the rails so they'll overlap in the mortises.*

2 Cut tenons in the rails. With a hand saw, cut half-tenons in the rail ends so that they overlap in the mortise. Cut tenons about 1 inch shorter than the width of the post. Tenons are not required where the rails join the end posts. For corner posts, cut mortises as shown.

3 Erect the fence. Set the first post, then set the next post loosely in place. Insert the rails, plumb and set the post permanently, and repeat the process.

Formal Post-and-Rail Fence 🔨🔨

Formal post-and-rail fences use dimensional lumber, typically 4x4s for the posts, and 2x6s or 4x4s for the rails. Depending on the fence height and look you want to achieve, you can attach one, two, or even three rails between the posts. Rails are either toenailed between posts or dadoed into them. The dado joint in this fence design provides a strong connection and is easier to make than the mortise-and-tenon joint used in the rustic post and rail fence. The fence will have a more finished appearance and will shed water if you chamfer the post tops, as shown.

1 Set the posts. Cut 1½-inch-deep dadoes in the posts (see "Dadoing Posts" on page 68). Dado adja-

3. *Set one post firmly, put in the rails, and then slip the second post over them.*

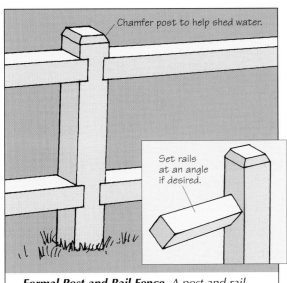

Formal Post-and-Rail Fence. *A post and rail fence made of dimensioned lumber has a dressier, more finished look.*

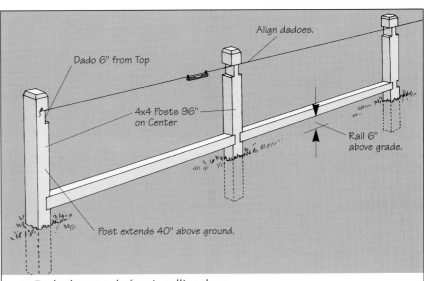

1. *Dado the posts before installing them.*

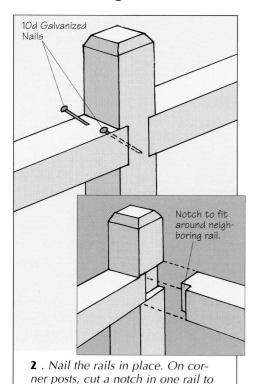

2 . *Nail the rails in place. On corner posts, cut a notch in one rail to house the other rail.*

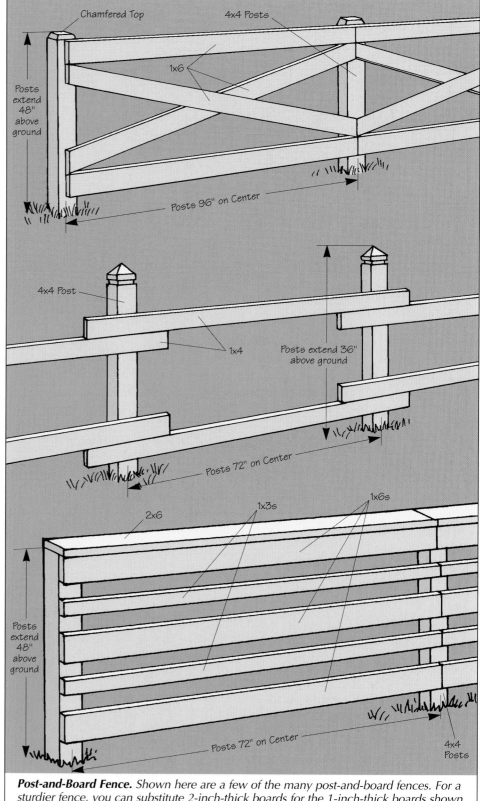

Post-and-Board Fence. *Shown here are a few of the many post-and-board fences. For a sturdier fence, you can substitute 2-inch-thick boards for the 1-inch-thick boards shown.*

cent sides of the corner posts. Set the posts to the same height on 96-inch centers. With a line level, make sure the dadoes in the posts are aligned properly.

2 **Add the rails.** Cut the rails to length, and slip them into the dadoes, tapping lightly with a hammer, if necessary, to fit them in place. Secure by toenailing two 10d-galvanized nails through the top of the rails. Where two rails meet at a corner, you will have to notch one of the rails to fit into the dado. Install the first rail, then notch one side of the second one to fit into the adjacent dado. (If your design calls for butting the rails between posts, you won't have to notch the corners.)

Post-and-Board Fence 🔨🔨

Because of their low, open design, post-and-board fences define boundaries while still providing good views from both sides of the fence. They are also easy to build and use less lumber than most other fences. This type of fence commonly consists of two, three, or four 1x4 or 1x6 rails nailed to one side of the posts. Most residential versions are

36 to 48 inches high. Posts are typically spaced on 72-inch centers for one-by rails or 96-inch centers for two-by rails, with the rails spanning three or four posts. Joints between top and bottom rails are staggered.

1 **Prepare and set the posts.** In the fence shown, the center and bottom rails are dadoed into 4x4 posts. Position the dadoes so that the boards will be spaced equally. The bottom board should be at least

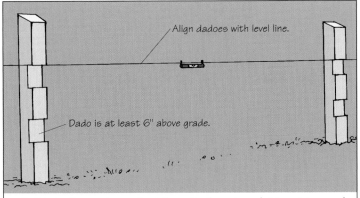

1. Dado the posts, and set them in the ground. Use string and a line level to make sure the dados are all at the same height.

Align dadoes with level line.

Dado is at least 6" above grade.

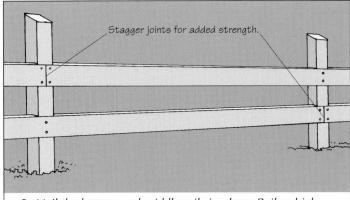

2. Nail the bottom and middle rails in place. Rails which span more than two posts add strength to the fence.

Stagger joints for added strength.

6 inches above grade. Set the posts at equal heights on 72-inch centers.

2 Install the middle and bottom rails.
Cut the 1x6 rails to length, and attach them to the posts with 8d galvanized nails or 2-inch galvanized all-purpose screws. For extra strength, you can cut the rails 12 feet long (to span three posts), then stagger the rail ends so that joints do not occur on the same post, as shown.

3 Add the top rail and cap.
Fasten the 1x4 top rail even with the tops of the posts. Fasten the 1x6 cap board to the post tops so that it is flush with the front of the top rail. Use four 10d nails or 2½-inch deck screws at each post. If desired, you can angle the post tops to provide a slanted cap that sheds water and keeps youngsters from walking on top of the fence.

Plywood Fences 🔩🔩

Plywood fences create a solid, opaque barrier that provides much the same privacy as a masonry wall. You should use only exterior-grade plywood (designated "ext") for these fences. Plywood with an "X" in its name, such as CDX, is not meant for outdoor use; the "X" simply means that the plywood may be left exposed for a short while until it is covered with siding, roofing, or other material. A popular type of exterior plywood, T1-11, has channels routed in the face to mimic tongue-and-groove boards.

Even exterior-grade plywood can peel apart, so protect the edges with caulk

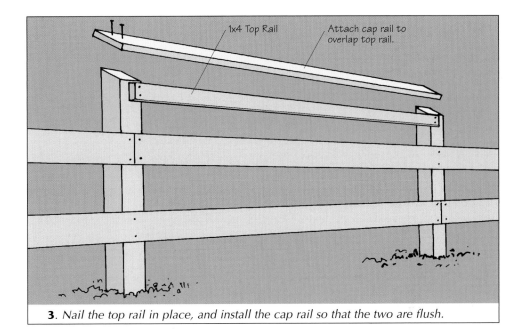

1x4 Top Rail

Attach cap rail to overlap top rail.

3. Nail the top rail in place, and install the cap rail so that the two are flush.

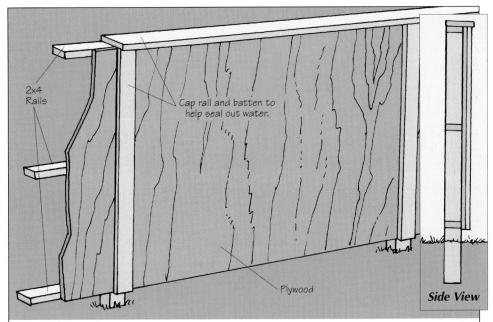

2x4 Rails

Cap rail and batten to help seal out water.

Plywood

Side View

Plywood Fence. *An economical solid fence, this plywood fence can be painted or covered with house-siding materials, such as shingles or stucco.*

and 1x4 battens. You should also install a 1x6 cap board to protect the top edges.

Plywood fences usually look best painted to match your house. They also can be covered with other materials, such as stucco or shingles. The plywood is typically ⅝- or ¾-inch thick 4x8 panels. If the fence is sub-ject to strong winds, a fence 48 inch-es high should have 4x6 posts set at least 24 inches into concrete collars in the ground.

1 Build the frame. The fence shown here consists of 4x4 posts set at equal heights on 96-inch centers. The 2x4 top and bottom rails are installed with the wide dimension up. A third rail is centered between them, also with the wide dimension up. Attach the framework with galvanized 10d nails or 2-inch deck screws.

2 Add the panels. With a helper, attach ¾-inch, 4x8 plywood pan-els to the fence frame, using 8d gal-vanized nails or 1½-inch galvanized deck screws, spaced about 6 inches

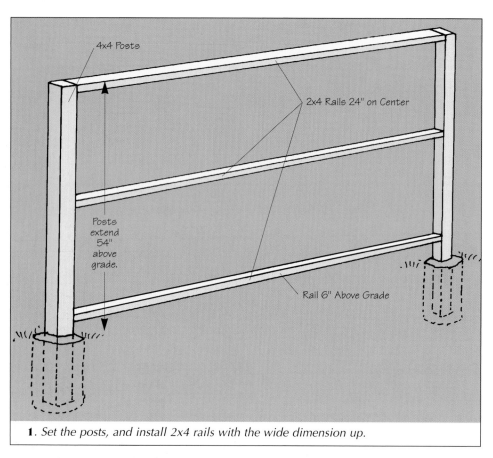

1. Set the posts, and install 2x4 rails with the wide dimension up.

2. Attach plywood to the rails with nails or screws.

Using Other Panels

You can substitute fiberglass or various types of plastic panels for plywood. These panels come in a variety of thicknesses, colors, surface textures, and degrees of translucency or opacity (ability to transmit light). Acrylic and PVC panels come in clear, obscure, textured, and colored forms, but they are easily scratched. Colored panels eventually fade when exposed to sunlight. For these reasons, the panels require careful placement to protect them from the weather.

Fiberglass panels come in flat or corrugated versions. Both types admit light while obscuring views. As with plastic panels, colors fade over time.

The thickness of the panels you choose depends on their overall size; the larger the panel, the thicker it must be to withstand winds. Large (4x6 or 4x8 foot) sheets may require additional bracing within the fence panel to prevent excessive flexing in high wind conditions.

Although you can cut plastic and fiberglass panels with a fine-tooth hand saw, a band saw, or a table saw equipped with a fine-tooth blade, it is easier to have the dealer precut the panels. To attach the panels to a wood frame, drill slightly oversized pilot holes in the panel edges and attach with aluminum twist nails and neoprene washers. Leave ¼-inch expansion gaps between panel edges.

apart. Start at one top corner and work your way across. Do the same for the next panel. Leave a ⅛-inch gap between the panels.

3 Add the battens and cap. Attach the 1x6 cap board so that it's flush with the back edge of the post. Caulk the ⅛-inch gap between plywood panels with a good exterior latex or silicone caulk. Nail 1x4 battens over the gaps with 6d galvanized finishing nails. Set the nail heads and fill the holes with exterior-grade wood putty. Nail a second batten to the end posts as shown in the inset.

Wood-and-Wire Fence

Welded- or woven-wire mesh can be attached to a wood frame to make an attractive, lightweight, and economical fence. Low wire fences are an excellent choice for enclosing children's play areas or defining garden areas; a taller fence provides security and can act as a trellis for climbing vines.

Welded wire comes in a variety of gauges and mesh sizes, typically in 36-, 48-, and 72-inch widths, in 50- or 100-foot rolls. It is best to choose the heaviest-gauge wire available; lightweight wire is easily deformed and prone to rust. Most wood-and-wire fences use a 2x2- or 2x4-inch welded-wire mesh, either galvanized or vinyl-coated. Vinyl-coated wire comes in a limited range of colors: White and forest green are the most common. Green blends well into the landscape, making the fence nearly invisible; use white when you want to define an area or provide contrast to surrounding landscape features.

Because the wood-and-wire fence shown here is more than 48 inches high, it has a center rail for extra stability. Fences less than 48 inches high don't require a center rail. You can add a pressure-treated kickboard to keep children and animals from crawling underneath the fence; the 1x6 cap board is optional but recommended because it covers exposed wire tips.

1 Build the frame. Construct the framework with 4x4 posts spaced on 96-inch centers, and 2x4 top and bottom rails. Position the rails so the distance between the top of the top rail and the bottom of the bottom rail is 48 inches. Fasten the top rail to the post tops. Fasten the bottom rail between posts.

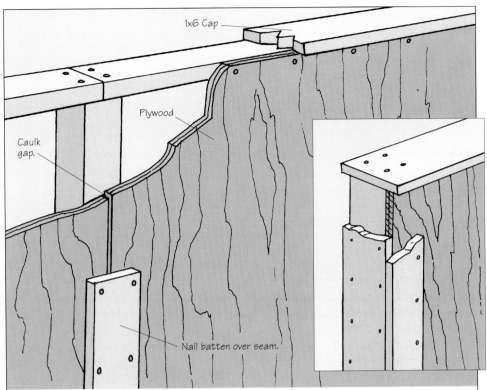

3. Cover the edges of the plywood with a top batten, and with another batten at the seams between the plywood.

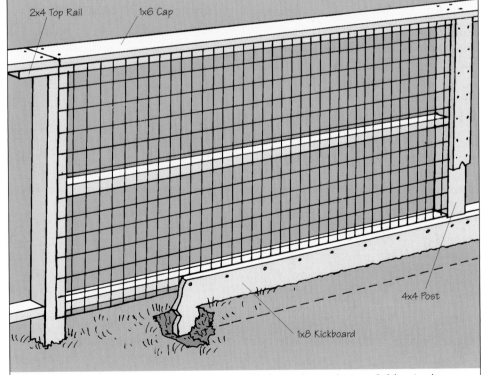

***Wood-and-Wire Fence.** This fence is a good choice for enclosing children's play areas because you can see through it. Be sure to cover all wire ends with battens, a cap board, and a kickboard.*

2 **Attach the wire.** With a helper, unroll enough wire to cover the first fence section. Hold the end about 1 inch back from the edge of the post, and align the top edge of the wire with the top rail. Fasten the top corner with a ¾-inch U-staple. While your helper holds the wire even with the top rail, staple the wire every 6 inches, first working your way down the post, then across the top rail, followed by the bottom rail and the next post. Have your helper stretch more wire across the next section, and repeat the stapling process.

3 **Splice the wire.** If you run out of wire before you reach the end of the fence, cut back the wire to the nearest post. Start the new roll by overlapping the ends. When you reach the end of the fence, cut the wire 1 inch short of the edge of the post and staple down any loose ends.

4 **Add the battens (optional).** Adding 1x4 battens to the posts gives the fence a finished appearance, helps secure the wire to the posts, and covers any protruding wire ends. Cut battens to span from the bottom to the top rail, and attach with 8d galvanized nails or 2-inch galvanized deck screws. Add a 1x6 cap board to protect the batten ends.

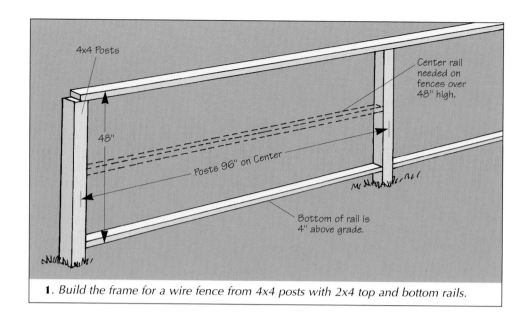

1. Build the frame for a wire fence from 4x4 posts with 2x4 top and bottom rails.

2. Unroll the fence and staple it to a post. Staple along the top rail to the next post; then staple the bottom rail before nailing fence wire to the next post.

3. If you run out of wire, splice it at the nearest post, and staple down loose ends.

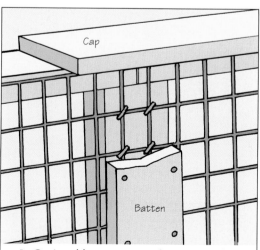

4. Optional battens cover the posts and the top of the fence.

OTHER FENCE DESIGNS

Obviously, not all fences are made of wood. The three most popular fence alternatives are ornamental metal fences, vinyl fences, and chain link fences. There are also a variety of simple, temporary fences that use a combination of wood and other materials. A note of caution concerning chain link fences: Installation requires some special equipment. Low chain link fences are easy to install. For taller fences, consider hiring a qualified fence contractor to install the fence. Most retail outlets that carry chain link fence supplies also offer installation services.

ORNAMENTAL METAL FENCES

The earliest ornamental metal fences were made of wrought iron that was hammered on anvils and twisted into classic forms. Although a few crafts-

men still work in wrought iron, most ornamental metal fencing today is made of cast iron, tubular steel, or aluminum. You can choose from a variety of prefabricated designs and install the fence yourself, or you can have a fence custom-made and installed.

Prefabricated Metal

Prefab metal fences are sold through fence suppliers, who can also deliver the fence to your home and install it. Styles range from ornate Victorian reproductions to sleek, modern designs. Most companies that make prefabricated fences also offer matching gates and the hardware necessary to mount them on the fence.

Most prefabricated steel and aluminum fences come with a durable factory-applied finish, typically a polyester powder coating. Colors commonly available include black, white, or brown. Check the manufacturer's warranty to see how long the fence is guaranteed against rust and corrosion. If the fence you choose requires on-site painting, use a high-quality, rust-resistant paint. It is easier to paint the components before installing them.

Post Options. With a helper or two, prefab metal fences are easy to install. The prefabricated panels typically come in 72- to 96-inch lengths (and various heights) and fit neatly into prepunched holes in the metal posts. You can also buy prefabricated sections and attach them to wood posts or masonry columns with mounting brackets (supplied by the manufacturer), lag screws, and masonry anchors.

No matter which route you go, spacing between posts depends on the size of the prefab panels, which must fit snugly between them. For this reason, it is best to erect the fence section by section, attaching prefab panels after two posts are in place. Use these instructions along with those provided by the manufacturer for the specific fence you are installing.

1 Locate and dig the postholes.
Carefully lay out the postholes according to the length of the prefab

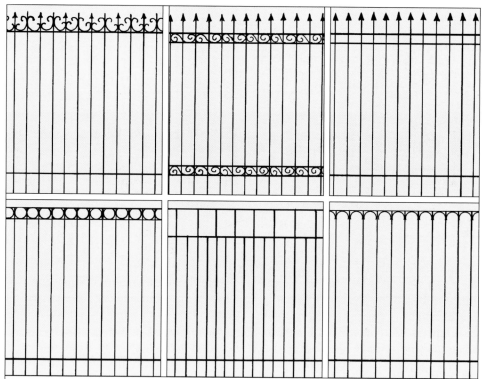

Ornamental Metal Fences. *Shown are several popular styles of prefabricated ornamental metal fence sections. Custom designs can be fabricated.*

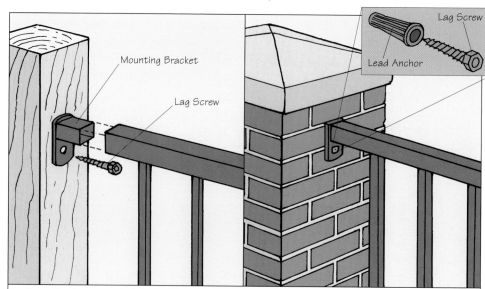

Post Options. *Manufacturers provide special brackets for attaching metal fence sections to wood posts or masonry columns.*

panels and prefab gate, if you're using one. Then dig the postholes. If you're planning to install a custom-built gate, you can set the posts and build the gate to fit the opening. For more information on layout, see Chapter Four, "Setting Posts," beginning on page 51.

In warm climates, postholes for metal fences 48 inches or less should be at

least 18 inches deep. For 60-inch fences, dig holes 24 inches deep. For 72-inch or taller fences, dig holes 30 inches deep. In cold climates, set the concrete below the frost line.

Before installing the posts, separate them according to function: Line posts have holes punched on opposite sides to accommodate the fence sections; end posts have only one

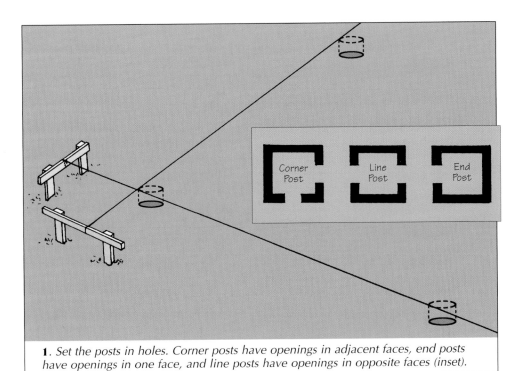

1. *Set the posts in holes. Corner posts have openings in adjacent faces, end posts have openings in one face, and line posts have openings in opposite faces (inset).*

mix.) Set the post all the way into the hole, positioning it along the line you set up to lay out postholes. After a few minutes, raise the post to the correct level. Make sure the holes that hold the fence sections clear the ground enough to allow installation. The exact height varies among manufacturers, so check the instructions that come with the fence. Temporarily brace the fence posts until the concrete sets, and check frequently with a level to make sure the posts remain plumb.

3 Install the fence sections. After the concrete sets slightly for the first post, install a second post, and then insert the rails of the first prefab section into the holes punched in the first post. Slide the rails into the holes in the second post. Attach with the screws, rings, or clips provided by the manufacturer. Check the posts and first section for plumb and level, and then install the third post and second fence section. Continue in this fashion for successive sections.

4 Special situations. If the last section of fence is shorter than the panel, cut the rails shorter with a hacksaw. If the rail ends are notched, cut notches to fit into the punched holes

side punched; corner posts are punched on adjacent sides.

2 Set the first post. In most cases, you set the posts one at a time, filling in panels as you go. If post caps are provided, install them before setting the posts in the ground. Starting at one end or corner, set the first post in concrete. (To speed things up, you can use a fast-setting concrete

Drive end caps into post before setting post.

Concrete extends below frost line. Minimum depth is 18".

2. *Set the first post, checking with the local building department about frost depth and footing requirements.*

Set first post plumb.

Slide rails into post and set second post plumb.

3. *Work your way down the fence, first installing a post and then a fence section, followed by a post and then another section. The fence sections attach with clips or screws supplied by the manufacturer.*

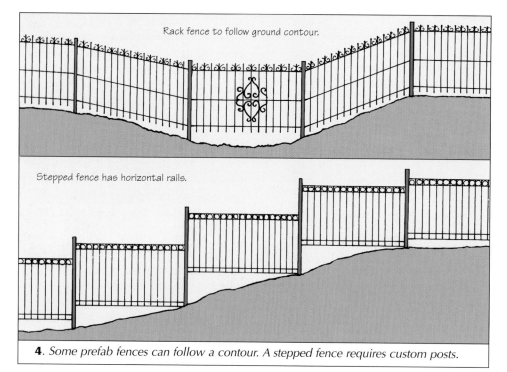

Rack fence to follow ground contour.

Stepped fence has horizontal rails.

4. *Some prefab fences can follow a contour. A stepped fence requires custom posts.*

Vinyl fencing must be directly from manufacturers or their distributors. The fences come in limited colors—usually white, brown, and tan. Since the color runs throughout the material, however, vinyl fences never need painting. Vinyl fences won't rust, decay, or peel and are impervious to wood-boring insects. Although vinyl fences are more expensive than the same styles in wood, the manufacturers say their higher initial cost should be offset by longer life and lower maintenance costs.

Usually you buy the fence material in kit form, with precut posts, rails, and siding. The rails fit into mortises or holes cut into the hollow posts and are secured with screws, clips, or lock rings. The rails are also hollow and may be channeled to accept simulated boards or mortised to accept pickets.

Many prefab panels can be racked to follow gentle contours and slopes. For steep slopes, you can order 45-degree sections with posts designed to accept them. If the fence follows a contour, set all the posts at the same height above ground. If you are building a stepped fence, you will probably need posts of varying lengths. These posts usually must be custom-made.

VINYL FENCES

These prefabricated fences are made of PVC plastic, the same material as vinyl siding, although fence material is usually a heavier gauge. Vinyl fences imitate a wide variety of fence styles, including board, rail, picket, lattice, and ornamental metal. A few of the more popular designs are shown.

Building a Vinyl Fence

Use these directions along with the manufacturer's assembly instructions to install your fence. Many manufacturers also provide matching gates and mounting hardware. The components usually come in precut lengths, but you can cut them with a fine-tooth hand saw.

Vinyl Fences. *Vinyl fences are manufactured to look like wood or metal, but they require less maintenance. Several other styles are available.*

1 Assemble the rails and pickets. In the design shown, pickets or boards are fitted into slots cut in bottom and top rails. For easier handling, use a wood support stand to help you assemble the sections. Foam inserts plug the open ends of the rail sections. If inserts are not provided, cover each rail end with a piece of duct tape. In a few designs, PVC cement may be required to secure various components.

2 Install the posts. Lay out and dig postholes. Most manufacturers recommend a 12-inch diameter hole. The depth of the hole is determined by the fence height and is also recommended by the fence manufacturer. Place a 4-inch layer of sand or pea gravel in the hole, and insert the post (the idea is to keep the concrete from sealing the bottom of the post). Backfill with concrete, and jab it with a shovel handle to remove any air pockets. With a trowel, slope the top of the collar so that water will drain away from the post. Plumb the post with a level.

The fence is installed one of two ways, depending on the design. On some fences, set all of the posts at one time, then attach the panels or rails between them. On other fences, you install a post, a panel, then a post, another panel, and so on. Follow manufacturer's installation procedures for the style you've chosen.

3 Attach the panels. With a helper, fit the panels or rail assemblies between the posts. The rails fit into holes in the posts. The top rail is usually secured with screws, and the lower rails are secured with plastic lock rings or clips, which must be inserted into the rail ends before they go into the posts.

There's no need to wait for the concrete to set around the posts before you attach the panel. Pour the concrete in a half dozen or so postholes, stick the posts in, and slip the panels between them before the concrete sets up. Then adjust the posts so that they are level and plumb. Hold them

in position with temporary braces until the concrete hardens.

4 Reinforce the end and gate posts. Vinyl bends much more easily than metal, so on many designs, the end and gate posts are reinforced

with two lengths of $1/2$-inch rebar and mortar. Reinforcing is usually done after the panels are installed and after the concrete in the postholes has cured for about two days. Typically, the rebar is about half the length of

1. Attach the rails to the pickets before the fence is installed. A wood stand helps hold the fence while you work on it.

2. Sand at the bottom of the hole keeps cement from filling the cavity in the post and allowing water to build up.

3. Install panels before the posthole concrete hardens.

the post. After inserting the rebar where shown, make a pourable mortar mix and pour it into the top of the post. (Use a coffee can with the rim bent to form a spout.) It's best to pour in enough mortar to fill the posts; that way you'll keep water out.

5 Finish the fence. Use post caps to prevent water from accumulating inside. On the design shown, the cap is secured to the post with a small screw. On other designs, you glue the cap on with PVC cement. (Be careful not to get any cement on exposed surfaces.) After the fence is assembled, immediately clean it with water and a plastic scouring pad or soft cloth. Do not use steel wool pads or abrasive cleansers because they will mar the vinyl surface.

6 Special situations. Some vinyl fence panels can be pushed out of square (racked) to follow a slope.

You may have to miter the ends of the rails and pickets, as shown. Ends can be mitered with a back saw and adjustable miter box, a power miter saw equipped with a fine-tooth blade, or by simply marking the angle on the rail end and cutting with a fine-tooth hand saw. If the slope is greater than a 2-inch rise per 12-inch run, the holes in the posts may need to be enlarged to accept the slanted rails. You can enlarge the holes with a straight bit in a router. Guide the cut with the router's fence attachment.

Certain vinyl-fence designs can also be stepped, but you will need longer posts than you would use for a conventional fence. Order end posts, which have holes on one side only, for all of the fence posts that will step down the hill. Rout a pair of holes on the blank side using a template (available from the supplier) to guide a router with a $1/8$-inch straight bit.

4. Vinyl bends easily, so reinforce the gate and end posts with rebar and mortar.

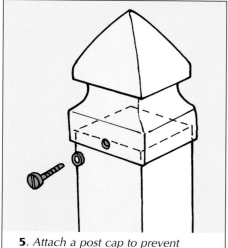

5. Attach a post cap to prevent water from collecting in the post.

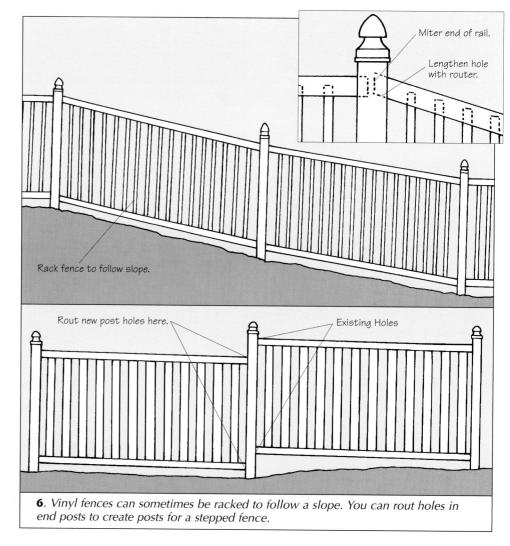

6. Vinyl fences can sometimes be racked to follow a slope. You can rout holes in end posts to create posts for a stepped fence.

CHAIN LINK FENCES

Chain link fences are durable and can provide excellent security. Because these fences don't block views, they are a good choice for keeping an eye on pets and small children. Most home centers, lumberyards, and fence suppliers stock all of the parts required, including the chain link mesh, posts, rails, and hardware. Just tell the dealer how long and how tall you want the fence to be. He or she will help you select necessary components to build the fence. Specify whether or not you want to include a chain link gate in the project.

The chart, Chain Link Fence Components, shows the materials required to construct a chain link fence.

Types of Chain Link

Chain link mesh may be galvanized with zinc, or it may be aluminum coated for an even more durable fence. You can also buy vinyl-coated chain link, usually in white, black, brown, or green. Dark colors generally blend into the surroundings, making the fence less visible. Matching vinyl sleeves are also available to cover the tubular metal posts and rails. Galvanized mesh is usually the least expensive, but durability (and price) depend on the quality of the galvanized coating. Vinyl chain link is the most expensive, but offers more design choices, and generally outlasts galvanized or aluminum mesh. Aluminum is generally better than galvanized because it looks nicer and lasts a bit longer than galvanized mesh.

Chain Link Inserts. When choosing chain link mesh, look at the link top. The wire ends can be either bent over or twisted upward to form barbs. The barbs are good for security but can cause injury. Where privacy is a consideration, you can weave slats of wood, metal, or plastic into the mesh, as shown on the next page. Plastic and metal inserts come in a wide range of colors, which can be mixed and matched to achieve different design effects. The inserts can be installed either vertically or diagonal-

CHAIN LINK FENCE COMPONENTS

Fence Hardware		Use
Terminal post		Placed at fence ends, corners, and gates
Line post		Placed at intervals between terminal posts
Tension band		Attaches fence to terminal post
Brace band		Slips over terminal post and attaches to rail end.
Post cap		Protects top of terminal post
Eye top		Supports top rail; protects top of line post
Top rail		Forms top of fence; helps support chain link mesh
Rail end		Supports rail at terminal post
Top-rail sleeve		Joins sections of top rail. Not necessary if one rail slips into the next.
Tension bar		Holds end of chain link mesh taut against terminal post
Chain link mesh		Attaches to posts and rails to create barrier
Tie wire		Secures chain link mesh to posts and intermediate rails

Gate Hardware		Use
Post hinge		Bolted to gate post; supports swinging gate
Gate hinge		Attached to gate by manufacturer; slips over pin on post hinge
Fork latch		Attached to gate by manufacturer; holds gate shut
Carriage bolt & nut		Variety of sizes supplied by manufacturer for attaching fence and gate components

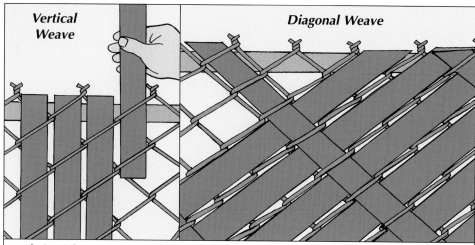

Vertical Weave

Diagonal Weave

Chain Link Inserts. *Inserts of wood, aluminum, or vinyl can be woven into the chain link to provide privacy.*

ly. For a more natural look, you can plant tall shrubs against the fence or raise vines on it. Chain link provides sturdy support for heavy vines, such as ivy, wisteria, or honeysuckle.

Building a Chain Link Fence

Chain link fences are not a popular do-it-yourself project. Many people are intimidated by the number of components and because the metal components are not as user-friendly as wood. Although tall fences are best installed by a fence contractor, low chain link fences (48 inches or less) are actually simple to install. Chain link mesh usually comes in rolls and must be cut to size, which is done simply by snipping the wire with lineman's pliers and undoing the wire strand.

The biggest challenge may be tracking down a fence puller, the tool that stretches the chain link mesh between the posts. A fence puller consists of a winch (known as a come-along), a chain, and a fence-pulling rod. You may have to check several tool rental shops before you find one that carries fence pullers.

1 Lay out and dig the postholes. Lay out the fence line and determine posthole locations, as described in Chapter 4, "Setting Posts," page 51. Space the posts no farther than 96 inches apart or as specified in the manufacturer's instructions and local building codes. Terminal (end and corner) postholes are typically 8 inches in diameter, and 18 to 30 inches deep. Holes for line posts are 6 inches in diameter and 18 to 24 inches deep, depending on the fence height and soil conditions. In colder climates, set the posts below the frost line. Check local codes.

2 Set the posts. Separate the terminal posts (end, corner, and gate posts) from the line posts (intermediate posts). Terminal posts typically have a larger diameter than line posts. All posts should be set in concrete. Use a fairly stiff mix, and frequently

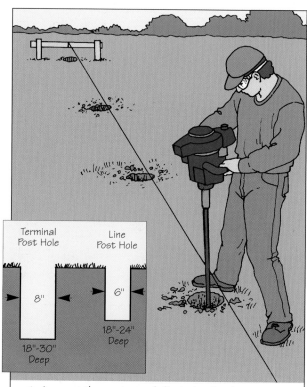

Terminal Post Hole

Line Post Hole

8"

6"

18"-30" Deep

18"-24" Deep

1. Lay out the posts, and dig holes for them no farther than 96 inches apart.

2. Set the end, or terminal, posts first, and stretch a string between them to mark the height of the lower line posts.

check the posts for plumb with a level. It's necessary to prop the posts with short lengths of lumber until the concrete sets.

Set the terminal posts first. Once the terminal posts are in, attach a leveled string between them marking the height of the line posts. (Line posts are usually about four inches lower than terminal posts because the rails cross over them. Check your manufacturers' specifications.) Set the line posts to this height.

3 Add the top rails. In one or two days, after the concrete has completely set, slide onto each terminal post the tension bands (three or four, depending on fence height), a brace band to anchor the top rail, and a terminal post cap. Gently tap the eye tops into the ends of the line posts using a hammer and wood block. Bolt the rail ends onto the brace bands on the terminal posts, and then install the top rails, slipping them through the eye-top connectors on the line posts and into the rail ends. Often, one end of each rail is reduced in diameter so that it can be fitted snugly into the rail preceding it. In other cases, rail sleeves may be required to connect rail ends. Rail-to-rail connections do not have to occur exactly above a post, although the installation will be stronger if they do.

4 Stretch the chain link. With a helper, unroll several feet of chain link mesh, and weave a tension bar into the end of the mesh. Attach the bar to the tension bands on the end or corner post using the carriage bolts provided. Next, unroll the mesh to the other end of the fence, pull the mesh tight by hand, and weave a fence-pulling rod into the mesh about 36 inches in front of the end post. The pulling rod has holes through which you attach a chain with S-hooks in the ends. Hook one end of a come-along to the pulling rod and the other end to the end post. Then crank the come-along to tighten the mesh. As you work, test for tautness by pinching the mesh shut. The fence is taut enough when the openings close no more than about ¹/₂ inch. Weave a tension bar

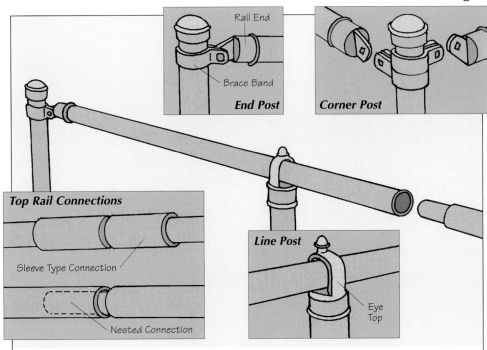

3. *After the concrete has cured, attach hardware to the end posts and to the top of the line posts.*

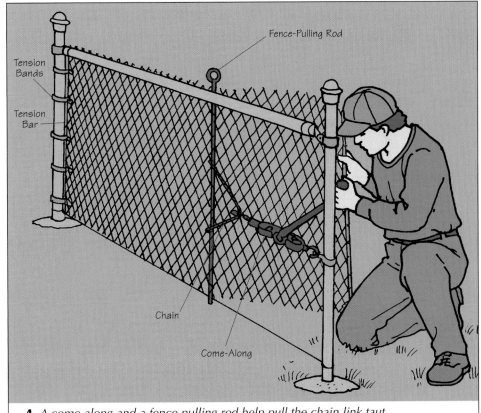

4. *A come-along and a fence-pulling rod help pull the chain link taut.*

into the mesh even with the end post. With lineman's pliers, cut the top and bottom links just beyond the tension bar. Undo the wire between the cuts to separate the mesh into two parts. Attach the tension bar to the tension

bands with carriage bolts. On short runs of fence with lightweight chain link, a come-along may not be needed. Simply have a helper stretch the mesh by hand as you fasten it to the posts. (See Step 5 on the next page.)

5. *The top of the chain link is attached to the fence with metal ties. The bottom sometimes has a cable woven through it that is then attached to the posts.*

6. *Stretch the chain link across the gate frame by hand, and hang the gate with the hardware that comes with it.*

5 Fasten the chain link to the rails. Attach the chain link mesh to the top rails and line posts with short pieces of galvanized wire or special wire ties, available from the supplier. Hook one end of the tie to the mesh, curl the tie over the post or rail, then hook the other end on the mesh. Space ties 24 inches apart on the rails and 12 inches apart on each line post. On some designs, a heavy gauge wire is woven through the chain link mesh at the bottom of the fence. It is attached to the end posts to provide additional stability and to keep the chain link from bowing. Attach the wire to one end post by forming a loop around the post and cinching it with a cable clamp to cinch the wire. Weave the wire through the links about 4 inches above the bottom edge of the mesh, stretch it tight, and attach to the opposite end post.

6 Install the gate. Gates usually come with hinges and latch attached. For an extra cost, you can have the gate set up with chain link mesh. If you choose to do it yourself, weave a tension bar in one end of the chain link mesh and attach it to the gate frame with tension bands. Stretch the mesh hand tight, weave a second bar even with the gate frame, cut the mesh just beyond the tension bar, and attach with tension bands. Attach the top and bottom of the mesh to the gate frame with wire ties. Next, determine which side of the gate will be hinged, bolt the hinge pins to the gate post, and hang the gate on the pins. Test the gate and adjust the hinges if necessary. You also may have to adjust the latch so that it is at a comfortable height; 36 inches is common.

QUICK, EASY FENCES

Sometimes, you may need to install a temporary fence or screen that can be removed later when plans change or when you build a permanent fence. Other simple designs can be permanent features in the yard.

Utility Fencing. Utility fencing consists of wooden slats wired together and is sold in large rolls, in heights from 36 to 72 inches. You simply

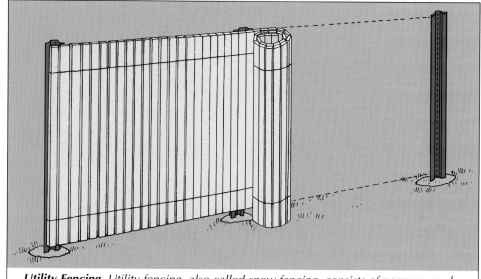

Utility Fencing. *Utility fencing, also called snow fencing, consists of narrow wood slats held together with wire.*

Wire Picket Fencing. *Wire picket fencing comes in rolls or in short, flat lengths. It is simply pushed into the ground.*

Reed and Bamboo Screening. *Reed and bamboo screening can dress up the frame side of a board fence, but the screening isn't very durable.*

unroll the fencing and nail or wire it to permanent or temporary wood or metal posts. While not especially attractive or durable, utility fencing provides a barrier to keep people and animals out of a designated area. Utility fencing is also called snow fencing because you can place it strategically to prevent snow from drifting across walks or driveways.

Wire Picket Fencing.
Wire picket fencing is also sold in rolls at home-and-garden centers and is used as a low temporary or decorative border around planting beds and walks. These welded-wire fences are either factory-painted or vinyl-coated and come in heights from 12 to 18 inches. To install, you simply unroll the wire and stick it into the ground. Low, pre-fabricated picket fence sections made of wood or PVC plastic are also available. These, too, are simply pushed into the ground and removed when your landscape plans change.

Reed and Bamboo Screening.
Reed and bamboo screening fences consist of a light reed or split bamboo material woven together with thin wire. Typically they are sold in 72- or 96-inch widths in rolls 25 or 50 feet

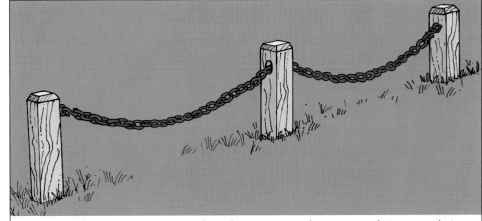

Rope or Chain Fences. *Rope or chain fences are mostly ornamental. Rope or chain is either threaded through holes drilled in the wood posts, or attached to eye screws anchored in the posts.*

long. The lightweight screening can be attached vertically to posts or a wooden frame to provide shade and privacy. It can also be used to dress up the frame side of a board fence. While bamboo and reed screening make attractive, natural-looking backdrops for informal gardens, they quickly deteriorate when exposed to the weather, so you can't expect them to last more than three to five years.

Rope or Chain Fences.
Rope or chain fences make attractive, economical boundary markers for large areas,

especially along paths, walks, long driveways, or roadsides. These fences are popular in coastal areas because they lend a nautical feeling to the landscape. To make one, you simply drill holes through low 4x4 or 6x6 posts and thread a length of chain or heavy rope through the holes. At end or corner posts, you attach the rope or chain to the post with large eye screws. Attach chain by putting an S-hook in the end. Attach rope by making a loop at the end, and cinching it with a wire clamp.

GATES

Gates can tell a lot about the people who live behind them. Gates can be simple or ornate, formal or informal, traditional or contemporary, inviting or forbidding. To call attention to an opening, choose a design that contrasts with the surrounding fence or wall. A low ornamental metal gate, for example, can soften the imposing mass of a solid masonry wall and has an open, inviting feeling. Similarly, you can call attention to the gate by changing the size, spacing, or direction of the siding materials used on the fence. Conversely, you may want a gate that provides a sense of security and privacy. Gates leading to side yards or backyards, for example, can be constructed from the same materials as the fence to lend the impression of an unbroken barrier. Garden gates can be designed simply so that they don't compete visually with other landscape features. Tall, heavy, solid gates send a clear message that the owners value their privacy.

GATE DESIGN AND FUNCTION

Most gates are made either of wood or ornamental metal. You can choose from a variety of prefabricated designs or create your own. No matter what design you choose, the gate must be sturdy and swing freely without sagging or binding. The most successful wood gates use lightweight, kiln-dried wood, heavy-duty hinges, and have sufficient bracing to prevent sagging.

Gate Size and Weight. Spacing between gate posts should be from 36 to 48 inches, depending on the gate's function and location. Posts for gates leading to a house's front door should be 48 inches apart, which allows room for two people to pass through at once. Posts for gates leading to backyards or side yards should be spaced no less than 36 inches apart so that lawn mowers, wheelbarrows, and other wheeled garden equipment may fit through the opening.

Even for low gates, you need to set the posts a minimum of 24 inches in the ground, or below the frost line in cold climates. Take extra care to plumb both posts so that they are exactly the same distance apart at the top and bottom.

If you're installing a prefabricated gate, space the posts to provide clearance on the latch side and hinge side. In most cases, you'll leave ½ inch of clearance on the hinge side and ½ to ¾ inches of clearance on the latch side; but you should use the clearances specified in the gate manufacturer's instructions. The clearances required for chain link and ornamental metal gates are usually determined by the type of hardware used to attach them.

Usually, gates are the same height as the fence or wall, but not necessarily. The gate's height depends on its function, and on the fence design. If a fence or wall provides security and privacy, you'll want to make the gate the same height and as difficult to climb as the wall.

Keep the weight of the gate in mind when choosing materials. The gate should be sturdy enough to stand up to continuous use and abuse, but not so heavy that it's hard to open and close. Large, solid-board gates tend to be heavy and may require three or even four hinges to support them. If the gate swings over a smooth, hard surface, such as a walk, you can install a wheel on the bottom of a heavy gate to relieve strain on the hinges and to keep the gate from sagging (see the drawing on page 102).

Selecting the Location. Usually, gates are located where a fence or wall will cross an existing or proposed walkway or entry. In a new landscape, these elements are planned simultaneously as part of the overall scheme.

If you are installing a front boundary fence directly next to a sidewalk (especially a busy one), it is good practice to jog the fence back 36 to

48 inches from the sidewalk and install the gate there. Setting the gate back from the sidewalk gives visitors a place to open the gate without having to stand in the middle of the sidewalk.

Direction of Swing. Entry gates traditionally open inward toward the house. (Your front door swings in the same direction, although there's no hard-and-fast rule about this.) The direction of swing depends largely on the gate location and features on either side of the gate. For example, if the gate crosses a sloping walk, it may have to swing downhill to provide clearance at the bottom of the gate. If a gate is located at the corner

Selecting the Location. *Place a gate 36 to 48 inches back from a busy sidewalk so that there is a clear place to stand while opening it.*

Direction of Swing. *When planning your gate, determine how the direction of swing will affect traffic through the gate. In most cases, a front yard entry gate swings inward, toward the house. Use adjacent walls or fences as places to mount hardware that will keep the gate open.*

of a fence, or at right angles to a wall, or other structure, it is usually best to have the gate swing toward the structure. You can attach a simple hook-and-eye screw to the structure and the gate to keep the gate open when necessary. The direction of swing will also influence the type and mounting location of hinges and latches and vice versa.

GATE HARDWARE

Hinges and latches range from utilitarian to ornamental. Choose a style that is appropriate for the fence design, and consider whether the hardware will be mounted on the face or edge of the gate. Some gates are designed to look like doors. These gates may call for concealed hinges, in which only the hinge pin is visible. In this case, utilitarian butt hinges will do.

Hinges. Hinges come in a wide variety of shapes and sizes, but there are four basic types: butt hinges, T-hinges, strap hinges, and hook-and-strap hinges. When choosing hinges, make sure they are designed for exterior use and are heavy enough to support the weight of the gate. Because most failures in gates result from inadequately sized hinges, choose the heaviest hinges you can install that are still in visual scale with the gate.

Gate Latches. You have many choices when it comes to gate latches. Some of the more popular styles are shown here. Many latches are designed to be fitted with a padlock, or you can install a separate lock and hasp. On seldom-used gates, a hasp alone may suffice. Formal door-style gates, such as those leading to a courtyard or front-entry enclosure, can employ conventional door locksets or deadbolts.

Other Hardware

On very wide or heavy gates, additional hardware may be required to keep the gate from sagging. Even if the gate you constructed doesn't feel very heavy, fasteners often work themselves loose in time. So it is always a good idea to install anti-sag hardware, which will keep the gate in good working condition for a long time.

Sag Rods. Sag rods or cables with adjustable turnbuckles can be used to keep gates from sagging or binding or to shore up a leaning gate post. The rods are easy to install. They are typically sold as kits that include a pair of threaded rods, a turnbuckle, and fastening hardware. A cable may be substituted for the threaded rods. If so, hooks in each end of a turnbuckle attach to the gate and to the cable.

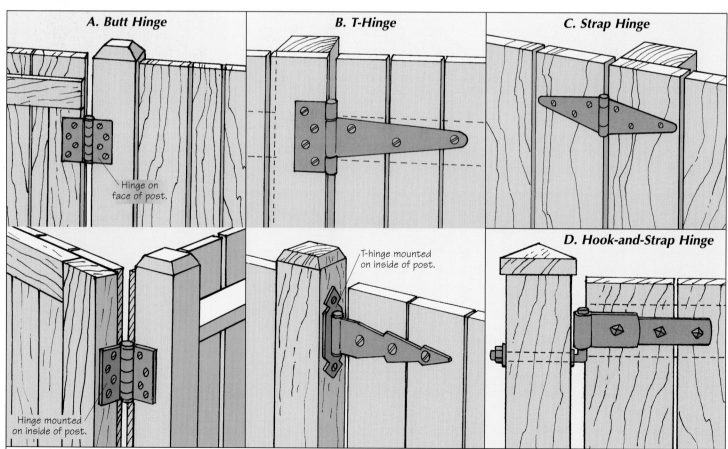

A. Butt Hinge — Hinge on face of post.

B. T-Hinge — T-hinge mounted on inside of post.

C. Strap Hinge

D. Hook-and-Strap Hinge

Hinge mounted on inside of post.

Hinges. Butt hinges (A) have two rectangular leaves joined by a hinge pin and are designated by the size of the entire hinge when open. Butt hinges may be mounted on the outside faces of the post and gate or concealed between the gate frame and post. T-hinges (B) are usually sized by the length of the long hinge leaf. This leaf mounts on the gate surface and can support more weight than a butt hinge. Strap hinges (C) are mounted on the outside faces of the gate and fence, and their long leaves make them even stronger than T-hinges. Strap hinges are commonly used on solid-board gates. Hook-and-strap hinges (D) consist of an L-shaped lag screw secured to the post and a leaf or strap fastened to the gate. These strong hinges can be used with square or round posts.

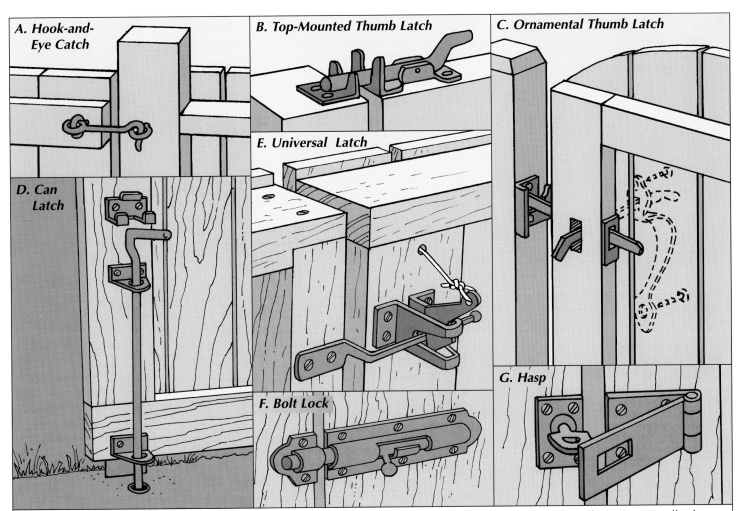

A. Hook-and-Eye Catch

B. Top-Mounted Thumb Latch

C. Ornamental Thumb Latch

D. Can Latch

E. Universal Latch

F. Bolt Lock

G. Hasp

Gate Latches. *Inexpensive hook-and-eye catches (A) are suitable for small garden gates but don't provide much security. Usually, the eye is screwed to the fence post and the hook is mounted to the gate. Thumb latches are available in two versions: top-mounted (B) and ornamental (C). Top mounted are used on low gates where the top of the frame is flush with the top rail of the fence. Ornamental latches are mounted in the gate. Can latches (D) are mounted vertically at the bottom of the gate. The bolt slips down into a hole drilled into a walk or driveway. Universal gate latches (E) come in several designs. The latch automatically captures the strike bar when you shut the gate. If you would like to be able to open the gate from the nonlatched side, attach a string to the latch, and run it through a hole in the gate. Bolt locks (F) come in various sizes and designs. A sliding bolt assembly attached to the gate fits into a U-shaped bracket attached to the post. A knob projecting from the bolt enables you to lock the bolt in an open or closed position. Hasp latches (G) have a hinged leaf that closes over a swiveling eye. These inexpensive latches are designed to be fitted with a padlock.*

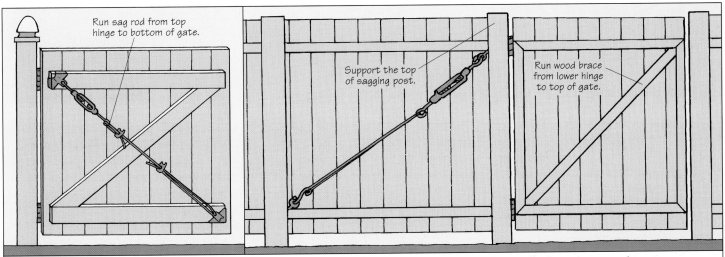

Run sag rod from top hinge to bottom of gate.

Support the top of sagging post.

Run wood brace from lower hinge to top of gate.

Sag Rods. *A sag rod or a wooden brace can keep a gate from drooping. The sag rod runs diagonally from the upper hinge to a lower corner. A post brace or wood gate brace runs in the opposite direction.*

On gates, sag rods and cables work by pulling up the sagging end. Install them diagonally with the high end at the top hinge and the bottom of the rod fastened to the bottom corner of the gate, as shown on page 101.

Fence posts are exactly the opposite. On fence posts, attach the rod so that it runs from the upper end of the leaning post to the lower end of its neighbor, as shown.

Casters. Where wide or heavy gates cross a relatively smooth, level surface, such as a walk or driveway, a wheel or caster installed at the bottom front corner of the gate frame effectively prevents sagging. If the siding extends below the frame, you may have to mount the caster on a block, as shown.

Gate Springs. You can make your gate close automatically with the

Casters. *If a gate is over a paved surface, a heavy-duty rubber caster will support the weight, preventing the gate from sagging.*

Making a Sliding Latch

This simple sliding latch lends itself well to rustic board fences and gates. It provides good security because it can only be opened from one side of the gate. If you want to operate the latch from both sides, cut a horizontal slot in the gate, and extend the dowel handle through the gate. Be sure to provide adequate backing for any loose fence boards.

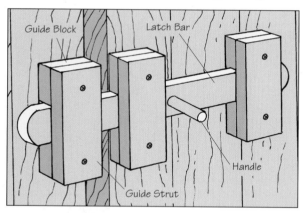

Cutting List

Qty.	Part	Dimensions	Comments
One	Latch Bar	$\frac{3}{4}$" x 1 $\frac{1}{2}$" x 11 $\frac{3}{4}$"	Cut from 1x 2
One	Handle	$\frac{1}{2}$" dia. dowel x 4"	Cut from $\frac{1}{2}$"-dia. dowel
Three	Guide Struts	$\frac{3}{4}$" x 1 $\frac{1}{2}$" x 4 $\frac{5}{8}$"	Cut from 1x 2
Six	Guide Blocks	$\frac{3}{4}$" x 1 $\frac{1}{2}$" x 1 $\frac{1}{2}$"	Cut from 1x 2
6	2-inch Screws		

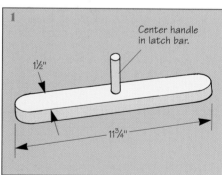
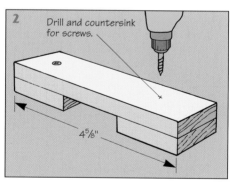
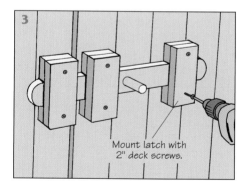

1 Make the latch bar. Cut the latch bar to size. Lay out the rounded ends using a compass set to a ¾-inch radius, and cut them with a saber saw or coping saw. Drill a ½-inch-diameter hole through the latch for the handle. Cut the dowel to length, and glue it in place with an exterior-grade wood glue.

2 Make the guide assemblies. Cut the guide blocks and guide struts to the dimensions in the cutting list. Because the supporting blocks are so small, you may find it easier (and safer) to cut them with a hand saw. Assemble the blocks and struts with construction adhesive. Drive a brad through the back of each small support block if you don't want to wait for the adhesive to set.

3 Assemble the latch. Next, tack the latch bar in level position across the gate using two finishing nails. The bar (tacked temporarily), will serve as the mounting guide for the blocks and struts. Hold each assembly over the latch bar, and drill two pilot holes about half the diameter of the screw shank as shown. Finish the job by driving screws through the pilot holes into the fence—one on the top and one on the bottom of each assembly—and then pull the tacks to release the latch bar.

help of a gate spring. A gate spring consists of a long, heavy spring and two brackets or eye screws, usually sold as a kit in hardware stores. One bracket or screw mounts to the gate, the other to the fence with the spring mounted to them.

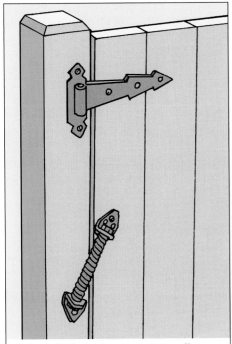

Gate Springs. *A gate spring pulls gates shut automatically. When combined with a self-latching universal gate latch, this combination will pull the gate shut and keep it shut—a good feature if you have pets or small children.*

BUILDING A WOOD GATE

Most wooden gates employ a braced frame of 2x4s to which you attach the siding of your choice. But before you start building, it is a good idea to spend some time with the posts that will support the gate.

With a level, double check to make sure the fence posts on either side of your gate opening are plumb. Then measure the distance between posts at both the top and the bottom, and make sure the distance is the same.

If a post is seriously misaligned, either reposition it with a sag rod, or take it out and reset it. Discrepancies of a ½ inch or less probably won't interfere with the gates operation or appearance. In that case, install the gate, and if necessary, correct the sag later.

Gate on Frame 𝑇

This is a simple, sturdy gate, which can be altered to match almost any fence design. To determine the gate width, measure the distance between the gate posts, then subtract 1 to 1¼ inches to allow clearance for the hinges and latch.

1 **Cut the gate frame.** Use straight, kiln-dried lumber for the gate frame. The ends can be either mitered or cut square: Mitered joints look better, but butt joints tend to be a little stronger. For the strongest, best-looking joints, make half-lap joints by notching the rails to accept the stiles. For more on cutting notches, see "Dadoing Posts," page 68.

In most situations, the horizontal frame parts are aligned with the fence rails. Cut the horizontal frame parts to run the entire width of the gate. Cut the vertical parts to a length that allows for your joinery and rail position.

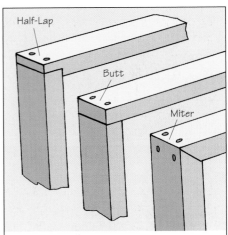

Half-Lap

Butt

Miter

1. *You can make the gate with a variety of reinforced joints. The half-lap is the strongest, followed by the butt, and then the miter joint.*

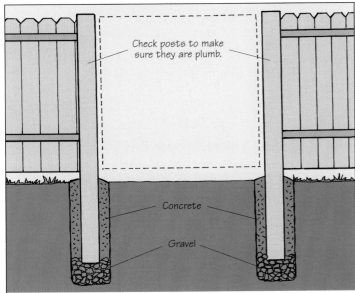

Check posts to make sure they are plumb.

Concrete

Gravel

Building a Wood Gate. *Check the gate opening with a tape measure and level before you build the gate to make sure the gate posts are plumb and parallel.*

Gate on Frame. *The most basic gate is a frame and a brace with fence boards nailed to it. It is strong and versatile enough to match almost any fence.*

2 Assemble the gate frame. Lay the frame members on a flat work surface, then join them with 10d galvanized nails or 2-inch deck screws to form four square corners. Metal brackets can be used to provide additional strength at joints.

3 Brace the frame. This gate is braced by a 2x4 that runs diagonally from the bottom of the hinge side to the top of the latch side. Lay the 2x4 diagonally under the frame and mark the cut line with a pencil. Cut the brace to fit tightly into the frame corners. Attach by toenailing the brace into the frame corners

with 7d galvanized nails or 2-inch deck screws. Predrill nail or screw holes to avoid splitting board ends.

4 Attach the fence boards. For solid-board designs, leave at least ¼-inch spaces between boards to allow for expansion during humid weather. Mark the board locations and spacing on the face of the frame, and use galvanized nails or deck screws to attach the boards to the frame and diagonal brace. On some gates, the siding on the latch side extends past the frame to serve as a gate strike (see next step). Frequently check that the frame remains square

and that the fence boards are perpendicular to the rails.

5 Attach the gate strike. A gate strike keeps the gate from swinging past its closure point and bending the hinges. Some gate latches, such as the universal latch shown in "Gate Latches," page 101, can serve as a gate strike. You'll need to install a strike board on the gate or the gate post. The location of the strike depends on gate design and the direction the gate opens. Design also dictates whether you install the strike before or after you hang the gate. Attach it with galvanized nails or screws.

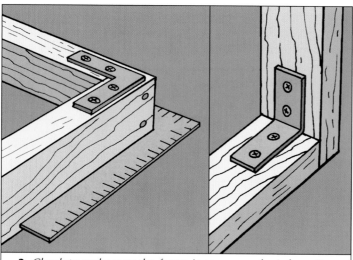

2. Check to make sure the frame is square, and reinforce it with metal brackets.

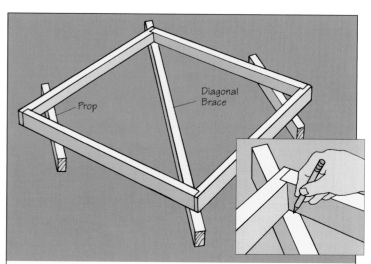

3. Mark the length of the brace and the angle at the ends by placing the brace under the frame and tracing with a pencil.

4. Attach the boards to the frame. Check often to be sure the frame has remained square.

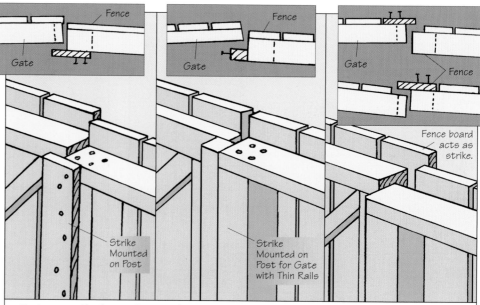

5. A gate strike keeps the gate from swinging past the opening when you close it. You can attach the strike to either side of the fence and to either the post or the gate.

Z-Brace Gate

This simple gate, reminiscent of rustic batten doors found on barns and other outbuildings, is easy to make and uses a minimum of lumber. Typically, a Z-brace gate is found on a solid-board fence, a masonry wall, or a breezeway between buildings.

The design shown uses 1x8 fence boards with dog-eared tops. Boards ranging from 1x4 to 1x10 would also work. If you want a thinner gate, use 1x6 instead of 2x4 for the braces.

1 Lay out the fence boards. Measure the opening and determine how many boards you will need. Allow for ¼-inch spaces between the boards. If necessary, rip boards to width. If possible, rip the two outside pieces so that you don't have a single skinny piece of one side of the gate.

Cut the dog ears. Lay the boards in position on a flat surface. Use scraps of ¼-inch plywood for spacers and make sure the gate is square.

2 Install the horizontal braces. Cut the 2x4 horizontal braces to be as long as the gate is wide. Position them on the siding so they will match the fence rails. If you are attaching the gate to masonry or a fence that has no visible rails, position the braces 8 inches from the top and bottom of the gate. Attach them by driving two 2-inch galvanized deck screws into each board. Stagger the screws as shown. Remove the plywood spacers.

3 Install the angled brace. To measure for the angled brace, place a 2x4 in position on top of the horizontal braces, and mark it for the cuts. Install by driving two 2-inch screws into each fencing board. Stagger the screws so that they do not follow along a grain line in the brace—otherwise, the brace may split.

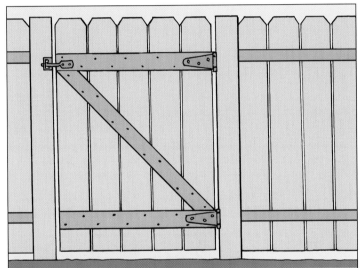

Z-brace Gate. *A Z-brace gate is simple to build and lends rustic charm to informal landscapes. Use T-hinges to fasten the gate to the fence post, as shown.*

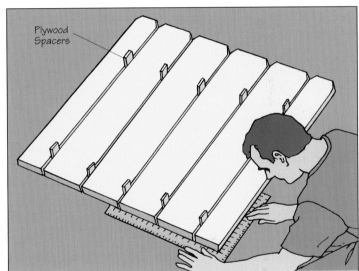

1. A Z-brace gate begins with the boards. Lay them on a flat surface and space them evenly.

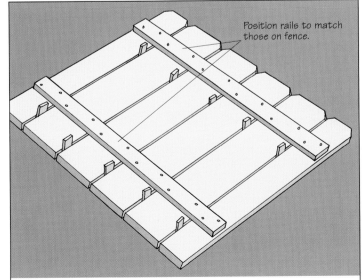

2. Attach the rails to the gate. Check frequently to make sure they stay aligned and correctly spaced.

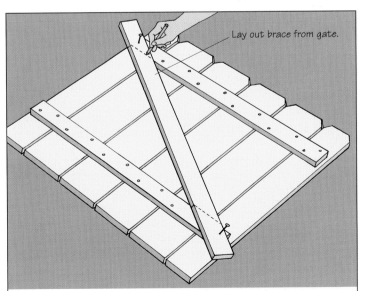

3. Place wood for the brace on the gate, and mark the length of the brace and the angles of the end cuts.

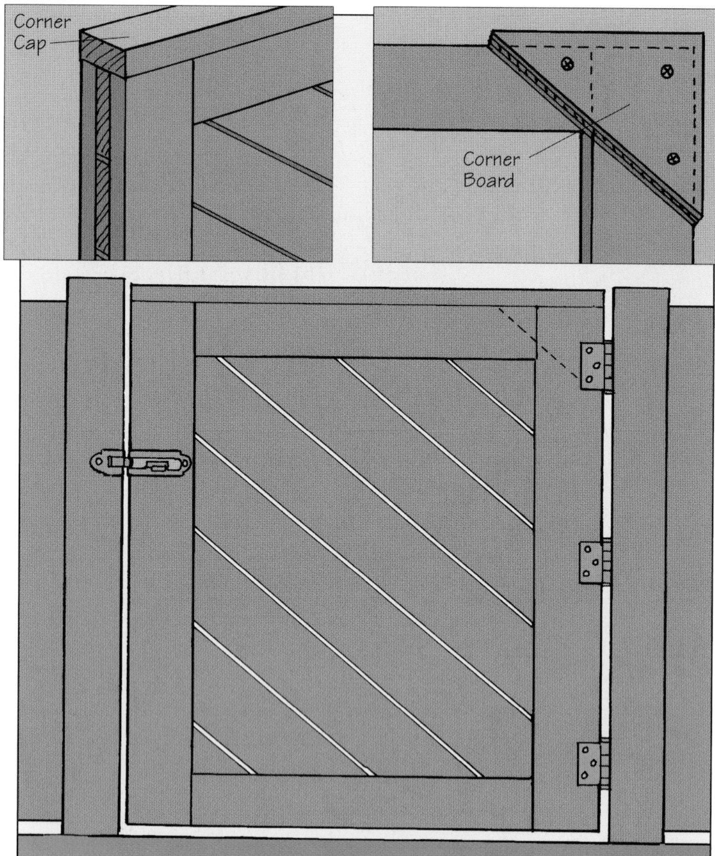

Diagonal-Board Gate. *Diagonal-board gates are sturdy and attractive, and may not require additional anti-sag bracing. On double gates, alternate the direction of diagonal boards on each section to make a herringbone pattern.*

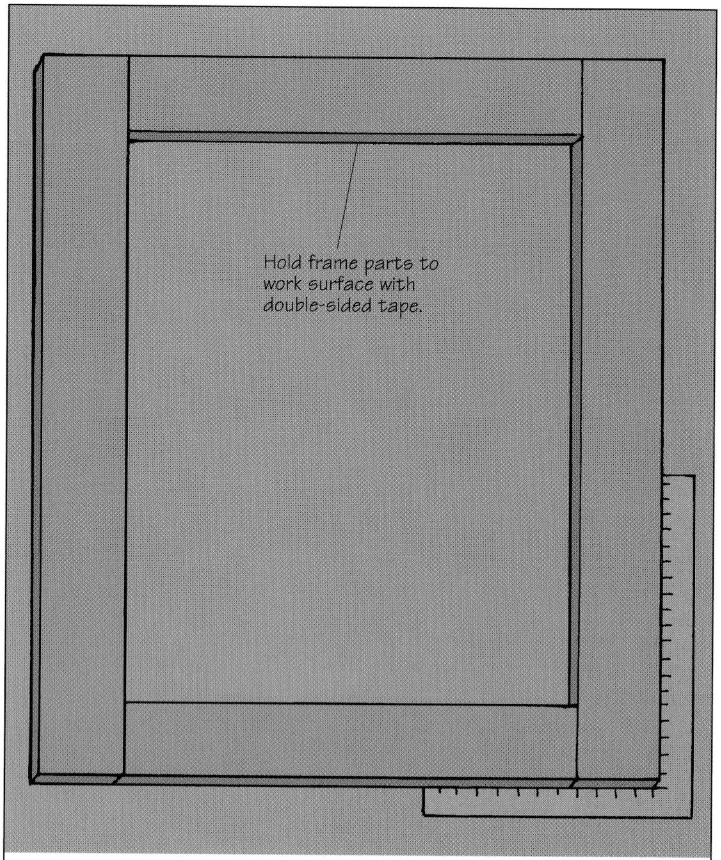

1. *Put double-sided carpet tape on the frame parts, and lay them on a clean work surface one at a time, making sure the assembly is square.*

Diagonal-Board Gate

Placing boards on an angle gives a gate extra strength. In this design, 1x8 tongue-and-groove cedar siding is sandwiched diagonally between two 1x6 frames, creating a solid entry gate that looks the same on both sides. A 2x3 cap rail protects the end grain of the siding pieces from the weather.

This design lends itself well to double gates. Hang the gates so the diagonals of each section run in opposite directions, creating a herringbone effect. For maximum strength, be sure the diagonal pattern runs from the top of the latch side to the bottom of the hinge side.

1 **Cut the frames.** Cut four pieces of 1x6 to the height of the gate, and four pieces to the width, minus 11 inches, to take into account the width of two pieces of 1x6.

Lay the pieces in place, as shown, on a flat surface. Make sure the unit is square. If possible, anchor the pieces in place to make construction of the gate easier. You can anchor them by taping them to a plywood work surface with double-sided carpet tape. If you don't anchor the pieces, periodically make sure they are square.

2 **Cut and install the first diagonal.** Cut a right-angle triangle from a piece of 1x6 tongue-and-groove siding so the groove is along the longest side of the triangle. You can do this by making two 45-degree cuts, as shown.

Fasten this piece to the top of the side that the hinges will go on so that the two shorter sides are flush with the edges of the frame. (If the hinges will go on the left, the piece will go in the upper left-hand corner.) Drill pilot holes to avoid splitting this small piece, and drive three $1\frac{1}{4}$-inch galvanized deck screws through the triangle and into the 1x6 frame.

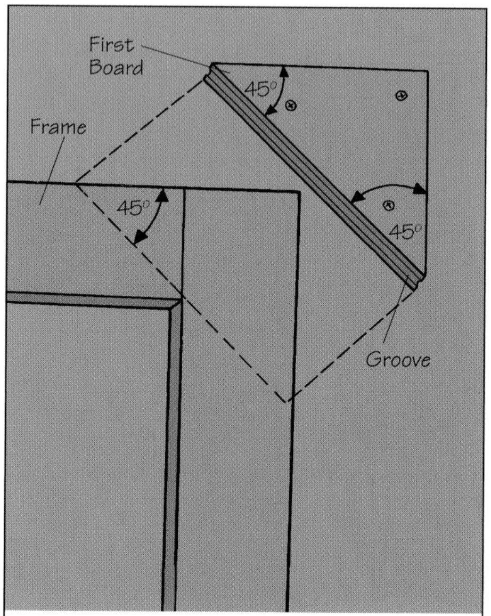

2. *Attach the first short board over the frame corner at a 45-degree angle using screws.*

3 **Cut and install the rest of the diagonals.** Fit another piece of siding against the first piece, and trace along the gate frame to mark it for

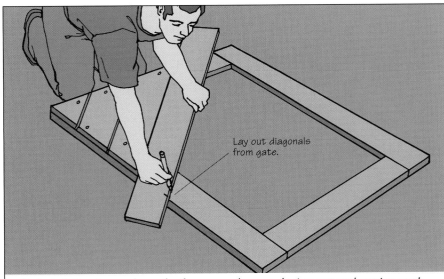

3. *Install the diagonals on the frame one by one, laying out and cutting each to fit as you go.*

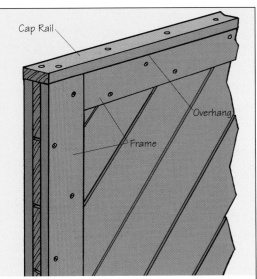

4. *Once all the diagonals are installed, attach the outer frame and the cap rail.*

cutting. Cut and attach to the frame, driving one 1¼-inch screw at each end. Repeat for all the other pieces.

4 Install other frame pieces and cap rail.
Attach the second set of 1x6s to the opposite side of the gate using 2-inch galvanized deck screws. Drive one into each piece of siding in an alternating pattern, as shown.

Cut a piece of 2x3 cap rail the width of the gate. Install it on the top of the gate, so it hangs over the same amount on either side. Drill pilot holes, and drive 3-inch galvanized deck screws every 6 inches in an alternating pattern so that the rail is attached to the framing pieces on either side.

Lightweight Picket Gate 🔨🔨

This gate is very lightweight, gaining strength from joinery rather than mass. It will blend in with your picket fence, or it can be used as a decorative feature in its own right. Use 1x3s or 1x4s for the pickets. For variations in the designs of the tops of the pickets, see "Picket-Top Designs," page 77.

Take your time when cutting the half-lap joint where the two cross braces meet. Mark and cut carefully, so the joint will be perfect. You may want to practice on a few pieces of scrap before cutting the real thing.

1 Construct the rectangular frame.
Cut two pieces of 2x3 to the exact width of your gate, and two pieces that are 14 inches shorter than the picket height. On a flat surface,

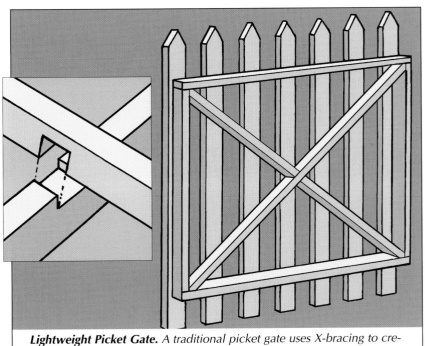

Lightweight Picket Gate. *A traditional picket gate uses X-bracing to create a sturdy frame. Cut a lap joint where the braces cross.*

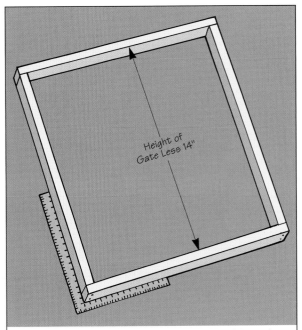

1. *Cut the frame parts to size and assemble with butt joints and screws.*

construct a simple box. Drill pilot holes and drive two 3-inch galvanized deck screws through each joint. Make sure the frame is square.

2 Cut the cross braces.
Set a piece of 2x3 at a diagonal on top of the frame. After making sure the frame is square, mark each end for a pointed cut so that the piece will fit snugly inside the box. Repeat the process for a diagonal crosspiece going in the other direction.

3 Cut the half-lap joint.
To do this, you will cut a notch in each brace at the point where they meet, so that they fit together. Slip one of the cross braces into position in the frame. Place the second brace in position on top of the first, and mark each to show where they meet.

Take the braces out, and place them on a good surface for cutting. Set your circular saw to cut exactly halfway through the width of a 2x3—make some experimental cuts to make sure you've got it right. For each board, cut to the inside of the two pencil lines. The distance between the two cuts will be 1½ inches, exactly the thickness of a 2x3. Then make a series of closely spaced cuts between the first two cuts. Knock out the waste, and pare the bottom of the notch clean with a chisel.

4 Attach the braces.
Slide the two brace pieces in position. They will fit snugly together. Attach them to the frame by drilling pilot holes and driving 3-inch galvanized deck screws at angles through the frame pieces and into the braces. At the half-lap joint, predrill and drive a 2-inch screw.

5 Install the pickets.
Attach one picket on either end of the gate, flush to the outside edges of the

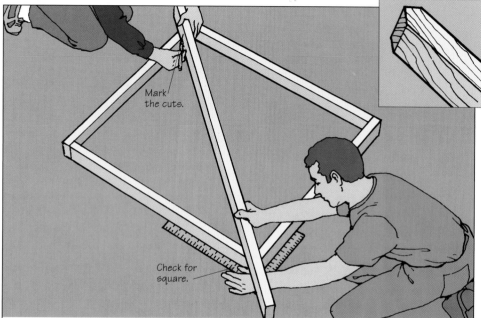

2. Lay out the length of the diagonal and its end angles by placing an oversized brace on the gate and tracing along the frame.

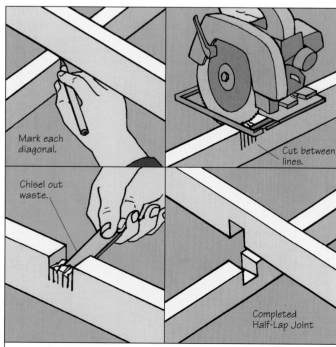

3. The two parts of a half-lap slip over each other. Lay the boards on top of each other to mark the width of the cut. Make repeated cuts with a circular saw to remove the waste. Clean up the rough spots with a chisel.

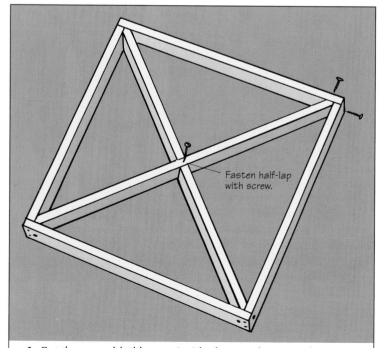

4. Put the assembled braces inside the gate frame, and screw them in place.

frame. Drill pilot holes, and drive 2-inch screws at 6-inch intervals.

Lay out the remaining pickets so that they will be consistently spaced. The spacing will probably differ from that of the fence. Drill pilot holes, and attach the pickets with two 2-inch screws in the upper rail, lower rail, and cross braces.

Lattice- and-Board Gate 🌴🌴🌴

Lattice-and-board fences and gates combine the open, airy feel of lattice with the security and privacy of a solid panel. This gate can be adapted to match an existing fence, or it can provide a pleasing contrast to a solid-board fence.

Because it combines two styles, this gate will take longer to build than other gates. However, no special skills or tools are required. The lattice section may get handled a good deal, so purchase a piece of the good stuff—¾ inch total thickness.

This is a heavy gate, so purchase strong hinges. If you want to make it lighter, use 2x3 instead of 2x4, or purchase light lumber, such as kiln-dried redwood or cedar.

1 Build a frame. Cut two pieces of 2x4 to the width of the gate. Then cut one piece to the width minus 3 inches, and two pieces to the height minus 3 inches. Lay the boards on a flat surface, and put them together as shown, spacing the rails to allow

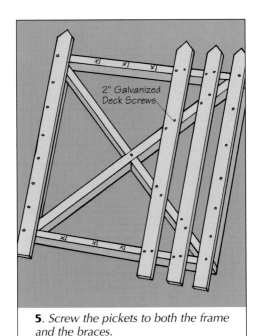

5. Screw the pickets to both the frame and the braces.

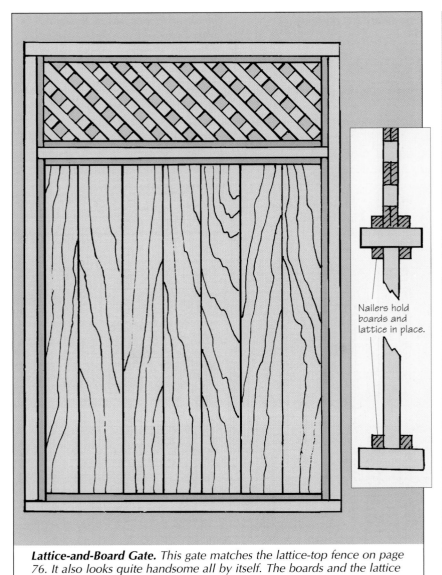

***Lattice-and-Board Gate.** This gate matches the lattice-top fence on page 76. It also looks quite handsome all by itself. The boards and the lattice are sandwiched between cleats, as shown.*

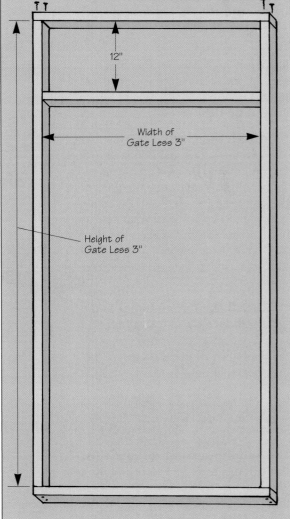

1. Cut the parts and screw the frame together. The short horizontal piece helps hold the lattice.

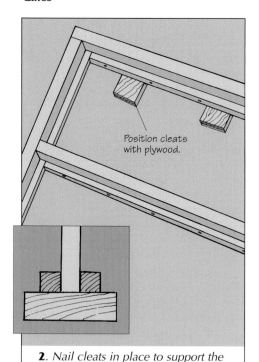

2. *Nail cleats in place to support the gate boards and lattice. Place scraps of ⅝-inch plywood under the gate to help position the cleats properly.*

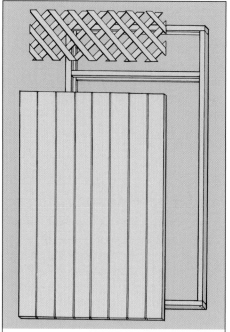

3. *Place the lattice and fence boards on top of the cleats, but do not nail them in place.*

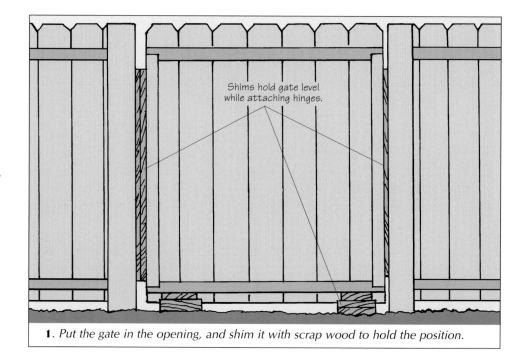

4. *A second set of cleats holds the lattice and fence boards in place. Nail them to the frame but not to the board or lattice.*

a 12-inch high area for the lattice section. Join the pieces together by drilling pilot holes and driving 3-inch galvanized deck screws.

2 Attach the cleats. The cleats will hold the lattice and boards in place on the finished fence. Cut pieces of 1x1 to fit snugly between the parts of the frame. Lay scrap pieces of ⅝-inch plywood down on the flat surface, and use them as spacers to keep the cleats a uniform ⅝ inch from the edge of the 2x4s. Attach with 4d galvanized finish nails.

3 Install the lattice panel and the boards. Cut a section of a lattice panel to fit, but not snugly. Set the lattice in place on top of the 1x1 cleats. Do not fasten it.

Cut 1x6 boards to fit—again, not snugly—in the lower section of the gate. Set them in place, and do not fasten.

4 Add the second set of cleats. Cut pieces of 1x1 to fit snugly, as with the first set of cleats. Push them into position so that they hold the lattice and the 1x6s fairly tightly. Attach them to the 2x4 frame only using 4d galvanized finish nails—do not attach them to the lattice or the 1x6.

HANGING A GATE

Whether you are hanging a custom or a prefab gate, you'll need a drill, some wood blocks, and some shims. Although it is possible for one person to do the job, it is always better to have a helper to hold the gate in position and keep it plumb while you attach the hardware.

1 Position the gate. Shim the gate to the right height with wood spacer blocks. Use wood shingle shims, if needed, to get exactly the right height. Use shims or wood strips to space the gate the required clearance from the gate posts. If you're hanging the gate by yourself, you can tack 1x4 cleats to the gate post, and temporarily nail the gate to the cleats with 6d nails to make

Shims hold gate level while attaching hinges.

1. *Put the gate in the opening, and shim it with scrap wood to hold the position.*

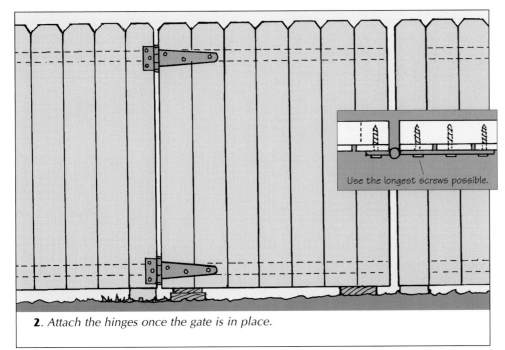

2. Attach the hinges once the gate is in place.

3. Attach the latch to the gate first, and then use it to position the strike.

Use the longest screws possible.

hinge installation easier. Otherwise, have a helper hold the gate in position while you attach the hinges.

2 Attach the hinges. Generally, butt hinges are installed about 4 to 6 inches from the top and bottom of the gate. T-hinges and strap hinges usually are installed at the top and bottom rails to provide additional backing for screws. With the gate propped in position, screw or bolt the hinges to the gate post first, according to instructions. Then attach the hinges to the gate. Screws should penetrate as far into the wood as possible without coming out the other side. Predrill all screw or bolt holes to make attachment easier and to avoid splitting the wood. Recheck the position of the gate and adjust it, if necessary. Make sure the gate swings freely. If it does not, remove it and trim the bottom as necessary.

3 Attach the latch. Attach the gate latch about 36 inches from the ground or according to instructions. In most cases, you attach the latch mechanism to the gate first, and then align and attach the strike to the fence. As with hinges, use the longest screws possible. Predrill screw holes.

Securing Gates to Masonry

When hanging gates on masonry walls or columns, the structure itself must be designed to support the weight of the gate, especially if it is heavy. For example, center cavities in brick columns or block walls should be filled with reinforced concrete a minimum of 12 inches back from the hinge location, or as specified by local codes. For new walls, plan for the location of the gate hinges when you design the wall. Masonry hinges, L-shaped bolts, or similar hardware used to mount the hinges are usually set into the mortar joints or fresh concrete when the wall is built.

For existing walls, bore holes with a carbide-tipped masonry bit. Locate the holes to accept screw anchors. You can bolt the hinges directly to the screw anchors, but it is easier to bolt a vertical 2x4 wood ledger to the wall and screw the hinges to the 2x4 ledger. When you insert the shield or anchor into the hole, it should fit snugly, requiring light tapping with a hammer or mallet. When a bolt or screw penetrates the anchor, it expands and holds the bolt in place.

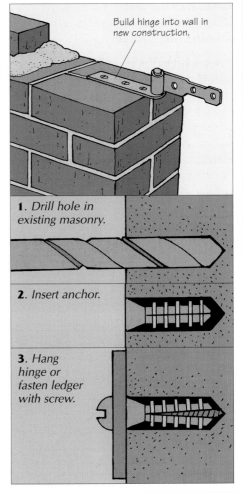

Build hinge into wall in new construction.

1. Drill hole in existing masonry.

2. Insert anchor.

3. Hang hinge or fasten ledger with screw.

TRELLISES

A trellis can be both an aesthetic and practical addition to your yard. From a designer's view, a trellis with climbing plants can make a yard feel less flat and more complete. As a practical matter, trellises also act to define spaces in and around your yard. Use a trellis to mark the boundary of your property, to divide your yard into areas of differing use, or to direct foot traffic.

Very often, a trellis is the best way to cover up something you don't want to see. Use a trellis to hide the garbage cans—it is less expensive, easier to build, and nicer looking than those box-like structures designed to house the trash cans.

Even if you don't have something to hide, a trellis simply looks great. Whether rustic or elegant, simple or elaborate, there is something peculiarly satisfying about light filtering through lattice and leaves: It makes for an atmosphere that is both relaxed and refined. Use a trellis to decorate a patio or deck.

PRACTICAL CONSIDERATIONS

On a practical level, a trellis can be a privacy screen. In designing your trellis, you can choose exactly how much privacy you want it to provide. You can weave lattice pieces into a mesh—like a wall, or you can space the pieces wide apart to create only a hint of a barrier. If you grow climbing plants on your trellis, you will find a small-leafed vine adds a light decorative touch, while a broad-leaved and bushy variety provides more privacy. If you plant annuals, you can have light filtering in during the spring, and increasing shade as the summer progresses and the days get hotter.

A trellis can function as a friendly version of a fence. Where a fence is clearly made to be a barrier, a trellis is more of an ornament that can provide privacy without hurting your neighbor's feelings. And even though they're made of thin pieces of wood, trellises can be surprisingly strong. It's not a good idea to make a trellis much longer than 10 feet, however. Longer trellises look awkward, and you'll probably be happier with a true fence.

Gardening

A trellis is very practical for the gardener with limited space. Put a trellis on a ground space of as little as 4 by 8 feet, and you can grow a variety of vegetables or decorative plants.

Many vegetables, fruits, and flowers will produce much greater harvests when allowed to climb into the air. And the quality of the produce often increases as well: A squash that is not lying on the ground is much less apt to rot. Trellis gardening means fewer bug problems because many insects live in and crawl on the ground.

Trellis gardening is easy on the knees and the back. There is little weeding. Most of the pruning and harvesting is done standing up, rather than stooping over.

DESIGN CONSIDERATIONS

Design a trellis that suits your yard and is strong enough for your purposes. Pick a modest-size structure. Trellises work best when they are accents, rather than the most prominent feature of a deck or yard. You're not building the Hanging Gardens of Babylon here. Match what you're

Plants that Climb

Some plants need only the slightest encouragement before they grab onto and climb up a trellis. Others need more help: You may have to tie an occasional branch, or weave tendrils around lattice pieces. And still others will never grasp the trellis at all—you'll have to tie or weave them in place with string. Before you choose your climbing plant, ask your garden supplier how much work it will require on a trellis.

Here are some of the most popular plants for trellises. For each, there are many varieties available to suit your climate and soil conditions.

Vegetables. POLE BEANS climb easily up almost any trellis. They have a long harvest time, and the more you pick the more will grow—so one or two plants will give you fresh beans for months. CUCUMBERS like partial shade, but require attentive watering. Choose either large or small varieties, and start picking after two months or so. SQUASHES, such as zucchini, grow very quickly—after less than two months, you will be able to pick new vegetables every few days. PEAS, PEPPERS, and EGGPLANTS also grow well on trellises.

Fruit. RASPBERRIES AND BLACKBERRIES will produce fruit for years, but usually require a good deal of attention in the first year or two, during which time they will produce little fruit. Trellises with lots of open space

work best. Once they grab the trellis, yearly trimming of unproductive canes and watering may be all that's required for you to have a plentiful harvest. Thorns will discourage young climbers. GRAPES are the trickiest fruit to grow—check with local experts before you start. Once established, however, they will be a most impressive part of your yard for years. STRAWBERRIES usually are set in mounds and allowed to trail on the ground, but a short (36 inches or so) trellis will work to keep the fruit off the ground and free from rot. Most varieties live for several years.

Decorative plants. Be careful not to get plants that go crazy and proliferate all over the place, or you will be consigned to lots of pruning. ROSES are the most popular trellis flower and for good reason. New varieties do not require much work and produce flowers all season long. Just prune them way back at the end of every season.

CLEMATIS, NASTURTIUM, CLIMBING HYDRANGEA, and other perennial climbers are widely available. IVY has a stately look, but may take years to grow enough for your trellis; VIRGINIA CREEPER is a faster-growing ivy-like plant. Although perennials may seem like the best option, many people prefer annuals, such as MORNING GLORIES and SWEET PEAS, because they can change them from year to year.

building with your yard. A 36-inch-wide trellis will look lost and lonely if placed in the middle of a large expanse of lawn. A large trellis can overpower a small area. Find the right size by temporarily propping up some posts on the spot where you want to put the trellis. Run some sort of webbing between the posts to get a sense of what it will look like when filled in (a volleyball net works fine), and stand back for a good look.

A trellis is usually an upright structure with distinctive plants growing on it. As a result, its size, shape, and perhaps color are different from the other structures in the yard. It is a pleasant interruption, a splash of something different. But you don't want it to clash with the rest of your yard. If possible, take a theme-and-variation approach: Make the posts the same size and color as your fence or porch posts. Or cut overhead pieces to a design that recalls elements of your house or deck. It may be possible to construct lattice sections that are made of the same lumber as your fence pickets, or that mimic the pattern of your fencing. Even the smallest gesture towards making your trellis fit in will make a difference.

If you are putting trellises on the side of your house, place them in pleasing relation to windows, doors, and sides: Either make them symmetrical or obviously nonsymmetrical, not something in between.

Will It Be a Jungle Gym?

You probably don't think of your trellis as a climbing structure, but any kids that happen to be around will. If children are a part of your life, you can either take steps to discourage climbing or build a trellis strong enough to withstand their weight. You'll find that either strengthening the arbor or discouraging kids is relatively easy.

Tight web-like lattice structures—factory-made lattice panels, for instance—are difficult to climb. Climbing plants will cause most children to stay off; plants with thorns will definitely deter them.

A trellis built to last is already a sturdy one. It may not take much more to make it withstand climbing youngsters. Because it uses so many pieces of wood, lattice can be surprisingly strong. By increasing the amount, or size of the pieces, and by taking extra care in fastening, you can increase its strength markedly.

Lattice Possibilities

Lattice need not be the simple crisscross grid pattern that people usually think of. Anything that filters light and allows plants to take hold will qualify. You can achieve a wide variety of effects by changing the pattern, materials, and finish of your lattice sections.

If you place your trellis near a deck, patio, house, or fence that is already interesting to look at, avoid visual chaos by building a simple trellis with a pattern of crisscrossing squares. Finish the trellis by painting or staining it to match the deck or siding. Where the surroundings are simpler, consider more complex trellises, such as the fan trellis or the gambrel-roof arbor on page 121 and page 128.

Rough-Sawn Lumber. Varying the construction technique and material used can change the look of a lattice. Make a rustic lattice with simple patterns and rough-textured, unpainted wood. Ready-made panels of cedar or pressure-treated lattice do the job quickly. You can also make ladder-like structures or widely spaced squares from 1x2 or 1x4. Visible nail or screw heads are no problem with this look. Rough-sawn posts complete the look, although milled posts also work well.

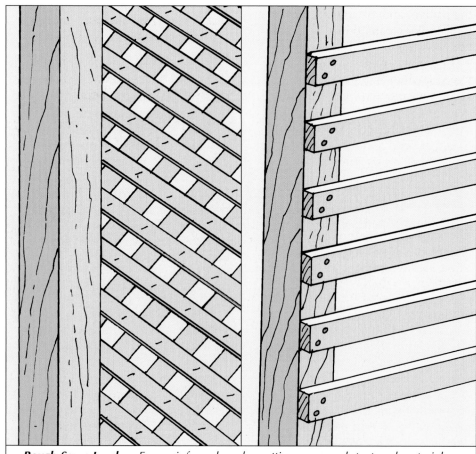

Rough-Sawn Lumber. *For an informal garden setting, use rough-textured materials such as rough-surfaced lattice panels or widely spaced rough cedar 1x3s.*

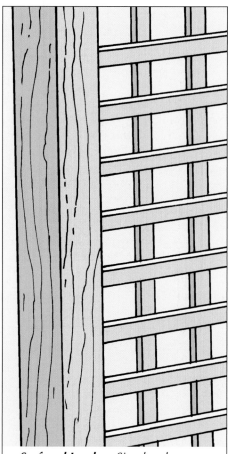

Surfaced Lumber. *Simple, clean lines combined with smooth materials create a formal look.*

Surfaced Lumber. For a more formal appearance, build the trellis from smooth-sided 1x2 or 1x1 crossed in a regular pattern of perfect squares. The smooth, clean surface of this material creates a much different feel than rough-textured wood. Use pieces with squared-off rather than rounded edges. Drive screws or nails from the back of the trellis so they won't be seen by most people.

Geometric Patterns. Geometric patterns and fairly large open spaces create an elegant look. Use smooth, unmarred wood, and give it a couple of coats with a glossy paint—white is the classic choice.

Lattice Materials. Often, the easiest way to put together a trellis is with ready-made lattice panels. These are available in 2x8 or 4x8 sizes at most lumberyards. Before you decide to buy panels, however, take a close look and test them for strength. The cheaper panels use lumber as thin as 3/16 inch, have cracked pieces, and are put together with staples that do not hold well. A better grade of lattice panel will use 3/8-inch lattice and will not collapse like an accordion when you pick it up on one end and give it a little shake.

There are ways to make a ready-made panel stronger and longer lasting: When you install it, support its edges by sandwiching it between two pieces of 1x4, 2x4, or 2x2. If the panel is longer than 72 inches, add a piece of 2x4, laid flat, in the middle. Give the panel a coating of sealer/preservative or paint before installing. Spray painting works better than brushing.

If you want a simple crisscross pattern made of rustic wood, by all means go with ready-made panels. These panels are somewhat limiting, however. You cannot vary the size of the openings or the pattern, and there is little choice of lumber. For greater design flexibility, consider making the lattice yourself, as explained in "Making a Lattice Panel," page 116. Building a lattice section is not as difficult as you may think.

TRELLIS PLANS

The trellises shown here range from small to large. But trellises are simple structures. The process of building or buying a screen and then attaching it to posts is pretty straightforward and makes for a project suitable to the skills of most homeowners. Modify the plans to suit your needs: Pick and choose your favorite features, and combine them in a lattice that's right for your yard.

Directions include both shopping and cutting lists. The shopping list includes everything you'll need when you go to the lumberyard or home center, including screws, nails, and hardware. Remember—a 2x4 measures only 1½x3½. The shopping list gives you the nominal dimension—2x4. The cutting list gives you the actual size of all the pieces but also tells you what to cut it from. Some pieces are cut to fit between two other pieces, so don't cut all the pieces in advance. Instead, refer to the cutting list as you work, measure, and cut each piece to size as you need it.

Choose a weather-resistant lumber for your project—cedar, redwood, or pressure-treated lumber.

Geometric Patterns. *Widely spaced geometric patterns add elegance to your trellis.*

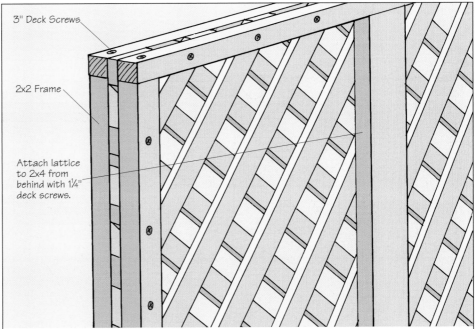

3" Deck Screws

2x2 Frame

Attach lattice to 2x4 from behind with 1¼" deck screws.

Lattice Materials. *This thin, prefabricated lattice panel has been reinforced by framing it with 2x2 stock. A 2x4 center support further strengthens the frame.*

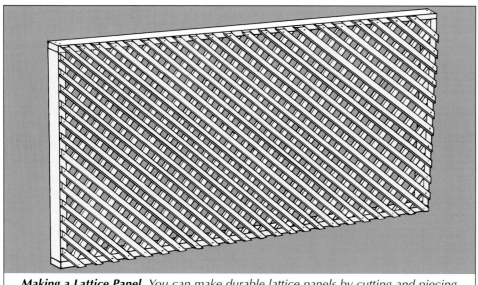

Making a Lattice Panel. *You can make durable lattice panels by cutting and piecing together one-by stock.*

Shopping List

☐ Three knot-free 1x8x8' ☐ Three 2x2x8'
☐ One 1x8x6' as a spacer

Fasteners

☐ 2 pounds of 1¼" screws or 4d galvanized nails
☐ 1 pound of 3" deck screws

Cutting List

Qty.	Part	Dimensions	Comments
Twelve	Lattice Strips	¾" x ¾" x 72"	Cut from 1x8x8'
Eight	Lattice Strips	¾" x ¾" x 48"	Cut from 1x8x8'
Six	Lattice Strips	¾" x ¾" x 24"	Cut from 1x8x8'
Two	Long Rails	1½" x 1½" x 96"	Cut from 2x2x8'
Two	Short Rails	1½" x 1½" x 45"	Cut from 2x2x8'

Making a Lattice Panel 🌱

This 4x8-foot section of lattice is made from 1x1 lumber, spaced 7½ inches apart, and attached to the frame at a 45-degree angle. To build this, you attach half the lattice strips to the outside of the frame. Then you cut the remaining lattice strips to fit snugly inside the frame.

Once you've built this panel, you can use it to screen off a porch or mount it against the house to hold plants. You can also substitute this design for the lattice used in any of the projects which follow.

1 **Make the lattice pieces.** If you have access to a good table saw or radial arm saw, rip the lattice pieces from the 1x8. Make them ¾ inch wide, so that they will be just as wide as they are thick. A sharp carbide blade will ensure smooth surfaces. You can also have a lumberyard rip the boards for you. There is usually a small cost for the labor.

2 **Paint or treat the pieces.** Cut the 1x1s and 2x2s to the lengths indicated and paint, stain, or treat them. (If you have a spray painter, you may want to wait until after the unit is assembled.)

3 **Construct the frame.** Slip the short rails between the long rails, and screw them together with 3-inch screws. Hold a framing square against

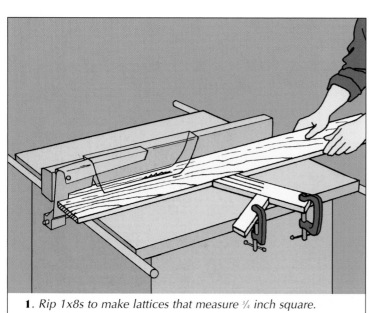

1. Rip 1x8s to make lattices that measure ¼ inch square.

2. Paint the lattice parts before assembly.

one corner and adjust the frame so that it is square. To keep the frame square while you work on it, attach a temporary brace to the corner, using 1¼-inch deck screws. Check the other corner for square and brace it, too.

4 Attach the first trellis strip.
Turn the frame upside down. Cut a short piece of lattice to the size and profile shown. Nail or screw it to one corner, so that the cut ends are flush with the outside of the frame. Drill pilot holes for the nails or screws. Use a single fastener at each joint.

5 Install the remaining strips on the frame's face.
Use a 1x8 as a spacer to position the remaining strips. The cutting list includes three lengths of lattice. As you work along the frame, attach the shortest lattice that will fit. Install it with the edges hanging over the frame. Don't trim the strips to exact length yet. It is easier to cut them once they are all attached.

6 Cut the trellis strips to length.
When all the pieces are installed, snap a chalk line along the strips. Position the line so that you will cut the trellis strips flush with the outside edges of the frame. Cut along the line with a circular saw, and paint the ends of the strips.

7 Install the remaining lattice strips.
The remaining strips don't overlap the rails. They nest between them, as shown, and have to be cut to fit as you attach them. Turn the panel over and cut the 1x8 spacer into two shorter spacers. Miter the ends of a trellis strip, as shown, to create a piece 5 inches long. Predrill and toenail or screw to the frame.

To lay out the length of the next piece, miter one end of the trellis strip. Position it with the spacer. Hold the mitered edge against the frame and trace along the frame to mark the other miter. Cut at the pencil line, screw it to the frame and to any lattice strips it crosses. Continue cutting and attaching lattice until you have filled the frame.

3. Square the frame and brace it.

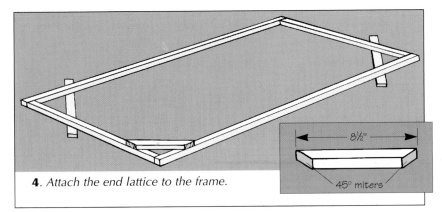

4. Attach the end lattice to the frame.

8½"

45° miters

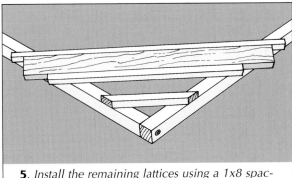

5. Install the remaining lattices using a 1x8 spacer to position them. Leave the ends long.

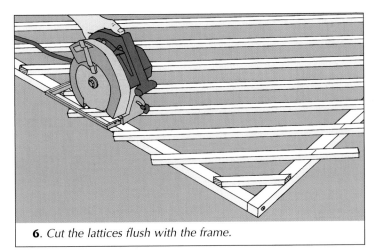

6. Cut the lattices flush with the frame.

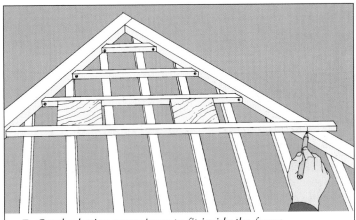

7. Cut the lattice crosspieces to fit inside the frame.

Simple Trellis T

A small, elegant unit like this can be used to hide the garbage cans or as a pleasant ornament located next to your entry door. Though it looks elaborate, it is actually very simple to build.

1 Set rear posts. Dig deep post-holes for the posts. They should be at least 32 inches deep to support poles this long, and the posts should sit 6 inches below the frost line. Check with your local building department to determine the exact depth required. Put 6 inches of gravel into each hole. Leave the posts 12 feet long for now, and trim them to length later.

Set the posts in place, and temporarily brace them so they are plumb in both directions and parallel with each other.

2 Attach the front lattice. Cut four pieces of 2x2 to 60 inches. Lay out the location of these slats on one of the posts, as shown in the

Shopping List

☐ Two 4x4x12'
☐ Two 2x2x10'

☐ Two post caps
☐ Six 2x2x8'

Fasteners

☐ 1 pound of 3" deck screws
☐ 1 pound of 2½" deck screws

☐ A small handful of 6d galvanized finish nails
☐ Ready-mix concrete, as needed
☐ Gravel, as needed

Cutting List

Qty.	Part	Dimensions	Comments
Two	Posts	3½" x 3½" x length to fit	Cut from 4x4x12'
Four	Front Lattice	1½" x 1½" x 60"	Cut from 2x2x10'
Two	Back Lattice	1½" x 1½" x 47"	Cut from 2x2x8'
Seven	Vertical Lattice	1½" x 1½" x 90"	Cut from 2x2x8'

illustration. These dimensions can be changed to suit your taste. With a level or chalkline and string level, transfer the layout to the other post.

Drill pilot holes in the lattice to avoid splitting the wood with the screws. The hole should be the diameter of the screw shank. Place a lattice in

position so that one end is flush with the post, and screw it in place with 3-inch deck screws. If necessary, pull the second post until the other end of the lattice is flush with it, and screw the lattice in place. Once you have installed the first lattice, install the others. Check for plumb, level, and parallel as you work.

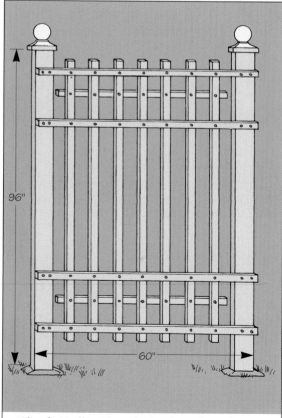

96"

60"

Simple Trellis. Though simple and quick to build, this trellis has an elegant feel and is perfect for fencing off an unsightly area of the yard.

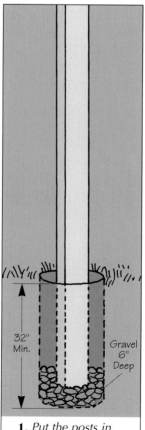

32" Min.

Gravel 6" Deep

1. Put the posts in their holes, and brace the posts so they remain plumb.

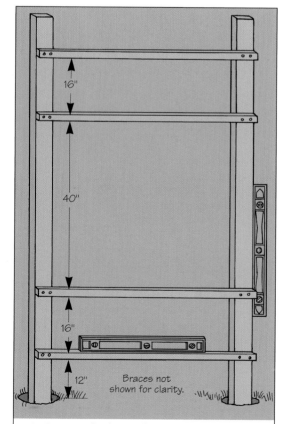

16"

40"

16"

12"

Braces not shown for clarity.

2. Lay out the lattice locations on the post, predrill the lattice for screws, and attach to the posts.

3 Attach the remaining pieces.

Cut the five vertical lattice slats to size. The pieces are evenly spaced. Lay out the location of the vertical slats on the slats you just installed. Space the lattice slats so there is $5\frac{5}{16}$ inches between each slat and between the end slats and the posts. Drill pilot holes and screw them in place with $2\frac{1}{2}$-inch deck screws.

Install the two short back slats, centering them between the front slats.

4 Finish the posts.

Cut the posts to height, 8 feet above ground and level with each other. Nail the post caps in place, and pour the concrete around the posts. See "Backfill with Concrete," page 61.

Planter Trellis 🌱🌱

This trellis, made of 2x2 verticals and 1x2 horizontals, rises up and outward from a box large enough to root almost any vegetable or decorative plant. It is designed to sit on a patio or deck.

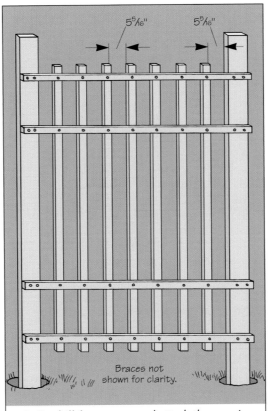

3. Predrill for screws, and attach the remaining lattice to the trellis. Backfill with concrete.

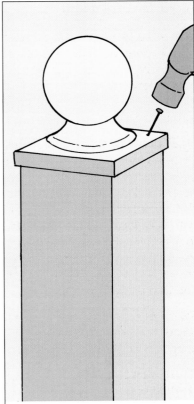

4. Nail a commercially made post cap to each post.

Shopping List

- ☐ Two 1x8x12'
- ☐ One 1x3x6'
- ☐ Two 2x2x12'
- ☐ Two 1x4x10'

Fasteners

- ☐ 1 pound of $1\frac{1}{4}$" deck screws
- ☐ 1 pound of $1\frac{5}{8}$" deck screws
- ☐ 1 pound of 2" deck screws

Cutting List

Qty.	Part	Dimensions	Comments
Two	Upper Sides	$\frac{3}{4}$" x $7\frac{1}{2}$" x 18"	Cut from 1x8x12'
Two	Lower Sides	$\frac{3}{4}$" x $7\frac{1}{2}$" x 17"	Cut from 1x8x12'
Four	Front/Back	$\frac{3}{4}$" x $7\frac{1}{2}$" x 37"	Cut from 1x8x12'
Two	Bottoms	$\frac{3}{4}$" x $7\frac{1}{2}$" x $34\frac{1}{4}$"	Cut from 1x8x12'
Four	Corner Trim	$\frac{3}{4}$" x $1\frac{1}{2}$" x 15"	Cut from 1x3x6'
Four	Wide Corner Trim	$\frac{3}{4}$" x $2\frac{1}{2}$" x 15"	Cut from 1x3x6'
Three	Vertical Lattice	$1\frac{1}{2}$" x $1\frac{1}{2}$" x 72"	Cut from 2x2x12'
Five	Horizontal Lattice	$1\frac{1}{2}$" x $1\frac{1}{2}$" x length to fit	Cut from 2x2x12'
Three	Bottom Supports	$\frac{3}{4}$" x $3\frac{1}{2}$" x $35\frac{3}{4}$"	Cut from 1x4x10'

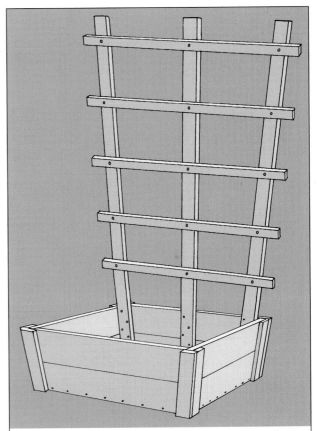

Planter Trellis. *A planter trellis is great on a deck or patio. Plant vines in the planter, and watch them climb up the trellis.*

1 Cut the front and side pieces. Cut the front and sides to the sizes listed in the cutting list. These pieces are slightly long to support the saw when you cut them to the shapes illustrated. To obtain the proper angle, first lay out the top of each piece. With a framing square, draw a line connecting the top corner to the bottom of each piece. To locate the bottom corner, measure inward ³/₈ inch and make a mark. Draw a line connecting the two corner marks, as shown. Lay out and cut the pieces to the sizes shown.

2 Assemble the box. Drill pilot holes and screw the box together with 2-inch deck screws as shown.

For the bottom, cut two pieces of 1x8 to fit. There will be a gap of about ¹/₈ inch between the bottom pieces, which allows excess moisture to escape. Drill pilot holes, and screw the bottom in place.

3 Add trim and bottom slats. Trim the sides with 1x2 and 1x3, as shown. Cut the trim to the size given in the materials list. Attach the 1x2 first, positioning it flush with the corners of the box. Attach the 1x3 next, positioning it flush with the 1x2.

Attach three pieces of pressure-treated 1x2s to the underside of the box, using 1¼-inch deck screws. Set the two outside pieces ³/₈ inch back from the front and back edges of the box, so they won't be visible.

4 Attach trellis pieces. Cut the three vertical trellis pieces to size. Attach a trellis piece to each of the back inside corners and a third trellis piece to the center of the box. The outer pieces will follow the angle of the box. Attach the center trellis so that it is square to the box. The horizontal pieces overhang the slanted trellis by 1¹/₂ inches, as shown. Measure and cut to fit. Slight variations in the cutting of the box could cause the angle to change substantially. Attach the lattice pieces every 11 inches on center with 1⁵/₈-inch deck screws.

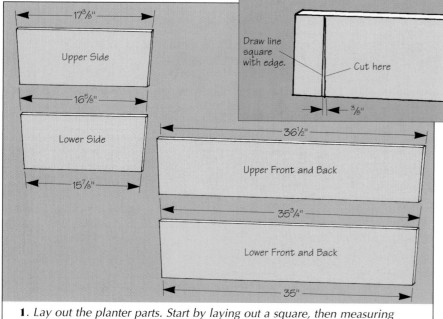

1. Lay out the planter parts. Start by laying out a square, then measuring back from the corner at the bottom of each piece.

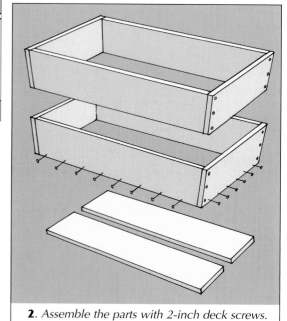

2. Assemble the parts with 2-inch deck screws.

3. Attach 1x2 and 1x3 trim to the corners, and screw slats to the bottom of the box.

4. Screw a trellis piece to each of the inside back corners. Attach a third trellis piece to the middle of the back.

Fan Trellis

This trellis is sophisticated-looking, but amazingly easy to make. A stake holds the bottom in place, but the trellis needs a building or fence to lean against for support.

The hardest part may be coming up with the wood pieces—thin strips of clear redwood or cedar that are ¾ inch wide by ⅜ inch thick. If your lumberyard can't produce them for you at a reasonable price, you can cut them on a table saw or radial arm saw.

1 Cut the pieces. Begin with a knot-free 1x4. Knots will cause the wood to break when you flex it to create the fan. On a table saw or radial arm saw, rip the 1x4 into seven pieces that are

⅜ inches thick. Cut the fan pieces and the top, center, and lower crosspieces from this stock to the dimensions given in the cutting list.

2 Bolt the fan pieces together. Clamp the five fan pieces together, and drill two ¼-inch holes through them near the bottom. Fasten the pieces together with two ¼-inch by 2½-inch machine bolts with washers and nuts.

3 Attach the top piece. Mark the top piece as shown. Attach the top piece to one of the outside fan pieces, drilling a small pilot hole for one 4d galvanized nail. Working from one side to the other, nail the top to the other fan pieces, spacing them as shown.

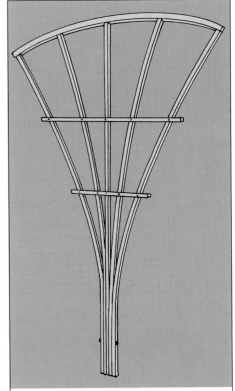

Fan Trellis. *A fan trellis requires few materials and assembles quickly.*

Shopping List

☐ One knot-free 1x4x8'   ☐ One pressure-treated 2x2x4'

Fasteners

☐ Four machine bolts, ¼" x 2½", with washers and nuts
☐ 1 pound 4d galvanized box nails

Cutting List

Qty.	Part	Dimensions	Comments
Five	Fan Pieces	⅜" x ¾" x 80"	Cut from 1x4x8'
One	Top Crosspiece	⅜" x ¾" x 51½"	Cut from 1x4x8'
One	Center Crosspiece	⅜" x ¾" x 38"	Cut from 1x4x8'
One	Lower Crosspiece	⅜" x ¾" x 24"	Cut from 1x4x8'
One	Stake	1½" x 1½" x 3"	Cut from 2x2x4'

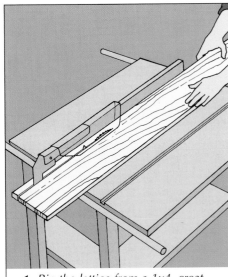

1. Rip the lattice from a 1x4, creating strips ⅜ x ¾ inches.

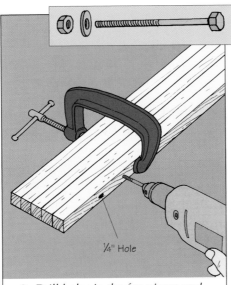

2. Drill holes in the fan pieces and bolt them together.

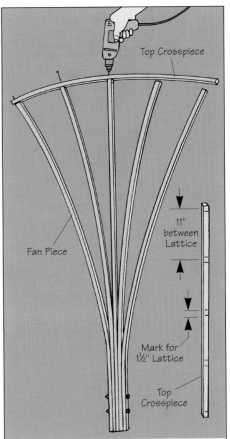

3. Mark the top piece to show where it meets the fan. Nail it to the fan with 4d galvanized nails.

4 Attach crosspieces and stake.

Measure 16 inches down from the top, and attach the first crosspiece. Measure down another 16 inches and attach the second crosspiece. Drive a 4d nail through each crosspiece into each fan piece, predrilling holes to avoid splitting the wood.

Make a stake by cutting one end of a pressure-treated 2x2 to a point, then cut the stake to length. Drive it into the spot where you want your trellis until only 8 inches are above the ground. Hold the trellis against the stake, drill two ¼-inch holes through both the trellis and the stake. Bolt them together with 2½-inch bolts with washers and nuts.

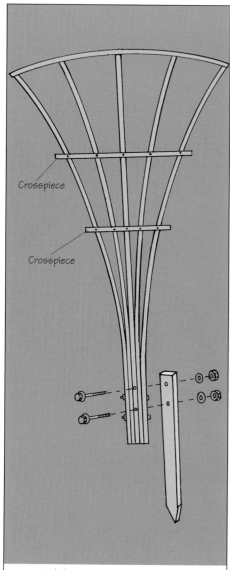

4. Nail the remaining crosspieces in place. Drive the stake in the ground and bolt the assembly to the stake.

Trellis Wall 🔩🔩🔩

This trellis has two octagonal openings for hanging flower pots, so you can show your best-looking potted plants to full advantage. Customize the design by adding or moving the openings.

The trellis grid is easier to construct than you may think: First you lay out

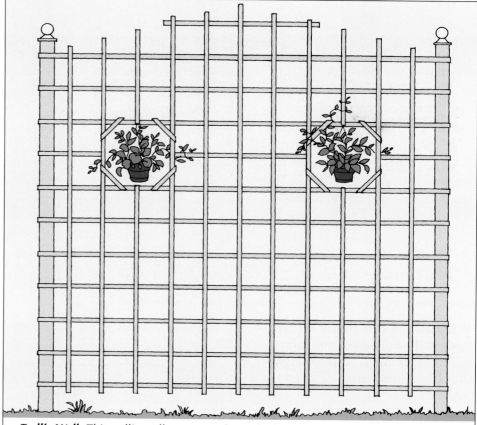

Trellis Wall. *This trellis wall accommodates climbing vines and lets you hang other plants in the openings as well.*

Shopping List

☐ Two 4x4x12'
☐ Four 1x8x8'

☐ Four 2x4x8'
☐ Two post caps

Fasteners

☐ 3 pounds of 1¼" deck screws or 4d galvanized nails
☐ Ready-mix concrete, as needed

☐ Gravel, as needed
☐ Eight 6d galvanized finish nails

Cutting List

Qty	Part	Dimensions	Comments
Two	Posts	3½" x 3½" x 12'	Cut from 4x4x12'
Eleven	Horizontal Lattice Slats	¾" x ¾" x 96"	Cut from 1x8x8'
One	Top Lattice Slats	¾" x ¾" x 36¾"	Cut from 1x8x8'
Two	Vertical Lattice Slats	¾" x ¾" x 84"	Cut from 1x8x8'
Two	Vertical Lattice Slats	¾" x ¾" x 86"	Cut from 1x8x8'
Two	Vertical Lattice Slats	¾" x ¾" x 88"	Cut from 1x8x8'
Two	Vertical Lattice Slats	¾" x ¾" x 90"	Cut from 1x8x8'
Two	Vertical Lattice Slats	¾" x ¾" x 92"	Cut from 1x8x8'
One	Vertical Lattice Slats	¾" x ¾" x 94"	Cut from 1x8x8'
Eight	Angled Trim Slats	¾" x ¾" x 7"	Cut from 1x8x8'

a normal square grid. To create the octagonal openings, you first attach lattice slats around the outside of the cut out, then you cut the openings with a hand saw.

The trellis as described is strong enough to support hanging plants and climbing vines, but not strong enough for children to climb on. If you want a firmer structure, use 1x2 or even 2x2 instead of the $^3/_4$x$^3/_4$-inch lattice specified.

1 Set the posts. Dig two postholes at least 32 inches deep, throw 6 inches of gravel into each, and set the posts in. Building codes vary, so check with your local building department to make sure the hole puts the post far enough below the frost line. Attach temporary braces, as shown, to hold the posts firmly plumb and parallel with each other. Fill the holes with gravel, and tamp the gravel firmly in place.

2 Install the horizontal lattice slats. Remove the temporary bracing, and cut the posts to height—8 feet 3 inches above the ground and level with each other. Attach the post caps. Cut the 11 horizontal lattice slats to size, and drill a single pilot hole two inches from each end. Attach the first lattice slat 3 inches from the top of the post by driving a 1$^1/_4$-inch screw through the pilot holes. Measure down from the installed slat, and make a mark every 8 inches to show where the tops of the other horizontal slats will go. Install the remaining 10 slats.

3 Install the vertical lattice slats. Cut the vertical slats to the dimensions given in the cutting list. Mark the top and bottom horizontal slats every eight inches to show where the vertical slats are attached. To keep the bottoms of the slats aligned, temporarily install a guide board: Nail or screw a straight 2x4 to the posts, 2 inches below the lowest horizontal slat. Rest the slats on this guide as you install them.

Work from one post toward the center, installing the slats with 1$^1/_4$-inch deck screws. Attach the pieces from the back so the screw heads will not

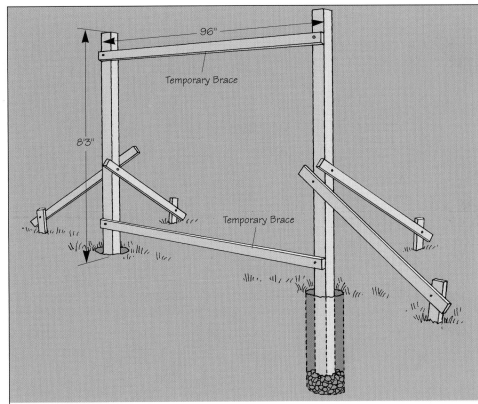

1. Dig postholes, backfill with about 6 inches of gravel, and set the posts in place. Backfill the rest of the hole, bracing the posts if necessary.

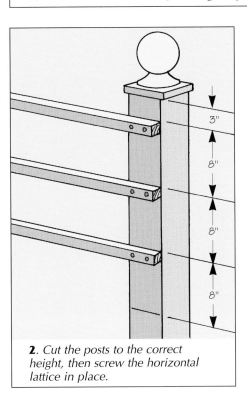

2. Cut the posts to the correct height, then screw the horizontal lattice in place.

3. Mark the top and bottom lattice to show the location of the horizontal lattice, and screw them in place.

show and drill pilot holes for each screw. The materials list gives several lengths for the vertical slats. Install the shortest slat first, and then the next longest one. As you work, install progressively longer slats until

you reach the center of the screen. Then work from the other post toward the center, again installing progressively longer slats. Install the center slat last, centering it between its neighbors.

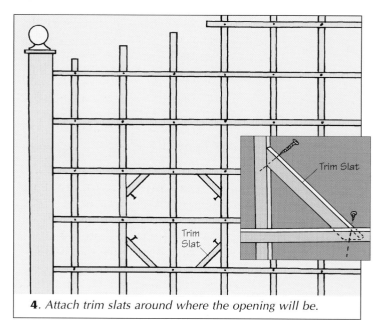

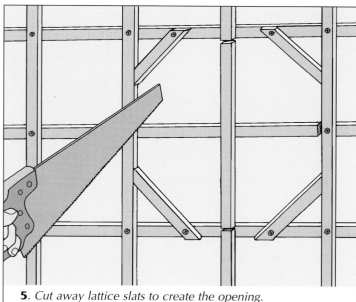

4. Attach trim slats around where the opening will be.

5. Cut away lattice slats to create the opening.

4 Attach the top and angle pieces.
Cut the top horizontal slat to 36¾ inches, and attach it as shown. Cut the eight angled trim slats: Each end is cut at 45 degrees, and the longest side is 7¾ inches. Position the angled trim slats, and install each slat with two screws as shown.

5 Cut the openings.
With a hand saw, cut away lattice slats to make the lattice as shown. Hold the flat part of the saw against the adjoining slat to make a flush cut.

Trellis with Arched Entry ⚘⚘⚘

This stately entryway provides privacy and a large area for climbing plants. A gently curved arch frames the top of the entry. With solid 4x4 posts on either side, the entry is ready for a gate, should you want to add one. The design is a bit tricky to build: The curved arch and the post caps take time, but no special skills.

1 Set the posts in postholes.
Lay out the and dig the holes, as explained in "Plotting a Straight Fence," page 52. The holes should be at least 36 inches deep; check with your building department to make sure this is far enough below the frost line. Set the posts in their holes.

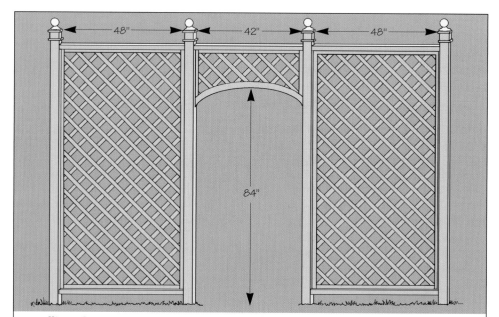

Trellis with Arched Entry. *The entry to this trellis is reminiscent of an arbor, but has broad flat surfaces that are easier to build.*

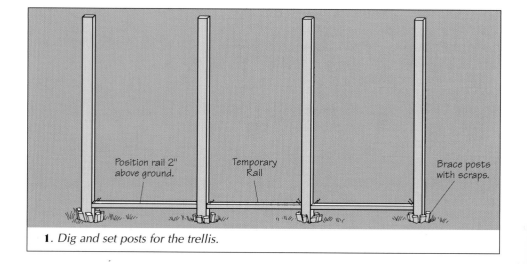

1. Dig and set posts for the trellis.

Shopping List

- [ ] Four 4x4x12'
- [ ] Seven 2x2x8'
- [ ] Seven 1x2x8'
- [ ] One 1x6x8'
- [ ] One 1x12x8'
- [ ] Two 4'x8' lattice sheets
- [ ] One 2'x4' lattice sheet
- [ ] Four post caps

Fasteners

- [ ] 1 pound of 3" deck screws
- [ ] 2 pounds of 2½" deck screws
- [ ] Ready-mix concrete, as needed
- [ ] 2 pounds of 2" deck screws
- [ ] 1 pound of 4d galvanized finishing nails
- [ ] Gravel, as needed

Cutting List

Qty.	Part	Dimensions	Comments
Four	Posts	3½" x 3½" x 12"	Cut from 4x4x12'
Four	Rails	1½" x 3½" x 48"	Cut from 2x4x8'
One	Rail	1½" x 3½" x 42"	Cut from 2x4x8'
One	Temporary Rail	1½" x 3½" x 42"	Cut from 2x4x8'
Eleven	Nailers	1½" x 1½" x length to fit	Cut from 2x2x8'
Eleven	Lattice Trim	¾" x 1½" x length to fit	Cut from 1x2x8'
Sixteen	Post Moldings	¾" x ¾" x 5"	Cut from 1x4x6'
Four	Post Platforms	¾" x 5½" x 5½"	Cut from 1x6x4'
Two	Arches	¾" x 11¼" x 40"	Cut from 1x12x8'

Position the posts exactly with the help of the rails. Cut the rails to size, and screw the bottom rails and the temporary rail in place, as shown. To keep the posts fairly plumb and solid, temporarily shove pieces of scrap wood into the holes as you work.

2 Plumb the posts and install top rails. Using a framing square and a level to align the structure so that it is square and plumb in both directions, attach temporary bracing stakes and crossbraces made of 1x4, 2x2, or 2x4 to hold it firmly in position.

There are 8 feet between the top and bottom rails. Measure 8 feet from the top of the installed rails, and mark the post for the bottom of the top rail. Attach the rails as before.

3 Attach nailers and lattice. The lattice is nailed against 2x2 strips attached to the post and rails. Cut pieces of 2x2 to fit, and nail them in place with 4d nails, flush with the rear of the posts. In the middle section, cut a 2x2 nailer to fit between the posts on the top rail. Then cut two 2x2x12 nailers, and nail them to post just below the top rail. No nailer is needed across the bottom of the arch.

The lattice panels will fit between the posts and rails. Nail them in place with 4d nails.

4 Cut the arches. The arch is actually made from two pieces stacked back to back. Lay out the arch on a 1x12. Begin by driving nails to mark three points on the lower curve, as shown. Flex a piece of ¼-inch lattice against each of the nails, and trace along it to draw the curve. To draw the upper curve,

2. Plumb and brace the structure before installing the top rails.

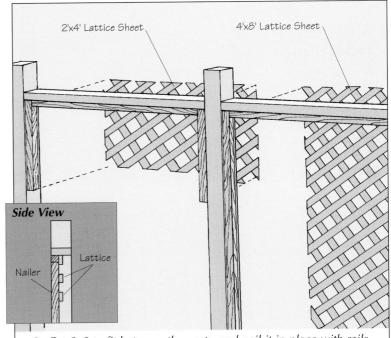

3. Cut 2x2 to fit between the posts, and nail it in place with rails to support the lattice.

reposition the nails, as shown. Cut out the arch with a saber saw. Sand out the saw marks, and use it as a pattern to lay out an identical arch.

5 Attach the arches.

Attach the front arch piece, positioning it as shown. Drive two 2½-inch screws at each end so that they go through the face of the arch, through the lattice, and into the nailers.

The rear arch fits between the nailers and is slightly shorter as a result. Mark the proper length by tracing along a scrap of nailer held against the end of the arch, as shown. Cut along the lines, slip the arch in place, and screw

it to the front arch and the lattice with 2-inch screws every 6 inches.

6 Cut off lattice and nailers in the middle section.

Use a saber saw, reciprocating saw, or hand saw to cut the lattice and nailers flush with the bottom of the arches. Cut very carefully, so as not to damage the arch or the posts. Remove the temporary piece of 2x4 at the bottom of the middle section.

7 Add 1x2 trim.

In the completed trellis, the lattice is sandwiched between the nailers and a piece of 1x2 trim. Cut the trim to fit, and attach it with 2½-inch deck screws.

8 Cut and trim the post tops.

Cut the four posts to the same height—6 inches above the top rails. Cut the post platforms to the size given in the materials list. Screw them in place with 2-inch galvanized deck screws. Nail the post cap in place with 6d nails.

To lay out the molding that runs around the posts, measure down 4 inches from the top of the post and mark a square line running all around the post. Miter a 1x1 to fit. Attach the molding with 4d galvanized finishing nails. Backfill the postholes with concrete.

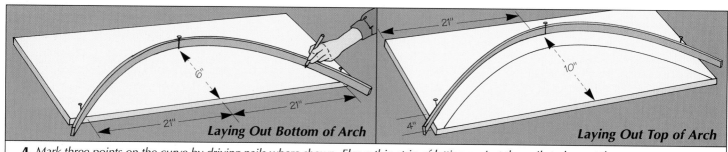

Laying Out Bottom of Arch   *Laying Out Top of Arch*

4. Mark three points on the curve by driving nails where shown. Flex a thin strip of lattice against the nails to lay out the curve.

5. Nail the arches in place between the posts.

6. Trim the lattice flush. Cut carefully to protect the arches.

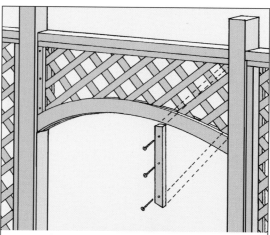

7. Apply trim over the lattice, and then sandwich the lattice between the trim and the nailers.

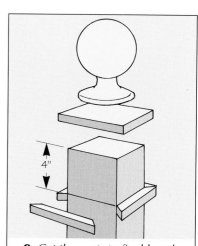

8. Cut the posts to final length, and attach decorative trim.

CHAPTER 9

ARBORS

An arbor is the big brother to a trellis. Like a trellis, an arbor consists largely of lattice supported by rails and posts. Like a trellis, an arbor lends itself to climbing plants. An arbor can be used as a privacy screen or perhaps to set off part of your yard. The big difference, of course, is that a trellis is a wall and an arbor has a roof.

While a trellis can be light, an arbor requires sturdy construction. Set the posts in deep holes, with gravel in the bottom for drainage, and concrete around the post for strength. The depth of the hole depends on local conditions and codes. As a general rule, one-third the total length of the post should be underground. There should be 6 inches of gravel in the bottom of the hole, and the bottom of the post should be 6 inches below frost line. Check with your building department to see what local requirements are. Many arbors are built with ready-made lattice panels. While they will work nicely on an arbor, the arbors shown here have shop-made lattice for sturdier construction and design.

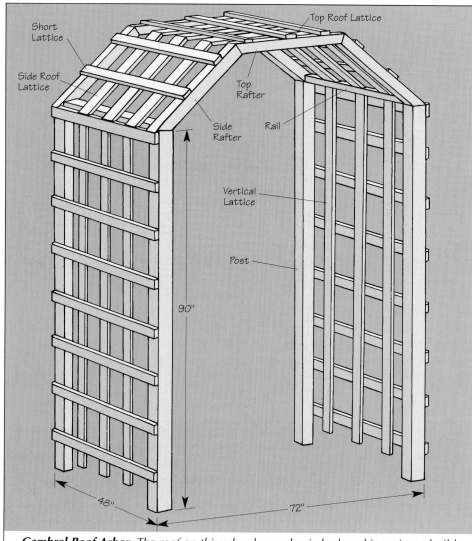

Labels in figure: Short Lattice, Side Roof Lattice, Top Roof Lattice, Top Rafter, Side Rafter, Rail, Vertical Lattice, Post, 90", 48", 72"

Gambrel Roof Arbor. *The roof on this arbor has a classic look and is easier to build than an arbor with an arched roof.*

Shopping List

☐ Four 4x4x12'
☐ Twenty-one 1x2x8'

☐ Four 2x4x8'

Fasteners

☐ 1 pound of 3" deck screws
☐ 1 pound of 1¼" deck screws

☐ 1 pound of 2" deck screws
☐ Concrete, as needed.
☐ Gravel, as needed.

Cutting List

Qty.	Part	Dimensions	Comments
Two	Top Rafters	1½" x 3½" x 33"	Cut from 2x4x8'
Four	Side Rafters	1½" x 3½" x 29¾"	Cut from 2x4x8'
Two	Rails	1½" x 3½" x 45"	Cut from 2x4x8'
23	Short Lattice	¾" x 1½" x 48"	Cut from 1x2x8'
Four	Posts	3½" x 3½" x 12"	Cut from 4x4x12'
Six	Vertical Lattice	¾" x 1½" x 87"	Cut from 1x2x8'
Six	Side Roof Lattice	¾" x 1½" x 29¾"	Cut from 1x2x8'
Three	Top Roof Lattice	¾" x 1½" x 33"	Cut from 1x2x8'

BUILDING ARBORS

Take time in laying out an arbor. Make sure the posts are not only in line with each other, but that they are plumb and the structure is square. The techniques are not at all difficult. In fact, they're the same ones used for setting fence posts. For information on laying out post holes, see "Plotting a Straight Fence," page 52. To review backfilling with concrete and gravel, see "Choosing Backfill Materials," page 63.

Gambrel Roof Arbor

Here's an entry to your yard or garden that is both solid and graceful. It stands more than 9 feet high and has a walkway that is nearly 72 inches wide. You can place it in the middle of a fence run, or let it sit alone in your yard as a decorative feature. Put a seat or two in it, and you have a pleasant, semi-shaded place to relax.

Building this arbor is pretty straightforward. The trickiest part is getting the angles right for the rafters. If you have a radial arm saw or a power miter saw, this will be no problem; doing it with an angle square and a circular saw requires good carpentry skills. Have a helper on hand, especially for installing the roof on top of the posts.

1 Cut the rafters, rails, and short lattice. There are six rafters—two top rafters and the four side rafters which angle up to meet them. Cut the rafters to the length and angles shown in the drawing. Cut the rails and the 23 short lattice pieces to the dimensions in the materials list.

2 Build the roof. On the ground, carefully attach two side rafters to each top rafter with screws driven at an angle. Drill pilot holes for each screw to avoid splitting the lumber. Next attach seven short lattice pieces across the rafter assembly, spacing them as shown.

3 Set the posts. Lay out the postholes using the 3-4-5 triangle method. (See "Establish a 90-degree Corner," page 52.)

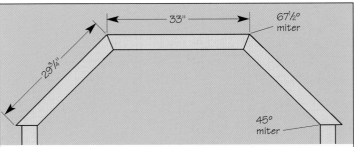

1. Cut four side rafters with a 45-degree angle on one end of each and a 67½-degree angle on the other end. Cut two top rafters with 67½-degree angles on each end.

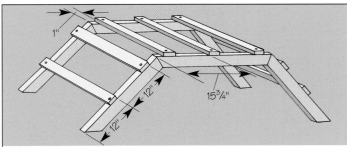

2. Working on the ground, assemble the rafters and install seven short lattice pieces across the rafters.

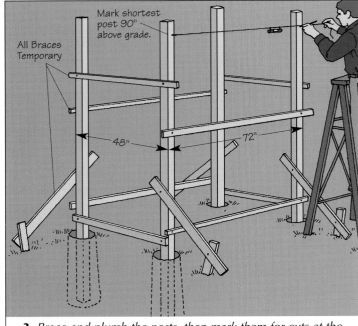

3. Brace and plumb the posts, then mark them for cuts at the same level.

4. Remove the side braces, then install lattice on the side of the arbor.

This structure calls for holes a minimum of 50 inches deep with the ends of the posts set 6 inches below the frost line. Check with your building inspector for requirements in your area. Place the posts in the holes, and install temporary bracing, making sure the posts are plumb. Measure the distance from the ground to the top of each post. Cut the shortest post off at 84 inches from the ground. Transfer the height of the cut post to the other posts and cut them all off level.

5. Screw the rails to the post tops, lift the roof into place, and screw it into the posts and the ends of the rails.

4 Attach short lattice to the post. Position the first two pieces so that their top edges are flush with the top of the posts. Drill pilot holes and attach the lattice to posts with 2-inch deck screws. Measure from each piece to determine the location of the other pieces, following the pattern shown in the drawing. Drill pilot holes and attach with 2-inch deck screws.

5 Attach the rails and roof. Using two 3-inch deck screws for each connection, attach the rails across the top of the posts so that they overlap the post tops by 2 inches. Check that the rails are level and the posts are plumb. Adjust the posts if necessary.

With a helper and two step ladders, put the roof into position. Attach it with 3-inch deck screws through the lower rafters into the posts and rails.

6 Attach the remaining lattice.
Cut the six vertical lattice to the size given in the materials list. Drill pilot holes and attach them, spaced as shown, butting them under the rails.

Cut the side roof lattice to the length in the materials list with miters on each end as shown. Use 1¼-inch deck screws to attach the side roof lattice to the bottom of roof short lattice spacing them as shown in the drawing. Measure for the top roof lattice pieces and cut them to fit. Attach them with 1¼-inch deck screws.

Arched Arbor 🔩🔩🔩

This tall entryway features a cross-hatch lattice design on the sides and a graceful curved arch overhead. It is a spacious 60 inches wide and 42 inches deep, so if you want to put a gate on it, use two hinged doors.

Construction is slightly different from the other arbors in this chapter. You'll actually build this while it is lying on the ground, then lift the assembled piece up and put it in the holes.

Make sure you have a heavy-duty saber saw for this arbor. A smaller model will not cut smoothly through two-by lumber. You'll want a helper when you build this and several helpers when it comes time to put the arbor in the ground.

1 Cut out the arches.
The front and back arches are each made of two pieces. To lay out the curve for the pieces, set two 2x12s on a flat surface to form a "T" as shown on page 131. Lay out the lines with a makeshift compass: Drive a nail in the base of the "T," 30 inches from the top. Firmly tie one end of a piece of string to the nail, and the other to a pencil, so that the pencil makes a mark exactly 30 inches away from the nail.

Draw the first curved line, which will be the top of the arch. Shorten the string by 3½ inches, and draw the second line, which will be the bottom of the arch. With your angle square, mark a 45-degree cut at one end of the curve, as shown. Make this cut

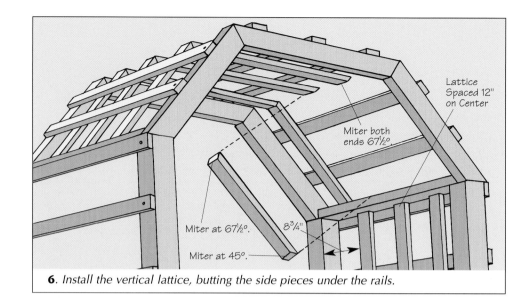

Lattice Spaced 12" on Center

Miter both ends 67½°

Miter at 67½°.

8¾"

Miter at 45°.

6. *Install the vertical lattice, butting the side pieces under the rails.*

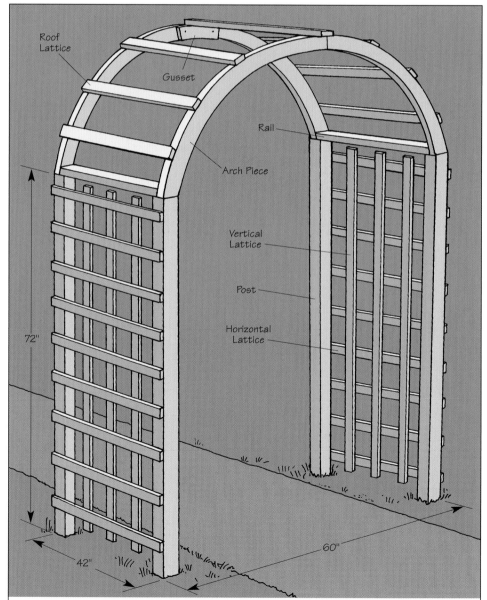

Roof Lattice

Gusset

Rail

Arch Piece

Vertical Lattice

Post

Horizontal Lattice

72"

42"

60"

Arched Arbor. *To simplify construction, this arbor is first assembled on its side, then lifted into the postholes dug for it.*

Shopping List

- [ ] Four 4x4x10'
- [ ] One 2x4x8'
- [ ] Fifteen 1x2x8'
- [ ] Two 2x12x12'
- [ ] Four 1x4x8'

Fasteners

- [ ] 1 pound 3" galvanized deck screws
- [ ] 2 pounds 2" galvanized deck screws
- [ ] 1 pound 4d galvanized finish nails
- [ ] 1 pound 2½" galvanized deck screws.
- [ ] 2 pounds 1¼" deck screws
- [ ] Concrete, as needed.
- [ ] Gravel, as needed.

Cutting List

Qty.	Part	Dimensions	Comments
Four	Posts	3½" x 3½" x to fit	Cut from 4x4x10'
Four	Arch Pieces	3½" x 1½" x 50"	Cut from 2x12x12'
Two	Rails	1½" x 3½" x 39"	Cut from 2x4x8'
Six	Vertical Lattice	¾" x 1½" x 69"	Cut from 1x2x8'
Eighteen	Horizontal Lattice	¾" x 1½" x 42"	Cut from 1x2x8'
Seven	Roof Lattice	¾" x 3½" x 42"	Cut from 1x4x8'

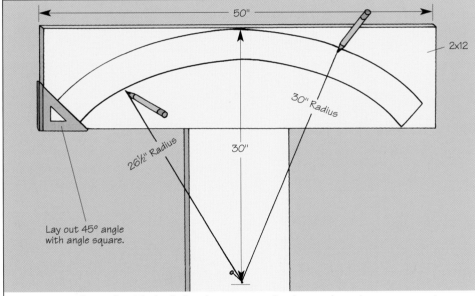

1. *Lay out the arch with the help of some scrap lumber and a string compass. Lay out the angles on the end with an angle square.*

with a circular saw, then cut out the arch with a saber saw. Lay out and cut three more arches using this piece as a pattern.

2 Assemble the arches. Butt two arch pieces together. The seam needs to be reinforced with a gusset, which you can make from a cut-off from the previous step. Take the cut-off, slip it under the arch, and trace along it with a pencil, as shown, to lay out a gusset at least 8 inches long. Cut along the line with a saber saw, and screw the piece to the arch with 2½-inch galvanized deck screws.

Repeat for the other arch, and sand the pieces smooth.

3 Join the arches and attach roof lattice. Begin by cutting two 39-inch rails from a 2x4. On a flat surface, screw them between the arches. Next cut seven 1x4s to 42 inches to make the roof lattice. Attach the top lattice, which spans the butt joints of the arch, first. Hold it in place, flush with the outside of the arch. Drill two pilot holes at each end, and attach with 2-inch deck screws.

Lay out and attach the remaining lattice, as shown. At each joint, drill two pilot holes and drive two 2-inch screws.

4 Attach the lattice to the posts. The overall length of the posts depends on the holes that will hold them. Check with your building inspector for the proper depth, and then cut the posts to extend 72 inches above the ground.

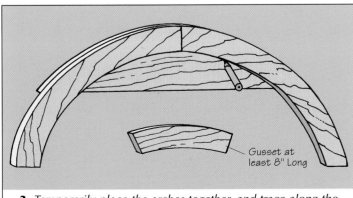

2. *Temporarily place the arches together, and trace along the arch to lay out a reinforcing gusset.*

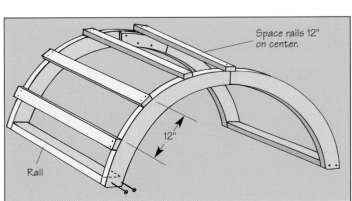

3. *Assemble the arches on the ground, and attach the rails and lattice which hold the top of the arbor together.*

Cut the lattice to the same length as the roof lattice—42 inches. Lay out their positions on all four posts. The top of the first piece is 4 inches from the top of the posts. The others are 8 inches on center, as shown. Drill pilot holes through the ends of the horizontals, and attach them to the posts with two 2-inch screws at each joint.

Next lay out the vertical lattice by marking their location on the top and bottom horizontal lattice. The verticals are spaced 10½ inches on center.

Attach them to the horizontals with one 1¼-inch screw at each joint.

5 **Attach arches to posts.** Have at least one helper for this part. Roll the crown on its side, and bring a side assembly in position next to it, as shown. Drill pilot holes through the rail and into the top of each post, then screw the two together with two 3-inch galvanized deck screws into each post. Repeat with the second side assembly.

6 **Brace the posts.** To stabilize the arch during assembly, cut four braces. Before attaching them make sure the posts are parallel. Screw the braces to the posts, as shown.

7 **Dig the postholes and install the arbor.** Lay out the postholes as shown. Dig holes to the depth required by the building inspector— this will be roughly 42 inches in most areas. Shovel 6 inches of gravel into each hole.

Have a helper grab each post, and stand the assembled arbor on its legs. Lift the arch slightly, carry it over to the holes, and place the posts in the holes. Check that the posts are plumb. If necessary, lift the posts back out of the holes, shovel in more gravel, and check again that they are plumb.

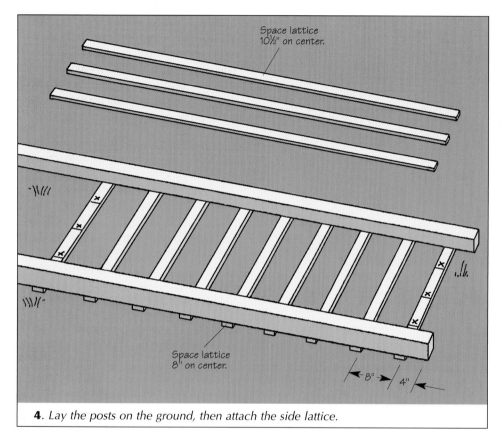

Space lattice 10½" on center.

Space lattice 8" on center.

8" 4"

4. Lay the posts on the ground, then attach the side lattice.

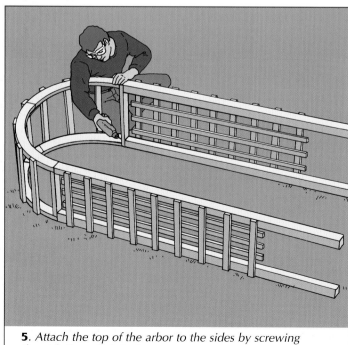

5. Attach the top of the arbor to the sides by screwing through the rails into the posts.

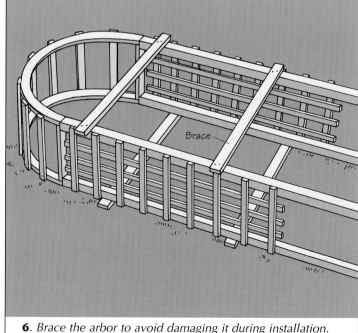

Brace

6. Brace the arbor to avoid damaging it during installation.

7. *Lift the arbor and place it in the holes. Pour concrete around the posts.*

When the arbor is plumb, pour concrete to fill the holes. For more information, see "Backfill with Concrete," page 61. Allow 24 hours for the concrete to set, and remove the temporary braces.

Deck Trellis 🔩🔩🔩

As designed, this trellis sits on a deck and creates a separate space that remains open to the rest of your deck. You also could build this as a free-standing unit somewhere away from the deck. If so, all four posts must be set in a concrete collar underground.

This structure is 84 inches long. You may increase the size up to as much as 14 feet, but use 2x6s instead of 2x4s for the rafters. You can adjust the amount of shade by placing the 1x2 lattice pieces, the 2x4 rafters, and the 1x2 top pieces closer together or farther apart. By placing these pieces closer together, you also allow smaller plants to climb.

1 Set rear posts. Dig deep post-holes for the two rear posts. The holes should be at least 54 inches deep to support posts this long, and the posts should sit 6 inches below frost line. Check with your local

Rafter · Crosspiece · Roof Beam · Front Post · Back Post · Lattice Rail · Vertical Lattice · Horizontal Lattice · 72" · 84" · 96"

Deck Trellis. *This trellis is designed to sit on your deck. You can also install this directly on the ground by lengthening the front legs and setting them in postholes.*

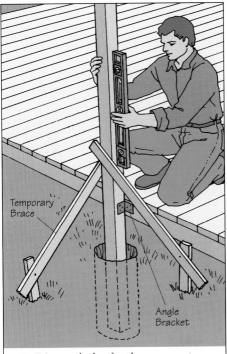

Temporary Brace · Angle Bracket

1. *Dig postholes for the rear posts. Brace and attach them to the deck.*

building department to determine the exact depth. Put 6 inches of gravel into each hole. Set the posts in place, and temporarily brace them so they are plumb in both directions and parallel with each other.

If you are building against a deck, attach each post with two 3x3-inch angle brackets. The posts should be a little higher than needed. Cut them to height later. You will pour the concrete when the whole structure is built.

Shopping List

- ☐ Two 4x4x8'
- ☐ Twelve 1x2x8'
- ☐ Nine 2x4x8'
- ☐ Four decorative wooden post caps
- ☐ Two 4x4' back posts. Length to equal 96 inches, plus the height of the adjoining deck or patio and the depth of the footing.

Fasteners

- ☐ 1 pound of 1¼" deck screws
- ☐ 2 pounds of 3" deck screws
- ☐ 12 lag screws, 4½x½-inch lag screws
- ☐ 4 angle brackets, 6 x 6 inches
- ☐ Concrete, as needed
- ☐ 3 pounds of 2½" deck screws
- ☐ 6 3x3 angle brackets
- ☐ A small handful of 6d galvanized finish nails
- ☐ Gravel as needed

Cutting List

Qty.	Part	Dimensions	Comments
Two	Front Posts	3½" x 3½" x 96"	Cut from 4x4x8'
Two	Rear Posts	3½" x 3½" to fit	Cut from 4x4
Two	Lattice Rails	1½" x 3½" to fit	Cut from 2x4x8'
Two	Roof Beams	1½" x 5½" x 84"	Cut from 2x6x8'
Five	Rafters	1½" x 3½" x 93"	Cut from 2x4x8'
Three	Horizontal Lattice	¾" x 1½" x 74"	Cut from 1x2x8'
Six	Vertical Lattice	¾" x 1½" x 45"	Cut from 1x2x8'
Six	Roof Crosspieces	¾" x 1½" x 81"	Cut from 1x2x8'
One	Center Support	1½" x 3½" to fit	Cut from 2x4x8'

2 Attach the vertical lattice to the rails.
Cut two 2x4 lattice rails to fit snugly between the posts, and cut the vertical lattice pieces. Lay down the rails on a flat surface. Then lay down two 2x2s as shown. These pieces automatically position the lattice on the rails. Put the outside edge of the first lattice 9 inches from the end of each rail. Predrill holes, and drive 3-inch deck screws through the rails and into the lattice.

Space the remaining lattice one at a time, with the help of a 10-inch spacer, as shown. Screw each in place before positioning the next.

3 Attach the horizontal lattice.
Cut the horizontal lattice to the dimensions in the cutting list. Make sure the structure is square and adjust if necessary. Lay the horizontal pieces in place, spacing them with a 10⅛-inch wide spacer as shown. Use a 2x4 spacer to align the ends of the lattice as shown so they will be 1½ inches away from the posts. Drive a 2½-inch deck screw at each lattice joint, as shown.

4 Attach the assembled lattice to the post.
Position the assembled lattice against the post, using temporary spacers, as shown. Make the spacers from a 2x4, and place them so the edge is 6 inches above

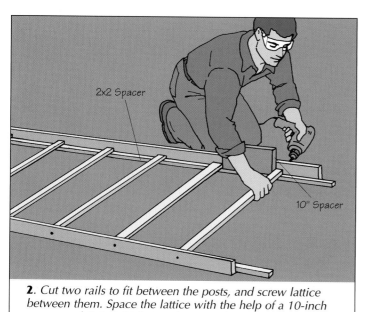

2. Cut two rails to fit between the posts, and screw lattice between them. Space the lattice with the help of a 10-inch spacer and 2x2s laid flat on the ground.

2x2 Spacer

10" Spacer

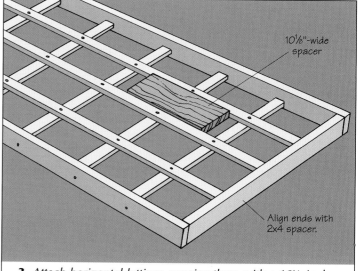

10⅛"-wide spacer

Align ends with 2x4 spacer.

3. Attach horizontal lattices, spacing them with a 10⅛-inch-wide spacer, and align them with a 2x4.

4. *Screw the rails in place between the posts.*

5. *Attach the beams with 4½ inch lag screws.*

the surface of your deck. Set the lattice on top of the 2x4 spacers. Drill pilot holes, and attach the section to the post with 2½-inch deck screws, driven on an angle. Attach the center support with 3x3-inch angle brackets. Nail it through the rail.

5 Install front posts and roof beams.
Cut the two roof beams to the dimensions in the cutting list. Cut the 22½-degree angle at each end as you cut the beams to length.

Lay the posts flat on the ground. Place a roof beam on one front post and the other beam on the second front post. Square the beams and posts. Tack the beams to the posts with 3-inch deck screws. Predrill ⁷⁄₁₆-inch diameter holes for the lag screws that will hold the rafters permanently. Drive three 4x½ inch lag screws through the rails and into each post.

Mark the spot on the deck where the post will go. Make sure it is square with the rest of the structure, using the 3-4-5 triangle method. (See "Establish a 90-degree Corner," page 52.)

Make up a temporary brace as shown, and have it within easy reach.

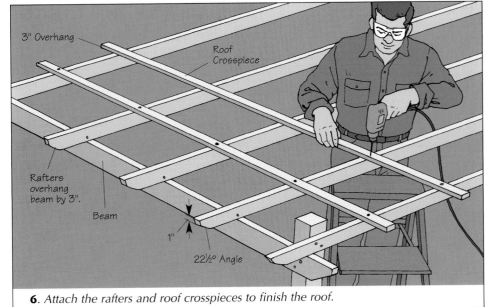

6. *Attach the rafters and roof crosspieces to finish the roof.*

With a helper or two and at least one good step ladder, carefully raise a front post-and-beam into position. Level the beam and attach it to the rear post as you did the front post. Attach the temporary brace to the post, tack it into the deck, and attach the second beam.

6 Attach rafters and roof crosspieces.
Attach the front rafter to the outside face of the front posts.

Attach the rear rafter to the outside face of the rear posts, driving two 3-inch screws at each joint. Space the other rafters evenly, and attach them to the roof beams with 2½-inch screws driven on an angle. Attach the roof crosspieces with 1¼-inch deck screws, making sure the rafters are straight while you work. If they are not, draw them in place by flexing them slightly as you drive the screws.

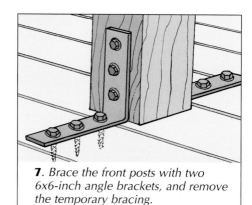

7. *Brace the front posts with two 6x6-inch angle brackets, and remove the temporary bracing.*

7 Cut posts to height. Cut the rear posts 2½ inches above the rafters. Install post caps with galvanized 6d finish nails. Pour the concrete for the rear posts, as explained in "Backfill with Concrete," page 61. Attach the front posts to the deck or patio with two 6x6-inch angle brackets and screws, then remove the braces. Attach decorative caps.

Privacy Screen with Overhead Lattice ⫪⫪

This freestanding lattice screen can provide a point of interest in your yard. It is sturdy enough for the heaviest of vines and will protect you from the wind as well as giving you a shady,

private spot. The screen has three panels of lattice set between four posts. A 48-inch wide panel and a 72-inch wide panel are set at 90 degrees to each other. A 24-inch wide panel runs at a 45 degree angle to the two larger panels. This modified L shape means the screen is open to the rest of the

Shopping List

☐ Four 4x4x12'
☐ Two 2x6x8'
☐ Forty-three 1x2x8'
☐ Fifteen 2x2x8'
☐ Six 2x4x8'

Fasteners

☐ 2 pounds 3" galvanized deck screws
☐ 12 lag screws, ½" dia. x 4½"
☐ 5 pounds of 2" galvanized deck screws
☐ Concrete as needed
☐ Gravel as needed

Cutting List

Qty.	Part	Dimensions	Comments
Four	Posts	3½" x 3½" x 12'	Cut from 4x4x12'
Three	Rails	1½" x 3½" x 72"	Cut from 2x4x8'
Three	Rails	1½" x 3½" x 36"	Cut from 2x4x8'
Three	Rails	1½" x 3½" x 48"	Cut from 2x4x8'
Four	Rafters	1½" x 5½" x 31½"	Cut from 2x6x8'
Eight	Rafter Supports	1½" x 1½" x 16"	Cut from 2x2x8'
Five	Long Roof Lattice	1½" x 1½" x 80"	Cut from 2x2x8'
Five	Short Roof Lattice	1½" x 1½" x 56"	Cut from 2x2x8'
Five	Angled Roof Lattice	1½" x 1½" cut to fit	Cut from 2x2x8'
Nine	Cross Lattice	¾" x 1½" x 31½"	Cut from 1x2x8'
Twenty	Long Side Lattice	¾" x 1½" x 72"	Cut from 1x2x8'
Twenty	Short Side Lattice	¾" x 1½" x 68"	Cut from 1x2x8'

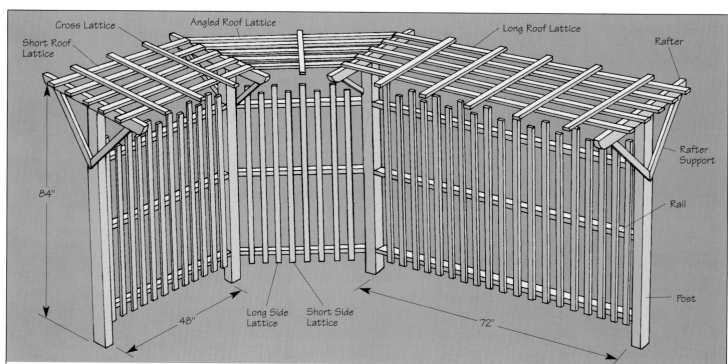

Privacy Screen with Overhead Lattice. *This screen is perfect for blocking off an unwanted view, segmenting the yard, or providing privacy from neighbors.*

yard while still having some of the feel of an enclosed space.

This is not a very difficult project, but it will probably take you and a helper a couple of days to put it together.

1 Dig the holes and set the posts. Begin by laying out an L with a 90-degree corner as explained in "Establish a 90-degree Corner," page 52. Locate a post 24 inches back from the corner along each side.

Dig holes at least 48 inches deep for the posts. Check with your local building department to make sure this is deep enough. Throw 6 inches of gravel into each hole, and place the 4x4 posts in them. Brace to hold them plumb and square, then pour concrete into the holes. Let the concrete cure for a day before proceeding.

2 Attach the rails. Because of slight variations in setting the posts, the rails may not be the exact size listed in the cutting list. Measure and cut the rails to fit. The rails for the middle panels are mitered 45 degrees on each end, as shown. Draw layout lines on the posts, so that the total distance from the bottom of the bottom piece to the top of the top piece is 64 inches.

Attach the rails to the posts, making sure it is square as you go. To attach the pieces, angle pilot holes into the ends of the rails, and drive 3-inch screws through the rails into the posts.

3 Cut the rafters. The ends of the rafters are rounded. To cut the rafters to size and shape, first cut them an inch longer than specified in the cutting list. Then lay out the

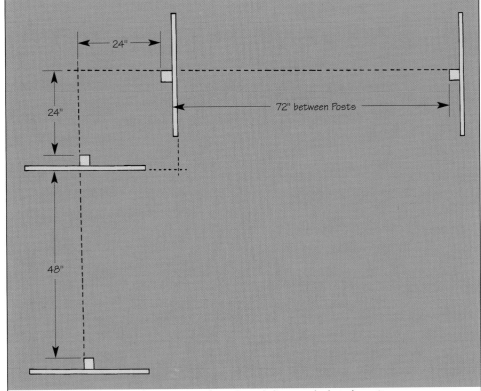

1. *Lay out an L-shaped pattern, and mark and dig post holes along it.*

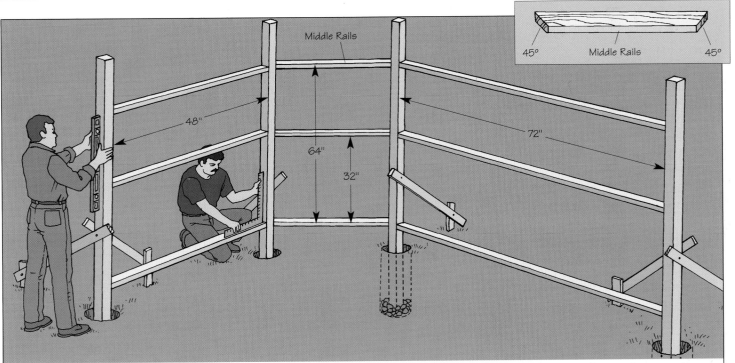

2. *Cut rails to fit between the posts, then screw them in place. Two of the shorter rails will have to be mitered to run between the rear posts.*

curve with a compass, set to a 2¾ inch radius. Cut each end with a saber saw, sand smooth, and use the first piece as a template to lay out the other three. Cut them out with a saber saw.

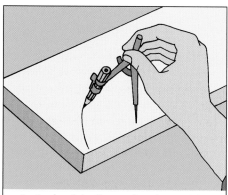

3. *Each of the four rafters has a 2¼ inch radius arc cut on both ends.*

4 Cut the posts and attach rafters.
On each post, draw a line 16 inches above the top of the top rail. With a square, transfer the line to each face of the post. Cut off at the line with a circular saw.

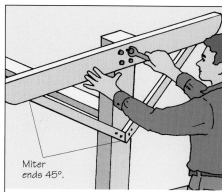

Miter ends 45°.

4. *Tack the rafters in place with deck screws, and attach permanently with lag screws.*

Temporarily attach the rafters with deck screws. Drill ⁷⁄₁₆-inch diameter holes for the lag screws that will hold the rafters permanently. Attach the rafters as shown with four ½-inch-diameter x 4½-inch lag screws.

Miter the 2x2 rafter supports to the dimensions in the cutting list, and attach to the posts and to the rafters with 3-inch screws. Drill pilot holes for all screws to avoid splitting the supports.

5 Attach roof lattice.
Attach the angled lattice first. Measure each piece individually, and cut a 45-degree angle on each end. Drill pilot holes; attach with 3-inch screws.

Cut the long and short roof lattice for the two side sections to the dimensions in the cutting list. These lattice

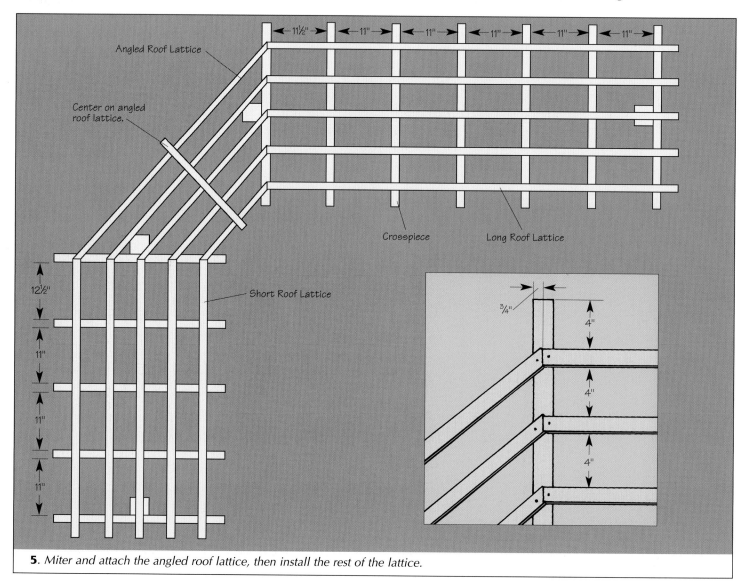

5. *Miter and attach the angled roof lattice, then install the rest of the lattice.*

6. *Attach the side lattice.*

pieces run the length of the two side sections. On the rafters, lay out the spacing as shown.

Set the lattice in place. One end of the lattice should overhang the rafters as shown. The other end goes only halfway across the rafter, as shown in the inset. Attach as before.

Cut the nine crosspieces to size. Mark layout lines for them on the top of the roof lattice pieces, and attach with 2-inch screws driven down through the top pieces. As you work, make sure the roof lattice pieces are straight and evenly spaced as shown.

Remove the bracing around the posts.

6 Attach the side lattice. Cut the side lattice pieces to size. Position them with the help of some spacers. First lay a two-by on the ground between the posts, as shown. Level it with shims, if necessary. The lattice will sit on

this board to align the bottoms. Also, cut a spacer 2 inches wide to get the proper spacing between lattice pieces.

Use the spacer to put the first lattice piece 2 inches away from a post. Attach each lattice piece by driving 2-inch screws through it into the rails. Use your spacers to align the other lattice pieces as well. As you attach every fourth or fifth piece, make sure it is plumb and make adjustments if necessary. As you near the end of a run, you may have to change the spacing slightly in order to make things come out evenly.

Grape Arbor 𝄞𝄞𝄞

Here's a traditional arbor, like those that once graced rural yards all over America. They were both pretty and practical. They provided gardening space for a popular crop, as well as shade and protection. If you are able

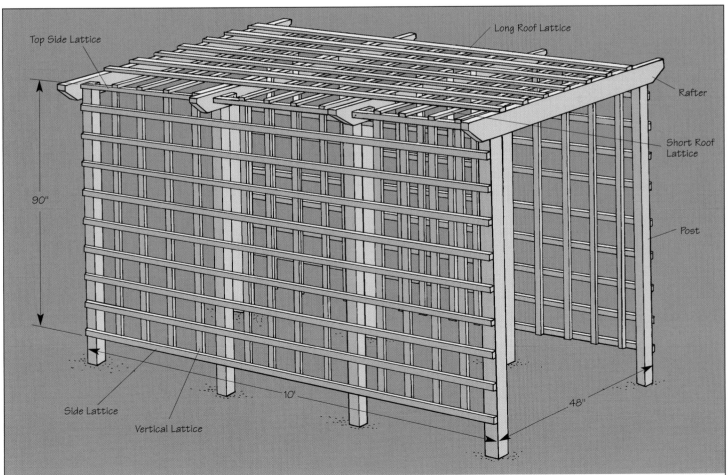

Grape Arbor. This old-fashioned grape arbor is the perfect touch for a country garden. While it is large and will take some time to build, the construction is straightforward.

Shopping List

- ☐ Eight 4x4x12'
- ☐ Twenty-four 1x2x8'
- ☐ Two 2x6x10'
- ☐ Seven 1x2x12'
- ☐ Twenty-six 1x2x10'

Fasteners

- ☐ 3 pounds of 2" deck screws
- ☐ 1 pound of 3" deck screws
- ☐ Gravel as needed
- ☐ 3 pounds of 1¼" deck screws
- ☐ 24 lag screws, ½" dia. x 4½"
- ☐ Concrete as needed

Cutting List

Qty.	Part	Dimensions	Comments
Eight	Posts	3½" x 3½" x 12"	Cut from 4x4x12'
Four	Rafters	1½" x 5½" x 60"	Cut from 2x6x10'
Eighteen	Side Lattice	¾" x 1½" x 120"	Cut from 1x2x10'
Four	Nailers	¾" x 1½" x 4"	Cut from 1x2x12'
Six	Top Side Lattice	¾" x 1½" x length to fit	Cut from 1x2x10'
Twenty-four	Vertical Lattice	¾" x 1½" x length to fit	Cut from 1x2x8'
Twelve	Short Roof Lattice	¾" x 1½" x 49½"	Cut from 1x2x10'
Seven	Long Roof Lattice	¾" x 1½" x 123"	Cut from 1x2x12'

to get grape vines to grow well, this structure will support a sizable crop.

Building this arbor requires no special skills, but make sure you take the time to get all eight posts perfectly aligned with each other.

1 Position the posts. Lay out and dig the postholes. The holes should be at least 51 inches deep, spaced as shown. Make sure the holes are deep enough to meet local building codes. Shovel 6 inches of gravel into the bottom of each hole, and put the posts in.

Temporarily brace a corner post with a two-by and a stake, so that it is plumb in both directions and firmly held in place. Measure off from this corner post and brace the other posts in their final position.

Attach two side lattice to each side of the arbor, as shown. Install the bottom lattice 16½ inches above the ground, and attach it to the posts so that it is level. Measure up 64 inches from the bottom lattice, and attach the upper lattice.

Double check to see that all the posts are correctly placed, and pour concrete into each hole. Allow the concrete to set firmly before going on to the next step.

2 Cut and notch the posts. Cut each post 8 inches above the top edge of the upper lattice. Then cut a notch to accommodate the rafters. You can cut the notch using a circular saw and hand saw or by first making a series of cuts 1½ inches deep, spacing the cuts about ¼ inch apart, then knocking out the waste with a chisel. Note that six of the posts have the rafters on the same side. One pair of end posts has the notch cut on the other side so that the rafters are on the outside of the arbor.

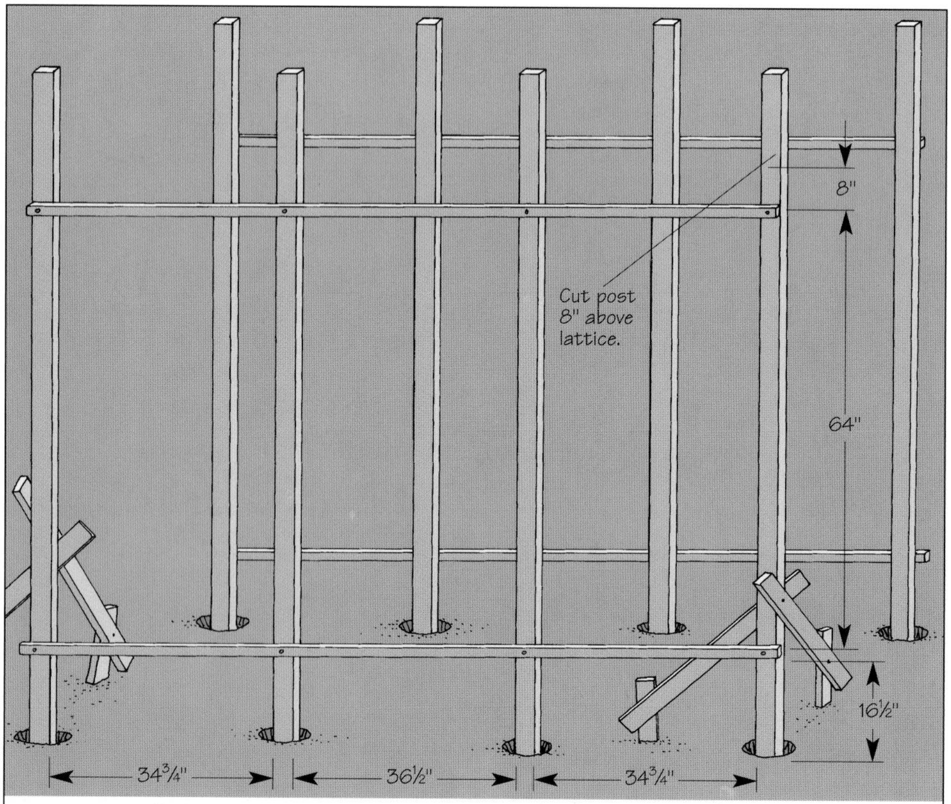

Cut post
8" above
lattice.

8"

64"

16½"

34¾"   36½"   34¾"

1. Dig postholes and brace the posts before pouring concrete.

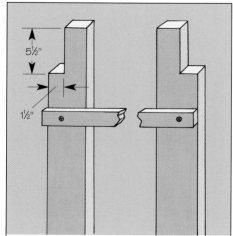

5½"

1½"

2. The rafters sit in notches cut in each post. Once the concrete has cured, cut a notch in each post.

3 **Cut the rafters.** Lay out the rafters, as shown. Cut them to length first, then cut the angles.

4 **Install the rafters.** Set each rafter in its notches so that the beginning of the angle cut overhangs the post by ¾ inch. If your posts are out of plumb or improperly placed, flex them into position if possible, or modify the overhang. Tack the rails in place with 3-inch deck screws. Drill ⁵⁄₁₆-inch diameter holes for the lag screws that hold the rafters in place. Attach with three ½-inch-diameter by 4½-inch lag screws in each post.

5 **Attach the side lattice.** Mark the center of an inside post. Lay out a lattice piece 8 inches on center to either side of the mark and every 8 inches on center thereafter. Predrill a ⅛-inch diameter hole 1½ inches from the end of each lattice piece, and attach by driving a 2-inch galvanized deck screw through each hole.

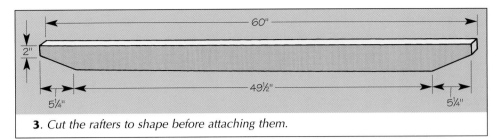

3. Cut the rafters to shape before attaching them.

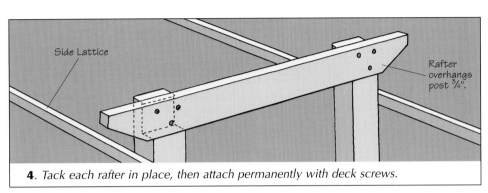

4. Tack each rafter in place, then attach permanently with deck screws.

The top side lattice pieces fit between the rafters. At four places on the arbor, they will not have anything to nail to. Cut four nailers to support them, and screw the nailers to the rafters, as shown. Cut the top side lattice pieces to fit, and attach them with 2-inch screws at each joint.

Cut 24 vertical lattice pieces so that they are long enough to span from the top of the top lattice piece to the bottom of the bottom lattice piece. Mark their positions—8 inches on center—on the side lattice. Predrill for screws as before, and attach with a 1¼-inch galvanized deck screw at each joint.

6 **Attach the roof lattice pieces.** Cut the short roof lattice pieces to fit—they should be 49½ inches

long, but measure and make changes if necessary for any variations. Predrill for screws, and set the lattice on top of the ends of the vertical lattice, as shown. Predrill again and attach with 2-inch screws at each end. Until you attach the long roof lattice pieces, they will be very weak, so work carefully.

Cut the long roof lattice pieces to size. Lay them out as shown, 8 inches on center. Predrill and attach to the rafters with 2-inch galvanized deck screws. Then attach them to the short roof lattice pieces with 1¼-inch galvanized deck screws. You may have to straighten out lattice pieces as you work—they don't have to be perfectly straight, but they should form consistent-looking squares.

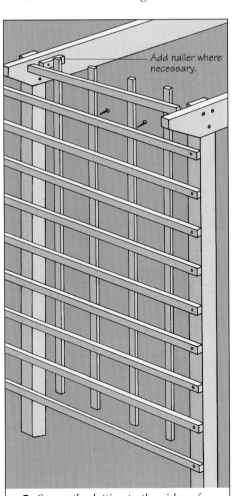

5. Screw the lattice to the sides of the arbor.

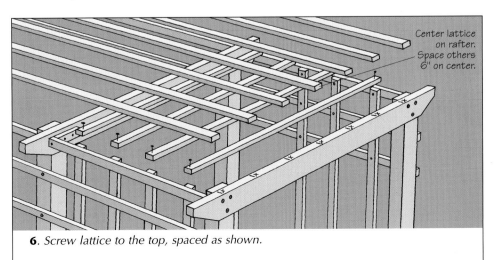

6. Screw lattice to the top, spaced as shown.

MAINTENANCE & REPAIR

A well-built fence, gate, or trellis will last years with a minimum amount of repair. But wind, rain, and weather do take their toll. Mold and mildew discolor the wood. Decay-producing organisms attack untreated areas, causing rot. Termites attack wood that comes in contact with the ground. Even pressure-treated wood will split, check, and weather.

Your best defense is a good finish. Wood preservatives, water sealers, paints, and stains all serve to slow down the decay process and reduce the effects of weathering. No matter how good the finish, however, be prepared to do some periodic maintenance. The finish will need to be periodically reapplied. Unless your project is built entirely of pressure-treated wood, you should check it once a year for rot and insect damage. And no matter what construction materials you've used, be prepared for the occasional repair. Storms, frost, and wind all take their toll on a fence, gate, or trellis.

CHOOSING A FINISH

In most cases, people choose a finish based on what they want a fence to look like. A redwood or cedar fence probably looks best with a clear finish. A picket fence, on the other hand, traditionally gets a coat of white paint.

But a finish does more than dress up your project. It provides a barrier against the weather. A good finish sheds water, discouraging decay. It seals the wood from the dirt, pollen, and pollution that cause it to turn gray. And because a good finish slows the expansion and contraction of wood caused by changes in humidity, checking and warping are minimized.

There is a wide variety of finishes to choose from, but all fall into one of four basic types.

Water Sealer. Water sealers are typically a wax dissolved in mineral spirits. The wax lodges in the pores of the wood, sealing it against water. The finish is clear, but like all finishes, will darken the color of the wood slightly.

Manufacturers of pressure-treated wood recommend a coat of water sealer once a year. Water sealers are generally applied to all above-ground parts when the project is built. Because the wax wears or is washed away, sealers are reapplied annually to maintain an even, natural wood color. Unfortunately, there are no products on the market that will preserve the color of freshly milled wood—all wood will eventually turn gray or brownish gray.

Stain. Taken by itself, stain does nothing more than color the wood. But some stains have been formulated to provide protection as well. Generally sold as "exterior" or "deck" stains, these are transparent, opaque, or somewhere in between.

Transparent stains are mixed with a preservative. Opaque stains offer more protection than transparent ones because their formula is closer to that of paint. While neither type of stain is as durable as paint, stains do not crack or peel as paint does. Better yet, when it comes time to apply fresh stain in a few years, you won't have to scrape and brush off the old finish. Read the label to make sure the stain is for exterior use and provides protection against mildew and UV rays.

Varnish. Varnish is a combination of an oil and a resin. It is extremely durable, though prone to cracking and flaking. Polyurethane resin varnishes dominate the market these days. Polyurethane is the toughest of the varnishes but not the best for exterior use. Direct sunlight can cause polyurethane to peel, and repairs are almost impossible. Aside from spar varnish, these finishes are best used indoors.

If you're going to use a varnish, choose a spar or marine alkyd resin varnish. Spar and marine vanishes have more oil than other finishes, creating a finish that moves with the wide range of expansion and contraction in wood used outdoors.

Paint. Paint is the most durable of the exterior finishes. It is an excellent wood preservative because it forms a surface film that seals the wood against moisture penetration. You have two choices in exterior paints: acrylic latex or oil. Latex cleans up with soap and water. Oil paints require paint thinner.

At one time, oil was considered much more durable than latex. But formulas have changed over time, and manufacturers now say a top-quality latex paint will hold up just as long as, if not longer than, oil. Both types come in flat, semi-gloss (satin) and gloss. Better exterior paints also include mildewcides that inhibit the growth of mold, mildew, and decay-causing organisms. Read the label to see what is in the paint you're considering.

Finishing Pressure-Treated Wood

Pressure treating protects wood from insects and rot and is the best thing to use for parts that will come in contact with the ground. It does not prevent checking, cupping or warping, however, so you should protect the wood with a finish. Unfortunately, pressure-treated wood presents some finishing problems. Although the wood has been kiln-dried before treatment, pressure treatment puts water back into the wood, often leaving a waterlogged surface that won't hold a finish. Don't apply a finish to any obviously wet wood. Before you apply a finish to pressure-treated wood, test it by sprinkling a few drops of water on it. If the wood absorbs the water, it is ready to finish. If not, wait. Air circulation will dry out the moisture.

Semitransparent oil-based stains work best on pressure-treated wood. In addition, you should coat the wood annually with water sealer. Manufacturers advise against painting pressure-treated wood with latex.

APPLICATION TECHNIQUES

Any finish or preservative can be applied by brush, roller, or spray gun. While brushing is the most time-consuming, it is often the best method for painting or staining fences with spaced boards or pickets. Rollers work well for fences with solid-board or plywood siding, but you'll still need a brush to catch areas that the roller misses.

Spray guns work well for designs that would be time consuming to paint with a brush and roller, such as those with latticework or basket weave. A spray gun will not save much time when painting an open design, such as a post-and-rail fence, and you'll end up wasting more paint than you would with a brush and roller. You'll also need to spread drop cloths to prevent overspray from getting on plants, adjacent buildings, patios, and other surrounding surfaces. So even though paint application is often much quicker with a spray gun, preparation and cleanup time takes much longer. If you have only a short section of fence to paint, it is probably fastest to use a brush or roller.

Redwood and red cedar can be stained or left to weather naturally. Many people actually paint these woods, especially if they're using a cheaper grade wood. Both species "bleed"; that is, the brownish-red

> **CAUTION**
>
> Some paints made before 1978 contain lead, which can be hazardous to your health if you try to remove the paint. Environmental laws are strict concerning the disposal of paint debris. If you suspect that a lead-based paint has been used, test it with an inexpensive lead-testing kit available at paint stores. Do not attempt to remove lead paint yourself. Hire a professional painting contractor to prepare the fence for repainting.

tannins in the wood will seep through light-colored paints, discoloring them. To prevent bleeding on freshly milled redwood or cedar, apply two coats of an oil-based, stain-blocking primer. (Latex stain blockers do not stop stains as well as oil.) A regular primer barely blocks stains at all. Have your paint dealer recommend a blocker that meets your needs.

If bleeding is not a concern, apply an oil or latex primer to all sides of any bare wood. To repaint previously painted fences, remove any peeling or flaking paint with a scraper or putty knife. If the surface is in very bad condition, old paint can be removed with a heat gun and putty knife or with a power sander. In both cases, wear a vapor respirator rated to avoid inhaling fumes or dust. Before repainting, scrub the surface with a solution of 1 pound trisodium phosphate (TSP) dissolved in 2 gallons of hot water. This treatment not only removes dirt, grime, and chalking paint; it also softens the old finish to provide better "tooth" for the new paint to stick to. Rinse the fence, gate, or trellis thoroughly after applying TSP.

Application Techniques. *Spray guns, at the top, can cover a large surface in a hurry, but make sure you cover adjacent plants and surfaces to protect them from over-spray. Brushes, left, make economical use of paint when working on short sections of fence. Keep a brush on hand for touching up spots that rollers or spray guns miss. Rollers, right, work well for flat surfaces. Rather than using a paint tray, buy a clip-on screen that fits into a 2-gallon paint bucket, as shown.*

MAINTENANCE

Other than the effects of weather, outdoor structures can be subjected to physical forces, such as frost heave, unstable soil, wind action, and young climbers, all of which can cause a project to sink or lean.

The best way to keep your fence, gate, or trellis in tip-top shape is to check for damage at least once a year. Add this chore to your spring garden cleanup list.

1 Check for rot. If your posts are set in gravel, dig around each post to a depth of about 4 inches. Check for decay, probing with an ice pick, knife, or other sharp object. Also check joints where rails meet posts, and where boards attach to rails. Check exposed ends, such as tops of posts and picket boards. If the tool sinks easily into the wood, the wood will have to be repaired or replaced. If decay is less than about ¼ inch deep into the surface, use a paint scraper or wide wood chisel to scrape out the decayed area down to sound wood, and then treat with several coats of a good wood preservative and water sealer.

Dry rot is caused by fungi that attacks wood under moist conditions,

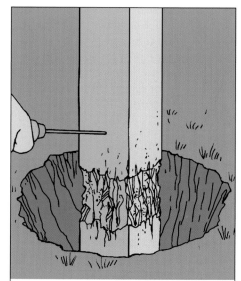

1. Check for rot by probing with an ice pick or knife. Decay less than ¼ inch deep can be scraped away. Deeper rot requires more significant repair.

2. *Weather or settling may have caused the posts to shift. Make sure they are plumb and that rails are square to them.*

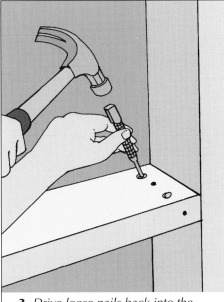

3. *Drive loose nails back into the post with a nail set.*

4. *Wash and scrub the fence to keep it clean. Dirt and mildew may require a commercial deck- or fence-cleaning mixture.*

leaving a dry powdery texture after the wood has dried out. Once the source of moisture is removed, no further decay will occur. Boards with small decayed areas can be scraped to remove the damaged portion and then painted or treated with a preservative to prevent future decay.

2 Check post alignment. Use a level to be sure posts are plumb and rails are square to the posts. Minor out-of-square conditions are normal. However, if the fence is dramatically leaning or out of square, consider correcting the condition before it gets any worse.

Grasp the fence near the top, and try to rock it back and forth. If the posts are loose, you should reset them. See if the panels have worked loose. You can add new posts or rails to shore up dramatically sagging panels.

3 Renail loose rails and siding. If any of the rails or siding boards have worked loose, renail them. First,

try to reset the original nails with a hammer and nail set. Provide additional strength with galvanized deck screws, which are less likely to pop out. Predrill to avoid splitting the wood. If this doesn't provide enough reinforcement, you'll need to add braces to the rails or replace the damaged rails or boards. If you're growing vines against the fence or trellis, make sure shoots or tendrils have not worked anything loose. Heavy vines may also cause the fence to lean. Keeping vines neatly trimmed will minimize such damage.

4 Clean the fence. If you'd like to restore that new look to an unfinished fence, apply one of the deck or fence cleaners available at the hardware store. It will remove dirt, mildew, and algae stains, and restore most of the old color to the surface.

If the fence has been painted or stained, it will still benefit from an occasional cleaning. During the summer, spray down the fence with a strong jet of clear water every few weeks to prevent dirt buildup. If you can't hose the dirt off the fence, rent a pressure washer and clean the fence with a mild detergent. To remove mold and mildew, mix a solution of 1 part chlorine bleach to 10 parts water and apply with a stiff bristle brush. Rinse

thoroughly. On painted and stained fences, test these solutions on a small area before doing the entire fence.

FENCE REPAIR

Some basic, relatively inexpensive repairs can extend the life of an old fence considerably. If the fence is too far gone, however, you may be better off tearing it down and replacing it. If you do decide to make repairs, consider not only the cost of materials and labor but also how the fence will look once the repairs are made. Most fence repairs involve repairing or replacing one or more damaged posts. If only a few posts are rotted and the rest are in good shape, it is worthwhile to replace the damaged ones. If most or all of the posts show damage, you may need to remove the siding and rebuild the entire fence frame. If the siding is still in good shape, you may be able to salvage it for the new fence or use the lumber for other garden projects.

1. To remove a rotten post, first dig around it, then cut off the rotted portion. If there is a concrete collar, break it up and remove it.

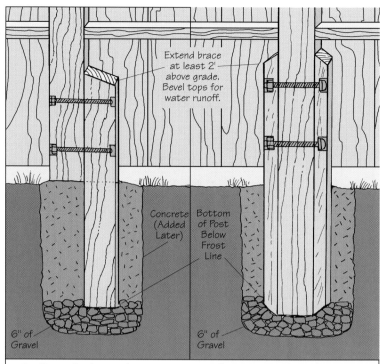

Extend brace at least 2' above grade. Bevel tops for water runoff.

Concrete (Added Later)

Bottom of Post Below Frost Line

6" of Gravel

6" of Gravel

2. Cut a single 4x4 brace or two 2x4 braces to replace the rotted section.

Repairing Damaged Posts

If the post is rotted at or below ground level, but the aboveground portion is still good, you may be able to install a brace instead of replacing it entirely.

1 Remove damaged portions of posts. Dig around the existing post down to the bottom. If the post has a concrete collar, break up the concrete with a pick or heavy pry bar and remove the pieces. If the concrete is difficult to remove, consider renting a hammer drill or rotary hammer to break the concrete. Cut off the damaged post about 1 to 2 inches aboveground, and remove the rotted portion. When installed, the brace will be in the ground, directly behind the location of the original post. If necessary, widen the hole to accept the brace.

2 Attach the brace. Cut a brace from a pressure-treated 4x4 to the length shown on the drawing. Bevel the top end to facilitate water runoff. Put the post in the hole, and attach the brace to the post with long carriage bolts. If your fence design

3. Plumb and level the post and set the brace or braces in concrete or gravel.

won't accommodate this type of brace or if you simply don't like the looks of it, you can attach pressure-treated 2x4 braces on each side of the post, as shown.

3 Set the brace. Align the post with the rest of the fence. Plumb the

post with a level, and then add a temporary 2x4 brace to keep the post aligned. Set the permanent brace in gravel and concrete, as you would a normal fence post. The concrete collar should extend about 1 inch above ground level and slope away from the post to allow water runoff.

1. To replace a post, first disconnect the rails and siding from it. Slip a piece of wood between the nail puller and the fence to avoid marring the fence.

2. Remove the post from the ground, breaking up the concrete collar if there is one.

Replacing Posts

Braces may be aesthetically out of place in some fence designs. If so, or if the post is damaged above ground level, replace the entire post.

1 Disconnect rails and siding. Remove the nails connecting the rails and siding boards to the post. A nail puller or small pry bar will give you better leverage and may work better than a hammer. Whatever you use, protect the fence by slipping a piece of wood between it and the nail puller. If necessary, prop up the top rails to keep the fence from sagging while you make repairs.

2 Remove the damaged post. If the post is set in earth, use a pry bar to lever the post out of the ground, as shown. If the post is set in concrete, dig around the collar to the bottom, and use a pick or pry bar to break up and remove the concrete. Then pull or pry the post out of the hole. Be sure to remove all rotted wood pieces from the hole because these can attract termites.

3 Add the new post. Dig deeper, if necessary, so that the hole is at least 30 inches deep. Put 6 inches of gravel in the hole. Place the new post in the hole, and slip it between the

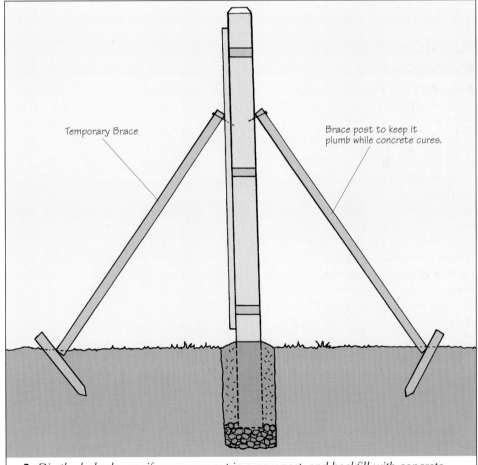

Temporary Brace

Brace post to keep it plumb while concrete cures.

3. Dig the hole deeper if necessary, put in a new post, and backfill with concrete.

rails. Plumb and brace the post to keep it plumb, checking it with a level. Fill the hole with concrete.

After the concrete sets, reattach the rails and siding to the new post using galvanized nails or deck screws.

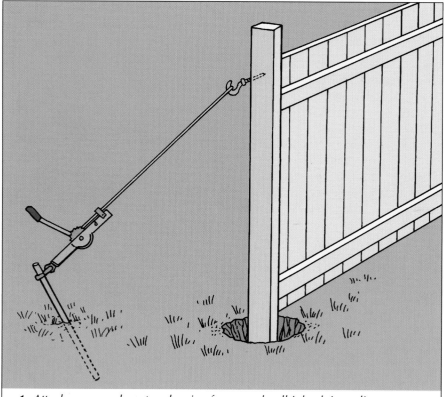

1. *Attach a come-along to a leaning fence, and pull it back into alignment.*

Hole Shown in
Cross Section

2. *When the post is plumb, brace it and fill the hole with gravel and concrete.*

Resetting a Leaning Post

If one or more posts are leaning or loose in their holes, you'll need to reset each one individually to bring the fence back into plumb. To do this, you'll need a tool called a come-along, which is essentially the same device used to stretch chain link fence. (See "Building a Chain Link Fence," page 94.) These can be rented at tool rental firms or purchased at a reasonable cost at home centers and hardware stores.

1 Pull the post into alignment. Dig around the post down to the bottom end. If the post is set in concrete, break it up with a pick or pry bar and remove the pieces. It is usually not necessary to detach the rails and siding from the post. Attach one end of the come-along to the top of the post, as shown, and the other end to a 36-inch length of $1/2$-inch pipe driven into the ground. Crank the handle on the come-along to bring the post back into alignment. Check the post frequently with a level while operating the come-along.

2 Reset the post. Once the post is plumb, secure it with temporary 2x4 diagonal braces, then backfill the hole with gravel and concrete. Once the first post is braced, repeat the procedure for other posts. Allow the concrete to cure (one to two days) before removing the brace.

Repairing Rails and Siding

As a rule, the bottom rails are more prone to decay because they are subjected to more moisture. Be sure to check the rail ends, which usually rot first. By spotting decay early, you can

Repairing Rails and Siding. *Damaged rails can be beefed up by installing a wood support block (left) or a metal T-plate (right). If too much of the rail end is rotted, you'll need to replace the rail.*

make simple repairs before it is necessary to replace the entire fence. A brace or mending plate is usually enough to reinforce the rail. If damage is severe, you'll need to replace the entire rail: Disconnect it from the post and siding boards, then add a new pressure-treated rail.

Fixing a Sagging Gate

Gates can sag or bind for a variety of reasons: leaning posts, a racked or out-of-square gate frame, loose or bent hinges, or a combination of any of the above. There are several ways to fix these problems.

Loose hinges are one of the most common causes of gate failure, especially if the gate sees heavy use. If the hinges have served the gate for a long time and are still in good shape, the screws may have just worked themselves loose over the years. However, premature hinge failure may be due

to hinges that are too small or screws that are too short. You can take the following steps to beef up the hinges.

1 Tighten loose screws. If the screws are loose, retighten them. If the screw holes are worn to the point that the screws no longer have a good bite, replace the screws with longer ones. If longer screws aren't feasible, epoxy small dowels or wooden match sticks into the old screw holes. When the epoxy dries, predrill new holes, and reattach the hinges. If necessary, you can remove the hinges and relocate them slightly above or below

their original position on the gate and post so that you'll be fastening to new wood.

2 Use larger or more hinges. Loose screws may also indicate that the hinges are too small. Bent hinges are a sure sign of this. Replace them with the largest size that will fit the gate frame and use the longest screws possible. If the gate has only two hinges, add a third hinge halfway between them. Mortising the hinges into the post and gate provides even more strength.

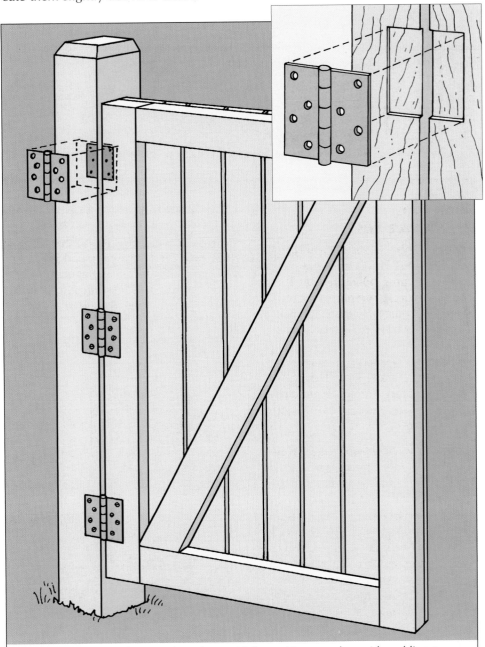

1. If the hinge screws are loose, fill the holes with epoxy and match sticks, or move the hinge to a slightly different location.

2. If the hinges are bent, replace them with larger hinges and consider adding a third one to help distribute the weight.

Fixing a Leaning Gate Post

A leaning gate post on the hinge side may be the cause of a sagging gate. If the post leans on the latch side, the gate may bind or the latch won't align properly with the latch strike.

To bring a leaning hinge post back into plumb, attach a sag rod. Sag rods are typically sold as kits that include a pair of threaded rods, a turnbuckle, and fastening hardware. Correct leaning fence posts as shown in the drawing, with the upper end of the rod attached to the upper end of the sagging post. Tighten the turnbuckle on the rod until the post is plumb.

Reinforcing Gate Posts

If the posts are sound but simply loose or unstable in the ground, reinforce them with concrete.

1 **Align the posts.** Dig a trench between the gate posts as wide and deep as the postholes. If the posts are not set in concrete, also dig around the post perimeters to add a concrete collar. Once the trench is dug, force the posts back into alignment and brace temporarily.

2 **Add gravel base.** Backfill the trench with 3 to 4 inches of compacted gravel or crushed rock.

3 **Place concrete.** Backfill the remainder of the trench with concrete until the concrete is level with the ground.

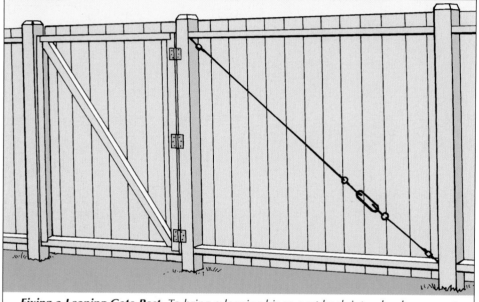

Fixing a Leaning Gate Post. *To bring a leaning hinge post back into plumb, connect a sag rod to the top end of the hinge post and the bottom end of the line post, as shown. Tighten the turnbuckle until the post is aligned and the gate operates freely. Generally, you don't have to remove the gate to make this repair.*

1. Dig between and around sagging gate posts before forcing them back into alignment.

2. Pour 3 to 4 in. of gravel into the trench and postholes if they are not filled with concrete.

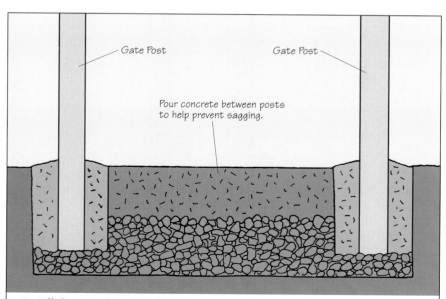

Gate Post   Gate Post

Pour concrete between posts to help prevent sagging.

3. Fill the rest of the trench with concrete. If necessary, pour concrete around the posts and form a collar.

Reinforcing a Gate Frame

Sometimes the gate frame itself may be the cause of binding. If the hinges are tight and the posts are plumb, make sure the gate is square. An out-of-square or racked gate may require bracing. If the gate-frame connections are weak, they'll need to be reinforced.

1 Reinforce the joints. If the gate structure is weak, you can reinforce the corner joints. First pull the gate into square. To do this, measure the diagonals of the frame. Run a clamp along the long diagonal, and tighten gently until the diagonals are the same length. Reinforce the gate with a metal bracket or plywood gusset. Fasten any loose boards or siding materials with galvanized deck screws.

2 Add diagonal bracing. To prevent further sagging, attach a sag rod between the top of the hinge side and the bottom of the latch side. You can also add a diagonal wood brace if the gate doesn't already have one. (See "Brace the Frame," page 104.) Unlike sag rods, wood braces are installed with the high end on the latch side and the low end on the hinge side.

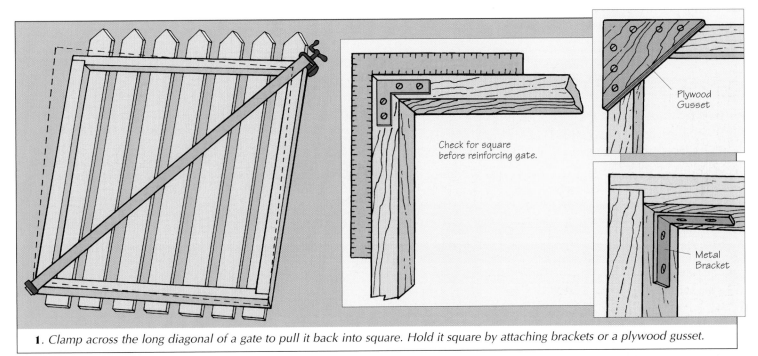

Check for square before reinforcing gate.

Plywood Gusset

Metal Bracket

1. Clamp across the long diagonal of a gate to pull it back into square. Hold it square by attaching brackets or a plywood gusset.

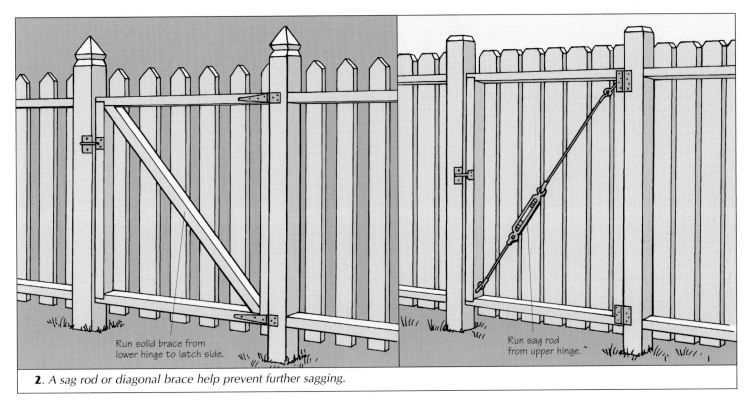

Run solid brace from lower hinge to latch side.

Run sag rod from upper hinge.

2. A sag rod or diagonal brace help prevent further sagging.

PHOTO CREDITS

p. 1:   Ben Aspen/Envision, New York, NY

p. 6:   Tom Rider; Architect: Peter Golze; California Redwood Association, Novato, CA

p. 7:   Phillip H. Ennis Photography, Freeport, NY

p. 8:   Bill Rothschild, Wesley Hills, NY

p. 9:   (top) Rufus Diamant; Architect: Bennett Christoferson; California Redwood Association, Novato, CA; (bottom) Susan Pashko/Envision, New York, NY

p. 10:   (top) John Schwartz, New York, NY; (bottom left) Andrew McKinney; California Redwood Association, Novato, CA; (bottom right) Dietrich Photography, Phoenix, AZ

p. 11:   (top) Ernest Braun; Designers: Christopher Klos, Westbrook Klos; California Redwood Association, Novato, CA; (bottom) Nancy Hill, Mount Kisco, NY

p. 13:   Ernest Braun; Designer: Timothy R. Bitts & Associates, Inc.; California Redwood Association, Novato, CA

p. 14:   (top) Dietrich Photography, Phoenix, AZ; (bottom left, right) Dietrich Photography, Phoenix, AZ

p. 15:   (left) Daniel Needham/Envision, New York, NY; (right) Susan Pashko/Envision, New York, NY

p. 16:   (top left) Jim Barrett, Pacific Grove, CA; (top right) Dietrich Photography, Phoenix, AZ; (bottom) Mary J. Peters/Jim Del Guidice, Convent Station, NJ

p. 17:   Tim Gibson/Envision, New York, NY

p. 18:   (top) Tom Rider; Designer/Builder: Mark O'Neil; California Redwood Association, Novato, CA; (bottom) Dietrich Photography, Phoenix, AZ

p. 20:   Tim Gibson/Envision, New York, NY

p. 21:   Heritage Vinyl Products, Assumption, IL

p. 22:   Bill Rothschild, Wesley Hills, NY

p. 24:   Makita U.S.A., La Mirada, CA

p. 27:   California Redwood Association, Novato, CA

p. 28:   American Plywood Association, Tacoma, WA

p. 35:   Ernest Braun; Designer: Douglas Fettling; California Redwood Association, Novato, CA

p. 36:   H. Armstrong Roberts, Philadelphia, PA

p. 37:   (top) Jim Barrett, Pacific Grove, CA; (bottom) Terry Wild , Williamsport, PA

p. 38:   (top) H. Armstrong Roberts, Philadelphia, PA; (bottom) Jim Barrett, Pacific Grove, CA

p. 39:   (top) Dietrich Photography, Phoenix, AZ; (bottom) H. Armstrong Roberts, New York, NY

p. 40:   (top left, bottom) H. Armstrong Roberts, New York, NY; (top right) Dietrich Photography, Phoenix, AZ;

p. 41:   (top and bottom) H. Armstrong Roberts, New York, NY

p. 42:   (top) H. Armstrong Roberts, New York, NY; (bottom) Dietrich Photography

p. 43:   (top) Tom Rider; Designer: Timothy A. Jones; California Redwood Association, Novato, CA; (bottom) Crandall & Crandall Photography, Dana Point, CA

p. 44:   Dietrich Photography, Phoenix, AZ

p. 45:   (top left) Ernest Braun; Designer: Timothy Jones; California Redwood Association, Novato, CA; (top right and bottom) Terry Wild Studio, Williamsport, PA

p. 46:   (top left) Jessie Walker, Glencoe, IL; (top right) Melabee M Miller, Hillside, NJ; (bottom left, right) Eric Roth Photography, Boston, MA

p. 47:   Melabee M Miller, Hillside, NJ

p. 48:   (top left) Crandall & Crandall Photography, Dana Point, CA; (top right) Terry Wild Studio, Williamsport, PA; (bottom) Eric Roth Photography, Boston, MA

p. 49:   (top left, right) Crandall & Crandall Photography, Dana Point, CA; (bottom) Bill Rothschild, Wesley Hills, NY

p. 50:   Melabee M Miller/Envision, New York, NY

p. 51:   Dietrich Photography, Wickenburg, AZ,

p. 64:   Ben Aspen/Envision, New York, NY

p. 87:   Terry Wild Studios, Williamsport, PA

p. 98:   H. Armstrong Roberts, Philadelphia, PA

p. 112: H. Armstrong Roberts, New York, NY

p. 127: Dietrich Photography, Wickenburg, AZ

p. 142: Crandall & Crandall Photography, Dana Point, CA

Back Cover:
   (top) Dietrich Photography, Phoenix, AZ
   (bottom) Tom Rider; Designer: Timothy A. Jones; California Redwood Association, Novato, CA

Air-dried lumber Lumber that is dried by being exposed to air, rather than an oven or kiln.

Arbor Garden structure that can support plants and serves as a transition between sections of a yard or as an architectural feature that complements the landscape.

Architectural grade lumber The best-looking and most expensive grade of lumber.

B-grade Like B-heart redwood, B-grade redwood contains limited knots. However, B-grade may also contain sapwood. Used for highly visible applications where the wood won't be subjected to rot.

B-heart Redwood grade that contains limited knots but no sapwood and is less expensive than clear all-heart.

Backfill Sand, dirt, gravel, or crushed stone used to fill the space around an excavation.

Battens Strips of wood placed over or between fence posts.

Batter boards Boards used to support cords that mark the position of a fence at the start of construction.

Blind corner Created when a fence is built on a corner lot and obstructs views at an intersection or sharp bend in the road.

Board foot A measurement of wood by volume; each board foot is equivalent to one-foot square and one-inch thick, or 144 cubic inches.

Borate-treated lumber Lumber preserved with borate salts. This method is effective against wood-boring insects, but not as effective against mold and fungus, so it is not recommended for posts or other ground-contact situations.

Box nail Used to nail thin dry wood close to the edge. In fence construction, they are used for fastening rails to posts and some types of siding to rails. Box nails are easier to drive and less likely to split than common nails.

Bracing Wood member used to support a structure. In fence building, bracing is usually only temporarily.

Buglehead screw Sharp-pointed screw that was named because of its bugle-shaped heads. They come with either coarse or fine threads; the coarse-threaded bugleheads are available as galvanized "deck screws" for outdoor use.

Casing nail Nail with small head that can be driven flush with or below the surface of the wood. Casing nails are similar to finishing nails, but are thicker for greater holding power.

Caster A wheel installed at the bottom of a gate to prevent sagging.

Chain link fence Prefabricated fence consisting of metal poles and chain-link mesh. These fences are durable and provide good security, but no privacy.

Clamshell digger Tool with shovel-like sides that is used to dig post holes.

Clear A grade of redwood that is free from knots and may contain sapwood. Clear wood is recommended for highly visible applications where the wood is not subject to rot.

Common nail Most widely used building nail; comes in lengths from 2d to 60d and may be galvanized to resist rust in outdoor use.

Creosote A wood preservative that is not available for use around the home because of its toxic nature.

Dado A rectangular groove cut at a right angle to the grain of a wood. Dadoes are most often used in joinery to receive another piece of wood.

Deck screw Galvanized, coarse-threaded screw that is often used in fence and deck construction.

Diagonal-board gate In this type of gate, boards are placed on an angle to give the gate extra strength without additional bracing.

Dry rot Decay from fungi that causes wood to become brittle and crumble to powder.

Duplex nail A nail with two heads used for temporary fastening. The lower head can be driven flush for a tight connection, while the upper head can be grasped with a hammer claw for easy removal.

Easement The right of access to property; a legal right to use property for a specific purpose, as the right to build a fence or run electrical power lines.

Fiberglass panel A substitute for plywood or plastic fence panels, these panels are either flat or corrugated and admit light while obscuring views.

Finial A decorative element at the top of a post. You can purchase posts with precut finials, cut your own, or purchase separate finials to attach to posts.

Finishing nail Nail with small head that can be driven below the surface of the wood, leaving a small hole that can be filled. Finishing nails are used when exposed nails would be unattractive for moldings and other decorative elements. Galvanized finishing nails, which are rust-resistant, are available for outdoor work.

Flathead screw Wood screw with a flat head that can be driven flush with or below the surface of the wood.

Frost line Depth at which the ground freezes. Posts must be placed below this line to avoid heaving when the ground freezes.

Galvanized mesh A material coated with zinc that is often used to make chain link.

Galvanized nail Exterior nail that is coated with zinc to prevent rusting.

Galvanized screw Exterior screw that is coated with zinc to prevent rusting.

Gate spring A device with a long, heavy spring and two brackets or eye screws that shuts a gate automatically.

Gate strike A piece attached to either side of the fence and to either the post or the gate. It keeps the gate from swinging past its closure point and bending the hinges.

Grape arbor An arbor that provides gardening space for a crop of grapes, as well as shade and protection.

Green lumber Often called garden-grade lumber because it is stacked outside in a lumberyard. Has a higher moisture content and is usually less expensive than kiln-dried or air-dried lumber. It is also easier to nail, but it will shrink as it dries, causing nails to loosen and gaps to appear between fence boards.

Heartwood Wood near the center of a tree that is harder, stronger, and usually more rot-resistant than wood closer to the outside.

High-density overlay (HDO) A resin-impregnated fiber bonded under high heat and pressure to one or both sides of a plywood panel. The tough overlay withstands severe exposure without the need for further finishing.

Kickboard A 1x8 or 1x10 piece installed along the bottom of the posts to strengthen a fence and prevent animals from crawling underneath it.

Kiln-dried lumber Lumber that is dried in a kiln, or a large oven, rather than by natural air currents.

Lattice Thin strips of wood that are crossed to make a pattern for a trellis or an arbor.

Louver fence A fence with boards installed either vertically or horizontally on an angle so that they serve as filters for wind and sunlight.

Masonry anchor Metal fastener used to hold wood structural members to masonry.

Medium-density overlay (MDO) Plywood panels that have a resin-impregnated overlay on one or both sides. The overlay has a texture designed for even paint application.

Merchantable heart grade The most economical all-heartwood redwood grade. Allows large knots and small knot holes, and is suitable for fences and posts. Used in some prefabricated fencing.

Post-and-rail fence Fence with posts that have one, two, or three rails toenailed or dadoed into them. Post-and-rail fences can be made to look rustic by butting rough-rounded rails or cutting them into half-tenons and inserting them in a mortise; they can be made to look formal with the use of dimension lumber.

Prefabricated fence Fence made with posts and panels that are prefabricated of wood, metal, or PVC plastic and come ready to assemble.

Prefabricated gate Gate made of metal or wood that can be purchased at a home center to save time in design and construction.

Pressure-treated wood Wood treated under pressure with chemicals designed to protect against termites and fungi.

Property-line fence Fence that is centered directly on the property line, meaning that tenants on both sides have ownership. Such fences are usually constructed in the "good neighbor" design so that they have the same appearance front and back.

Rough-sawn lumber Lumber that has not been planed; therefore, it lacks the uniformity of surfaced lumber. It has a splintery appearance that often shows saw marks.

Sag rod A rod or cable with an adjustable turnbuckle that is used like a wood brace to keep gates from sagging.

Segmented fence A fence consisting of short, straight sections attached to posts plotted along a curve.

Setback Code that requires structures to be built a certain distance from the street, sidewalk, or property line.

Spacer board A board ripped to the width between pickets that is used to make even spaces on a fence.

Trellis Garden structure on which plants and vines can grow.

Utility fencing Also called snow fencing because it prevents snow from drifting across walks or driveways, it consists of narrow wood slats held together with wire. It is sold in large rolls that are simply nailed to permanent or temporary wood or metal posts.

Variance A permit or waiver to build a structure that does not comply with zoning ordinances.

Vertical board-on-board fence Fence that is fully sided to provide privacy while not entirely blocking sunlight. Often built on a property line.

Vinyl fence Prefabricated fence made of PVC plastic that imitates a variety of fence designs, including board, rail, picket, lattice, and ornamental metal. It requires little maintenance but comes in only a few colors.

Wane A lumber defect that leaves wood missing from the edge of a piece.

Welded wire Woven wire mesh that is often attached to a wood fence to act as a trellis for climbing vines.

Wire picket fencing Rolls of factory-painted or vinyl-coated welded-wire fencing that come in heights of 12 to 18 inches. Used as a temporary or decorative border around planting beds and walks.

Wood-and-wire fence Welded or woven-wire mesh that is attached to a wood frame to make a lightweight, economical fence.

Z-brace gate A reinforced gate with a Z-shaped wood brace. It is found on a solid-board fence, a masonry wall, or a breezeway between buildings.

INDEX

METRIC CONVERSION TABLES

LUMBER

Sizes: Metric cross sections are so close to their nearest U.S. sizes, as noted at right, that for most purposes they may be considered equivalents.

Lengths: Metric lengths are based on a 300mm module, which is slightly shorter in length than an U.S. foot. It will, therefore, be important to check your requirements accurately to the nearest inch and consult the table below to find the metric length required.

Areas: The metric area is a square meter. Use the following conversion factor when converting from U.S. data: 100 sq. feet = 9.29 sq. meters.

METRIC LENGTHS

Meters	Equivalent Feet and Inches
1.8m	5' 10$\frac{7}{8}$"
2.1m	6' 10$\frac{5}{8}$"
2.4m	7' 10$\frac{1}{2}$"
2.7m	8' 10$\frac{1}{4}$"
3.0m	9' 10$\frac{1}{8}$"
3.3m	10' 9$\frac{7}{8}$"
3.6m	11' 9$\frac{3}{4}$"
3.9m	12' 9$\frac{1}{2}$"
4.2m	13' 9$\frac{3}{8}$"
4.5m	14' 9$\frac{1}{8}$"
4.8m	15' 9"
5.1m	16' 8$\frac{3}{4}$"
5.4m	17' 8$\frac{5}{8}$"
5.7m	18' 8$\frac{3}{8}$"
6.0m	19' 8$\frac{1}{4}$"
6.3m	20' 8"
6.6m	21' 7$\frac{7}{8}$"
6.9m	22' 7$\frac{5}{8}$"
7.2m	23' 7$\frac{1}{2}$"
7.5m	24' 7$\frac{1}{4}$"
7.8m	25' 7$\frac{1}{8}$"

Dimensions are based on 1m = 3.28 feet, or 1 foot = 0.3048m

METRIC SIZES (Shown before Nearest U.S. Equivalent)

Millimeters	Inches	Millimeters	Inches
16 x 75	$\frac{5}{8}$ x 3	44 x 150	1$\frac{3}{4}$ x 6
16 x 100	$\frac{5}{8}$ x 4	44 x 175	1$\frac{3}{4}$ x 7
16 x 125	$\frac{5}{8}$ x 5	44 x 200	1$\frac{3}{4}$ x 8
16 x 150	$\frac{5}{8}$ x 6	44 x 225	1$\frac{3}{4}$ x 9
19 x 75	$\frac{3}{4}$ x 3	44 x 250	1$\frac{3}{4}$ x 10
19 x 100	$\frac{3}{4}$ x 4	44 x 300	1$\frac{3}{4}$ x 12
19 x 125	$\frac{3}{4}$ x 5	50 x 75	2 x 3
19 x 150	$\frac{3}{4}$ x 6	50 x 100	2 x 4
22 x 75	$\frac{7}{8}$ x 3	50 x 125	2 x 5
22 x 100	$\frac{7}{8}$ x 4	50 x 150	2 x 6
22 x 125	$\frac{7}{8}$ x 5	50 x 175	2 x 7
22 x 150	$\frac{7}{8}$ x 6	50 x 200	2 x 8
25 x 75	1 x 3	50 x 225	2 x 9
25 x 100	1 x 4	50 x 250	2 x 10
25 x 125	1 x 5	50 x 300	2 x 12
25 x 150	1 x 6	63 x 100	2$\frac{1}{2}$ x 4
25 x 175	1 x 7	63 x 125	2$\frac{1}{2}$ x 5
25 x 200	1 x 8	63 x 150	2$\frac{1}{2}$ x 6
25 x 225	1 x 9	63 x 175	2$\frac{1}{2}$ x 7
25 x 250	1 x 10	63 x 200	2$\frac{1}{2}$ x 8
25 x 300	1 x 12	63 x 225	2$\frac{1}{2}$ x 9
32 x 75	1$\frac{1}{4}$ x 3	75 x 100	3 x 4
32 x 100	1$\frac{1}{4}$ x 4	75 x 125	3 x 5
32 x 125	1$\frac{1}{4}$ x 5	75 x 150	3 x 6
32 x 150	1$\frac{1}{4}$ x 6	75 x 175	3 x 7
32 x 175	1$\frac{1}{4}$ x 7	75 x 200	3 x 8
32 x 200	1$\frac{1}{4}$ x 8	75 x 225	3 x 9
32 x 225	1$\frac{1}{4}$ x 9	75 x 250	3 x 10
32 x 250	1$\frac{1}{4}$ x 10	75 x 300	3 x 12
32 x 300	1$\frac{1}{4}$ x 12	100 x 100	4 x 4
38 x 75	1$\frac{1}{2}$ x 3	100 x 150	4 x 6
38 x 100	1$\frac{1}{2}$ x 4	100 x 200	4 x 8
38 x 125	1$\frac{1}{2}$ x 5	100 x 250	4 x 10
38 x 150	1$\frac{1}{2}$ x 6	100 x 300	4 x 12
38 x 175	1$\frac{1}{2}$ x 7	150 x 150	6 x 6
38 x 200	1$\frac{1}{2}$ x 8	150 x 200	6 x 8
38 x 225	1$\frac{1}{2}$ x 9	150 x 300	6 x 12
44 x 75	1$\frac{3}{4}$ x 3	200 x 200	8 x 8
44 x 100	1$\frac{3}{4}$ x 4	250 x 250	10 x 10
44 x 125	1$\frac{3}{4}$ x 5	300 x 300	12 x 12

Dimensions are based on 1 inch = 25mm

Have a home improvement, decorating, or gardening project? Look for these and other fine Creative Homeowner books wherever books are sold. . .

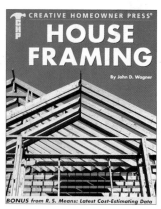

Designed to walk you through the framing basics. Over 400 illustrations. 240 pp.; 8½"x10⅞"
BOOK #: 277655

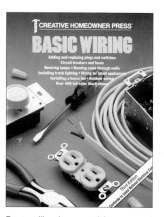

Best-selling house-wiring manual. More than 350 color illustrations. 160 pp.; 8½"x11"
BOOK #: 277048

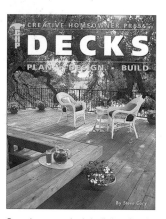

Step-by-step deck building for the novice. Over 500 color illustrations. 176 pp.; 8½"x10⅞"
BOOK #: 277180

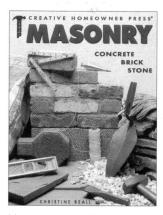

How to work with concrete brick and stone. Over 500 Illustrations. 176 pp.; 8½"x10⅞"
BOOK #: 277106

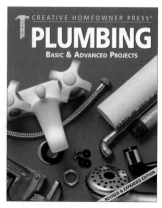

Take the guesswork out of plumbing repair. More than 550 illustrations. 176 pp.; 8½"x10⅞"
BOOK #: 277620

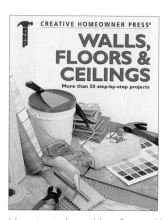

How to replace old surfaces with new ones. Over 500 illustrations. 176 pp.; 8½"x10⅞"
BOOK #: 277697

Install tile on walls, floors, patios, countertops, and more. Over 500 illustrations. 176 pp.; 8½"x10⅞"
BOOK #: 277540

How to convert unused space into useful living area. 570 illustrations. 192 pp.; 8½"x10⅞"
BOOK #: 277680

How to create kitchen style like a pro. Over 150 color photographs. 176 pp.; 9"x10"
BOOK #: 279935

How to work with space, color, pattern, texture. Over 300 photos. 256 pp.; 9"x10"
BOOK #: 279667

How to select and care for landscaping plants. Over 500 illustrations. 208 pp.; 9"x10"
BOOK #: 274238

Create more beautiful, healthier, lower-maintenance lawns. Over 300 illustrations. 160 pp.; 9"x10"
BOOK #: 274359

For more information, and to order direct, call 800-631-7795; in New Jersey 201-934-7100.
Please visit our Web site at www.creativehomeowner.com

INTRODUCTION TO
SOCIOLOGY

eighth edition